COPS vs. The Constitution

The Neo-Progressive Exploitation of Law Enforcement

Sheriff Clarke,
Best wishes to you sir.
Be safe.

4/15

Written by

Tim L. Smith, M.A.

Tim L. Smith

Independent Publishing

September 2014

Library of Congress Cataloging-in-Publication

ISBN - 13: 978-1502345950
ISBN - 10: 1502345951

Printed in the United States of America

For Jasmine and Avah

Contents

Hobbes vs. Locke

Spirited Debates

Civilized Society

Public Education

Rights

Equality

Give an Inch, a Mile is Taken

What is Property?

The Law

Blackstonian Theory

Redistribution of Wealth

Guns

Self-Ownership

Civil Asset Forfeiture

Introduction

When I was about seven years old I lived about a mile or so from school. Sometimes I would walk home because I'd miss the bus, for whatever reason. One day while walking home, a white station wagon, with wood paneled siding, pulled up next to me on the side of the road. A large white male was driving and he wore a large straw hat. I remember vividly. He opened the passenger door and yelled, "Jump in, I'll give you a ride." All I could think about at that moment was my mom telling me to never get into a car with a stranger, and why. I got scared and ran off, the other way. I didn't know what the man's intent was, it could have been perfectly innocent. Anyway, I got lost and soon found a park. So I got on the swings and stayed there a while.

Soon enough, two cops pulled up on the street. One was in a patrol car and the other on a motorcycle. They walked towards me and one yelled "Timmy!" So I ran up to them. One picked me up and asked me if I was lost. I said yes. He then told me my mom had sent them to find me. He then asked me if I wanted to ride in the police car or on the motorcycle. I chose the patrol car because I rode on the back of my uncle's motorcycle often. I had never ridden in a police car. It was cool. The cops took me home and my mom was very happy to see me. The cops were very kind and as a seven year old, I thought they were bigger than life. Since then I wanted to be a cop, or an astronaut. But, I didn't become a cop, or an astronaut. I became a high school Social Studies teacher instead. In time, however, I left teaching and went into law enforcement.

I became a Law Enforcement Officer to try and make the world a better place, to become a part of something bigger than myself, to go after those who harm others. I swore no allegiance to any man or agency, but to an ideology, which is that *We the People* are free and independent. My job was to secure and *preserve* that ideology, by protecting life, liberty and property. For me, to become a cop, was my own participation in the American Revolution against aristocracy, inequality and arbitrary violence. I held a very clear conscious in this regard.

Over the years I began to see past the legal system's smoke and mirrors. I began to feel that the appearance mattered more than the substance. And it did. We no longer respect, adhere to, nor seek to preserve our constitutional *Oaths of Office*. Rather, the Oath has become a mere formality. *We the People* have become over regulated, over taxed and our natural, fundamental rights have been undermined by legal privileges created by corporate interests, forced collectivism, a global and political financial agenda, and policies like the War on Terror, all having an indirect, negative effect on competent, law enforcement duties. In fact, I recall the planes hitting the Towers while I was sitting in my Communications block of instruction during Basic Law Enforcement Training (police academy). It was surreal, to say the least.

Apart from this, and likewise, subconsciously for most officers across this country, their rank, job security, and camaraderie, tend to deviate or distract one's perspective and motivation from fulfilling their genuine duty, in and of itself, into an effort to win over the praise of the ones who award or oversee their rank and/or job security. This is coupled with the falsification of self-empowerment and esteem that comes from "training." Many officers become "yes men" and tend to always lose sight of their Oath. Not all, but most. Ralph Waldo Emerson wrote that, "It is a lesson which all history teaches wise men, to put trust in ideas, and not in circumstances.... I much prefer that life be of a lower strain, so it be genuine and equal, then that it should be glittering and unsteady." In other words, many cops throughout this country lose sight of their *sworn* purpose by the distraction of "ruling" over others rather than "leading."

In addition, most law enforcement officers within America don't truly understand our system of government and they take for granted that secondary laws are legitimate at face value without any critical inquiry at all as to the law's constitutionality, even by the fact that laws that regulate the exercise of inalienable rights, for example, contradict each other from state to state. Cops, along side the public, also take for granted that those who enter into office to create secondary law do so in our best interest. From all this, the exploitation of force comes about, whereby the laws that make up the legal system uphold the will of the ruling classes and of the politically connected. These capricious secondary laws consist of, but are not limited to, congressional acts, public policy, statutes, orders, ordinances, codes and the like, making up the modern legal system, which has become fundamentally distinctive from the Founders' *Rule of Law*, or primary law. David Hume said, "Mankind are, in all ages, caught by the same baits: the same tricks played over and over again, still trepan them."

As a law enforcement officer myself, in around 2009, I began writing about what I was seeing and feeling. I began writing from a philosophical perspective, and it has turned into this book, which I've also heavily researched. I take the philosophical approach simply because I love philosophy. Philosophy is the foundation of all thinking, ideas and argument. Philosophy is the *Socratic Method* in action. Philosophy seeks to "know" what right and wrong *really* are. Philosophy helps one seek out the truth about something by asking the right types of questions, either within the context of a certain discipline, like politics, or within the context of how things really are, "out there," like in religion. Philosophy helps develop critical thinking skills, and reasoning skills. America, for example, *was* the instantiation of the founders' philosophical inquiry into "What is the just and moral role of government?" and "What is liberty?" Once the founder's convictions were set, they said to the King, "No More!" This book, then, is a philosophical inquiry into the new question of, "What is happening to this American liberty that the founders established?"

All my "formal" education is in philosophy. I did my undergraduate work (BA) in Philosophy and then I earned my Masters Degree (M.A.) in Philosophy. I could not afford to go back and get my PhD, which literally means Doctor of Philosophy. So, I figured writing this book will be my "dissertation." In the context of this book, for example, I use philosophy as a way to get to the truth behind the modern day legal system and its effect on Law Enforcement, given what I think I "know" at this time in my life. I am, however, always open to new information and sound evidence that may undermine what I think I "know." Until that happens, and as it relates to being a cop, I always return to the source, the US Constitution, and why it exists. For me, the Constitution is the Law in Law Enforcement. There are those who find this conviction troubling, however, as you will see. And, these people seek to demonize such a conviction's actualization through the legal system itself. These people are what I call *Neo-Progressive*.

In this book, I repeat myself often, on purpose, because there is a lot to take in. There are many serious points I make that I want the reader to soak in, to really remember. Philosophical writings generally tend to drag a bit and appear run on. And that's ok, just keep reading, even past the typos. I'm not writing an English paper here. I'm writing a philosophical rebuttal to a neo-progressive, political agenda. To illustrate, I often utilize the philosophical technique called *reductio ad absurdum*. It means to "reduce to absurdity." This is a technique that reduces someone's line of reasoning to absurdity by pushing their argument's premises or conclusions to their logical limits and showing how illogical the consequences would be, thus invalidating that way of thinking. This can apply to both deductive and inductive reasoning. A cop's authority, for example, is not authority in and of itself. So statements like "because I said so" or "if you have nothing to hide you have nothing to worry about" are absurd, in and of themselves, because such statements are authoritarian in nature and do not instantiate the actual *source* of authority in the officer, which is the *actualizing* of both the spirit *and* the letter of the Law. I show how cops, through social engineering and training, only focus on the letter of the Law. Michael Ellner said it best, "Just look at us. Everything is backwards, everything is upside down. Doctors destroy health, lawyers destroy justice, psychiatrists destroy minds, scientists destroy truth, major media destroys information, religions destroy spirituality and governments destroy freedom."

Why did I title this book *Cops vs. The Constitution*? Like a court case, I want to defend, in part, any negative consensus of Law Enforcement by arguing that things are not as they appear. Don't judge a book by its cover, so to speak. What I mean is that there are causal, philosophical elements at work within American society and its social engineering that directly exploit a cop's gun, or the government's monopoly on force, unbeknownst to the cops themselves. Cops don't get out there and simply decide to take people's stuff, or arrest children for pretending to play with guns on school playgrounds. Some do I suppose, but there are always going to be "bad apples" within every profession. It goes deeper than that, much deeper. This book attempts to take you behind the scenes to the real sources of "why?" And, those sources have their roots in philosophy, just as the Constitution itself, the Declaration of Independence, and the State Ratification debates, and the like, all have their roots in philosophy.

So before you dive into this book, let me share an example of what it means to actualize both the letter and spirit of the Law, from my own experience. I did not like to participate in drivers' license checkpoints. And, the men and women I worked with knew this and respected me for that. I would simply remain on the road when a checkpoint was set up. A license checkpoint is not the same as DWI checkpoint, however. State law heavily regulates DWI checkpoints, and for good reason. I did not like license checkpoints because I believe that the reasonable expectation of privacy supercedes a cop's "need to know" whether or not a driver has a license, unless reasonable suspicion attaches to a specific driver. Absent the minimum of reasonable suspicion, a forced stop violates the 4th Amendment rights of the driver. And, the US Supreme Court backs this up in *Delaware v. Prouse.* On the other hand, as long as there is *intent* to find information relating to a specific crime, then a license checkpoint is *lawful,* provided all vehicles are stopped. So to illustrate the *letter of the law*, it is lawful to set up a license checkpoint in an area where there have been a series of break-ins, in hopes to possibly find evidence that leads to a suspect, like a car with stolen items in it. As it relates to avoiding the *spirit of the law*, for example, it is unlawful to set up a license checkpoint just because cops are bored and want something to do.

The incompetence within all levels of American government today, as it relates to preserving the actual Rule of Law, is staggering. It's as though the only *real* principles anymore are to sustain the Legal System's design to protect itself from the Rule of Law. Therefore, consider this book philosophy in action, whereby, as someone who loves wisdom, as someone who seeks truth, as a former law enforcement official, and as I see it, I decisively analyze the conceptual apparatus behind the American Legal System and it's exploitation of our Law Enforcement.

"Nothing appears more surprising to those, who consider human affairs with a philosophical eye, than the easiness with which the many are governed by the few; and the implicit submission, with which men resign their own sentiments and passions to those of their rulers. When we enquire by what means this wonder is effected, we shall find, that, as Force is always on the side of the governed, the governors have nothing to support them but opinion. It is therefore, on opinion only that government is founded; and this maxim extends to the most despotic and most military governments, as well as to the most free and most popular."

– David Hume, Of The First Principles of Government

1

The Rise of Liberty and its Rule of Law

"Freedom, however, is not the last word. Freedom is only part of the story and half of the truth. Freedom is but the negative aspect of the whole phenomenon whose positive aspect is responsibleness. In fact, freedom is in danger of degenerating into mere arbitrariness unless it is lived in terms of responsibleness."

– Viktor Frankl

Freedom takes responsibility. Responsibility is something that must be cultivated and encouraged, not only by mistakes, family and customs, but also by non-capricious law. Laws within governments throughout the history of the world were, for the most part, designed only to secure and protect the interests of the state. Little to none of the laws were ever designed to secure individual liberty. Once American liberty surfaced from within the nearly 6000 years or so of modern human history, laws were established to do the opposite of what past laws have done, secure the interests, liberty and the property rights of the individual. The American founders knew history and philosophy very well. They were very familiar with the political theories of philosophical thinkers and all the pros and cons of the varying views. The founders were also very knowledgeable of the history of governments, the types of governments and how the idea of *law* or *decree* had generally been a means to not only secure the arbitrary will of the state, but to extract wealth from the people to serve and secure state needs and wants.

The founders were divided on the philosophical and political theories that they would adopt to establish the American Rule of Law, which would then attempt to secure liberty. This idea, in the face of past governments and England in particular, was hugely progressive. The Framers were at great odds, however, not only on how Law in America would secure individual liberty, but how the Law will restrict the negative aspects of human nature within government officials, secure property ownership, protect people from other people, and yet maintain the legitimate and limited power the state needed to do its job. The founders were all certain, in spite of their differences, that America and its government would be radically and progressively different from governments in the past. Individual liberty would be the new government's primary objective, the political paradigm by which the new government would operate. This *Rule of Law* in America would be designed as a moral force against the capricious and historical evils of human nature that have prolonged and sustained the authority of people in government for millennium, such as the greed for power and wealth, the desire to control other people and their property, the blatant use of violence to secure aristocracy and inequality, and the constant lust for war and empire. To undermine this historical motif became an enormous challenge for the new government. Thus, the founders would use an array of philosophical and political views as a frame of reference to determine how the new American government would be formed.

Hobbes vs. Locke

Where do these ideas about the moral role of government, inalienable rights, property ownership and individual liberty come from? These ideas have a history within philosophy, dating all the way back to Plato's *Republic*. The founders, in the main course of debate, wrestled with the political thought of primarily two Renaissance philosophers: Thomas Hobbes and John Locke. Both of these English philosophers asked the question, "What is the just and moral purpose of government?" And, both attempted to answer this question fundamentally different. Thomas Hobbes (1588–1679) believed that government was absolutely necessary to combat the *state of nature*. "It followeth, that in such a condition, every man has the right to every thing; even to one another's body. And therefore, as long as this natural Right of every man to every thing endureth, there can be no security to any man... of living out the time, which Nature ordinarily allow men to live."[1] The *state of nature* that Hobbes talks about was a natural human disposition, where strong people would go around and take weaker people's things, through violence. Thus, says Hobbes, life within this society is "solitary, poor, nasty, brutish, and short."[2] He argued that *Justice* would always be based upon the claims of those in power, that without there being a power source, a government, to define what actions are right and wrong, there would be no such thing as law or even *injustice*. "Where there is no common power, there is no law: where no law, no injustice."[3] According to Hobbes, Justice and Law is both the same thing, created by and defined by government, which is formed by the people coming together to protect themselves and their belongings from other people. For Hobbes, when people come together to create government as a means to live peacefully, they surrender some of their natural rights in exchange for laws, that some freedoms are sacrificed for security under a *social contract*. "Law was brought into the world for nothing else but to limit the natural liberty of particular men in such manner as they might not hurt, but assist one another, and join together against a common enemy."[4] Whatever the government does, it is just and right, says Hobbes. This also means that there are no limits on what government can and can't do. That the people can do whatever it wants through their government. In fact, Hobbes says that government creates the *idea* of justice.

> "Therefore before the names of Just and Unjust can have place, there must be some coercive Power, to compel men equally to the performance of their Covenants..., to make good that Propriety, which by mutual contract men acquire, in recompense of the universal Right they abandon: and such power there is none before the erection of the Commonwealth."[5]

Hobbes argues that personal liberty within a social compact is limited to the permissions of whatever the state prescribes within the context of its system of laws. "The liberty of a subject, lieth therefore only in those things, which in regulating their actions, the sovereign hath permitted: such as the liberty to buy, and sell, and otherwise contract with one another; to choose their own abode, their own diet, their own trade of life, and institute their children as they themselves think fit; and the like."[6] Personal liberties, therefore, and earning a living are created, defined and regulated by the state.

Hobbes believed in a big and powerful government, to protect people, not only from themselves, but also from foreign invasion. He argued that big government creates and defines what rights, property and liberties are. Hobbes believed that government should be the ultimate control over mankind, which also defines what is morally right and wrong, *all by force*, or by the threat of force. Human behavior, human innovation, and the like, are all limited to the welfare and interests of the state via collective subjugation to the will of those people who run the state. Sound familiar? Hobbes appears to be describing today's America, and other major countries around the globe. Hobbes called this type of government, the *Leviathan*. A leviathan is a huge sea monster that was originally described in the book of Job 41, in the Old Testament. Many of the founders liked this type of government and they argued for it as the foundation for the new American system of government, not only during the Convention, but also during the Ratification debates and within personal political dialogue. Yet, Hobbes' political theory lost the overall debates to another political view. The political philosophy in opposition to Hobbes' view of government actually became the premises within the founders' dialectic and in fact became the foundational principles of the new American system of government.

These foremost principles that became the foundational principles for our government here in the United States today derive from the political philosophy of John Locke (1632-1704), and *not* of Hobbes. It was John Locke who intellectually paved the way and advanced the building blocks for American liberty. Locke's view of government was very different from Hobbes. Locke emphasized three aspects of human freedom that are separate from law, separate from government and separate from other people: life, liberty and property. What does Locke say about the *state of nature*?

> "The state of nature has a law of nature to govern it, which obliges every one; and reason, which is that law, teaches all mankind who will but consult it, that, being all equal and independent, no one ought to harm another in his life, health, liberty, or possessions…there cannot be supposed any such subordination among us, that may authorize us to destroy one another…Every one, as he is bound to preserve himself, and not to quit his station willfully, so, by the like reason, when his preservation comes not in competition, ought he, as much as he can, to preserve the rest of mankind, and may not, unless it be to do justice on an offender, take away or impair the life, or what tends to the preservation of the life, liberty, health, limb, or goods of another."[7]

Both Hobbes and Locke argue two versions of the social compact. Hobbes argues for a government that holds absolute, central power and Locke argues for a government that is ethically constitutional and consensually limited. Locke says that mankind has a *natural law*, regulated by the light of *reason*, that government is created not only to secure what is morally right and wrong, but to also secure property, individual rights and to secure the *equality* between all people. Locke also discards noble and royal superiority that the history of the world has been *forced* to endure,

> "In races of mankind and families of the world, there remains not to one above another, the least pretence to be the eldest house and to have the right of inheritance: it is impossible that the rulers now on earth should make any benefit, or derive any the least shadow of authority from that, which is held to be the fountain of all power."[8]

In particular, Locke makes equal those people in government with those people not in government. Thus, genuine political power is not inherited, or aristocratic, but vested as an equal right between all people, under a social compact designed to secure people and their property from the harm of aristocracy. In addition, there is a necessary aspect of secondary legislation and its "enforcement" that comes from within the communities themselves, to help secure this moral, social compact,

> "Political power, then, I take to be a right of making laws with penalties of death, and consequently all less penalties, for the regulating and preserving of property, and of employing the force of the community, in the execution of such laws, and in the defence of the common-wealth from foreign injury; and all this only for the public good."[9]

Moral government, says Locke, lies in mutual and consensual equality between *all* people. Locke thus describes individual liberty as, "not to be subject to the inconstant, uncertain, unknown, arbitrary will of another man."[10] In addition, Locke says that, "freedom from absolute, arbitrary power, is so necessary to, and closely joined with a man's preservation, that he cannot part with it, but by what forfeits his preservation and life together."[11] The key word here is arbitrary. *Arbitrary* is *self-serving* and *illogical* actions. Arbitrary is also defined by Locke as the, "unlawful power of other individuals," that, "unlawfully harm the lives, health, liberty, or property of other individuals."[13] Well what does *lawful* mean, then? Black's Law Dictionary, 8th Edition, defines lawful as, "Not contrary to law, permitted by law." But then in the Treatise, Locke asks the question, "How came so many lawful monarchies come into the world?" Locke goes on to define what lawful government is, "in the consent of the people, which being the only one of all lawful governments." Black's definition of *lawful* as, "Not contrary to law, permitted by law," can virtually apply to any system of laws, either within a totalitarian regime, a theocracy, fascism, an oligarchy, a democracy, a republic, or of a King. Lawful means consent of the people and does not necessarily mean *implied consent*, as is the case within "representative" government today. Mass implied consent is illogical. Lawful, then, in Locke's view means *direct consent* and the direct adherence of secondary laws to the Law of the Land, which fundamentally secures the individual's inalienable rights to life, liberty and property.

The Law of the Land, or the Rule of Law, in the United States today is the US Constitution, which includes the Bill of Rights. Thus, *lawful* in America can be inferred as *direct consent* of the governed, by way of non-arbitrary laws designed to secure an individual's liberty, inalienable rights and property ownership. When secondary laws, or individuals within government act in contrast to the security of natural rights and individual liberty, those government officials and such secondary laws in likeness, are considered arbitrary and *unlawful*, because they work directly against the Law of the Land and against *direct consent* of the governed.

This does not mean, however, that the natural liberty of an individual within the *state of nature* is equal, or the same as the liberty of an individual within a governed society. Part of coming together within a social compact, or a civilized society, is compromise of the people in government with the people not in government. But, not compromise that surrenders or undermines an individual's life, liberty or property. Locke goes on further to describe the difference between natural liberty and individual liberty under a social compact, or individual liberty within a self-governed society,

> "The natural liberty of man is to be free from any superior power on earth, and not to be under the will or legislative authority of man, but to have only the law of nature for his rule. The liberty of man, in society, is to be under no other legislative power, but that established, by consent, in the commonwealth; nor under the dominion of any will, or restraint of any law, but what that legislative shall enact, according to the trust put in it. Freedom then is not... a liberty for every one to do what he lists, to live as he pleases, and not to be tied by any laws: but freedom of men under government is, to have a standing rule to live by, common to every one of that society, and made by the legislative power erected in it."[12]

The founders gravitated to Locke because Locke emphasized a moral balance within the social compact between those who are chosen by the people to govern with those who are governed. This balance encompasses limited government power that aims at securing as much of the natural liberty of individuals as possible, while making laws that are necessary to keep people from harming one another and to secure the well being of all people within the compact. Thus, the moral balance shifts with the exploitation of force behind laws that are created to self-serve government interests, expanding that natural inequality that the whole intent of self government was established to work against. Locke's philosophical attack on the historical, arbitrary power of traditional governments also included attacks on a state's arbitrary use of religion, because many "laws" had been created to respect and adhere to the establishment of religion, for the government's sake, which generally sought to oppress natural rights and was an excuse to extract property and wealth from the people, and to control behavior. Paradoxically, these laws were *lawful*, in accordance to that particular system of laws, which were based in that particular Law of the Land. But were they ethically sound? As it relates to religious freedom, Locke argues,

> "No one…neither single persons nor churches, nay, nor even commonwealths, have any just title to invade the civil rights or worldly goods of each other on pretence of religion. Those that are of another opinion would do well to consider with themselves how pernicious a seed of discord and war, how powerful a provocation to endless hatreds, rapines, and slaughters they thereby furnish to mankind. No peace and security, no, not so much as common friendship, can ever be established or preserved amongst men so long as this opinion prevails, that dominion is founded in grace and that religion is to be propagated by force of arms."[14]

Locke's position that morality, as it related to religion, should not be forced because it violates our natural right to reason, to figure things out for ourselves. That is liberty. This also directly influenced the founders, who were mostly made up of Anglo backgrounds, which included

Protestants, Catholics, Deists, Christian Deists and Agnostics,[14.5] though agnostic is a later term. The sentiments of agnosticism resounded, however. Locke's freedom of religion from force predisposed Thomas Jefferson's later idea of the separation of Church and State. Theocracies, historically, or any government that had forced religious dogma on people by way of violence, as a way to control behavior, had been extremely dangerous to many human cultures, human achievements and even basic survival under such authoritarian regimes, whereby any and all matters of actions, possessions and even thoughts were potentially criminal with brutal consequences, and which held the *blessings* of the religious majority. The religious majority sought to use or exploit a government's monopoly on violence to force their particular moral view on society as a whole. The founders said no more. Forced religious dogma is still dominant today in many countries. Fortunately, the founders were wise enough to secure a government that allowed people to worship, or not worship, as they see fit. Thus, we have the First Amendment, whereby this *codified moral force* prevents government officials in America from forcing religious dogma onto free people and the will of a religious majority does not prevail over the freedoms of the minority. Yet, even the very intent of forcing a "moral" view is in and of itself immoral. It is immoral because it deviates from the sound intent of the social compact, which secures the individual's natural rights, which includes their own moral approbation, provided such view is not itself harmful to others. Under Locke, therefore, real crime, essentially, derives from an individual's inability to adhere to another individual's natural rights, which are their life, liberty, which includes one's opposite religious views, and property. People come together, says Locke, to create government as a means to secure these natural rights and to punish those who violate such rights. Locke in this way helped established the idea of limited government, sovereignty of the people and emphasized individual *right of conscious*, and the right to be left alone (privacy).

In 1833, Supreme Court Justice Joseph Story, who authored *Commentaries on the Constitution*, described Locke as "a most strenuous asserter of liberty" who "helped establish in this country the sovereignty of the people over the government," "majority rule with minority protection," and "the rights of conscience." In 1839, John Quincy Adams', in *The Jubilee of the Constitution*, a Discourse, declared that, "The Declaration of Independence was...founded upon one and the same theory of government...expounded in the writings of Locke." Locke says in the 2nd Treatise of Government,

> "Any single man must judge for himself whether circumstances warrant obedience or resistance to the commands of the civil magistrate; we are all qualified, entitled, and morally obliged to evaluate the conduct of our rulers. This political judgment, moreover, is not simply or primarily a right, but like self-preservation, a duty to God. As such it is a judgment that men cannot part with according to the God of Nature. It is the first and foremost of our inalienable rights without which we can preserve no other."

Locke here says that holding government officials morally accountable is an act of "self-preservation." In addition, I think that one of Locke's most philosophical impacts on the American founding, in comparison to the history of governments, as it relates to the people's relationship to government, is that Locke's principles *equalize* the people in government to the people not in government. I will make reference to this quite often because it is absolutely essential to understanding the vivacity of the US Constitution. Thus, true equality is not only between the classes of people, but when the people in government are equal to the people not in government. This, I believe, is one, if not the primary reason the founders adopted Locke's political views. This is also, I believe, one of the primary reasons why many people are opposed to Locke's principles, especially those who argue for unlimited government, because they are conditioned upon being better than, and not equal to others. In addition, and very significantly, Locke was arguing his political views *tongue in cheek*, in reaction to the system of government that he existed under at the time, which was an oppressive Monarchy made up of nobles, royalty and peasants. In contrast to Locke, Thomas Hobbes wrote to actually validate the dictatorial, Divine right rule of King Charles II.

Benjamin Rush, who signed the *Declaration of Independence*, said Locke was, "an oracle as to the principles...of government."[15] Likewise, John Adams, another founding father, said of Locke's philosophy, "Mr. Locke...has steered his course into the unenlightened regions of the human mind, and like Columbus, has discovered a new world."[16] The founders rejected and were somewhat more silent on Hobbes because his views emphasized a more authoritarian, or totalitarian form of government. Hobbes believed that free people were incapable of governing themselves. Thus, Hobbes' political philosophy became more of a frame of reference on how not to create the new American government. Benjamin Franklin said that Locke was one of "the best English authors" for the study of "history, rhetoric, logic, moral and natural philosophy."[17] In 1872, historian Richard Frothingham said that Locke's principles produced the "leading principle of republicanism...summed up in the Declaration of Independence and became the American theory of government."[18] Here "republicanism" is not referring to a political party, but to the form of the

Federal government being a Republic, not a Democracy. In short, the American Revolution, with the intellectual help of Locke, was waged against the history of aristocracy, successfully, at first.

Spirited Debates

During the Constitutional Convention and the State Ratification debates, the founders were at odds over which type of government should replace the Articles of Confederation. The Articles had to be replaced due to a lack of financial and war powers allowed in Congress. Alexander Hamilton and George Washington generally supported the more Nationalist government idea, while Thomas Jefferson and James Madison supported the more strict Federalist government idea. Jefferson and Madison did eventually claim victory over Hamilton and Washington, even though Washington was not as verbal as Hamilton on the issues. Thus, the Convention concluded that the new government would remain Federal, as opposed to becoming National. The State Ratification debates then unpacked and articulated the actual meanings of the new US Constitution, as it related to the Federal government's increase in power from the Articles, the new role of the States, and their Compact with the new Federal government. During these ratification debates, a Bill of Rights was added to secure certain liberties, to restrict certain government powers and to secure certain State powers.

In spite of Madison and Jefferson's triumphant debates on how to interpret the US Constitution, Hamilton, with the support of banks and businessmen, formed the Federalist Party, where he would try to implement a more Nationalistic understanding of the Constitution. He succeeded temporarily under his *implied powers* ideology, whereby such Clauses as *Necessary and Proper*, and *General Welfare*, for example, could be interpreted loosely, thus allowing for the establishment of the first United State's Bank. In sound disagreement with Hamilton's scheme of implied powers, Jefferson and Madison broke away from the Federalist Party and formed the Democratic-Republican Party. Jefferson and Madison's arguments, that such Clauses must be directly tied to the specific Delegated Powers in Article 1, Section 8, became the sound standards of constitutional interpretation. Later as President, Madison reaffirms this in response to a Bill passed by Congress, which makes reference to various Clauses in the Constitution as authority for the Bill, and as a way to validate the Bill's intent and funding. Madison rebuttals that the Bill is based upon misinterpretation of the Constitution's Clauses and emphasized the following strict understanding,

> "To refer the power in question to the clause "to provide for common defense and general welfare" would be contrary to the established and consistent rules of interpretation, as rendering the special and careful enumeration of powers which follow the clause nugatory and improper. Such a view of the Constitution would have the effect of giving to Congress a general power of legislation instead of the defined and limited one hitherto understood to belong to them, the terms "common defense and general welfare" embracing every object and act within the purview of a legislative trust. It would have the effect of subjecting both the Constitution and laws of the several States in all cases not specifically exempted to be superseded by laws of Congress, it being expressly declared "that the Constitution of the United States and laws made in pursuance thereof shall be the supreme law of the land, and the judges of every state shall be bound thereby, anything in the constitution or laws of any State to the contrary notwithstanding."

...But seeing that such a power is not expressly given by the Constitution, and believing that it can not be deduced from any part of it without an inadmissible latitude of construction and reliance on insufficient precedents;...I have no option but to withhold my signature from it."[19]

Madison asserts here that if the Clauses in the Constitution, including the *Supremacy Clause*, are not specifically tied to the Enumerated Powers in Article 1, Section 8, then such interpretations of the Clauses, which then allow an increase in Federal power, are dependant upon "inadmissible latitude" and "insufficient precedents" and are thus withstanding to the Constitution itself. This is what Hamilton had done earlier as a way to establish a "National" Bank. If the *General Welfare* clause, for example, allowed Congress to create law outside of Delegated Powers, then such Delegated Powers would not have been constructed as a limitation in the Constitution from the start,

"Had no other enumeration or definition of the powers of the Congress been found in the Constitution, than the general expressions just cited, the authors of the objection might have had some color for it; though it would have been difficult to find a reason for so awkward a form of describing an authority to legislate in all possible cases. A power to destroy the freedom of the press, the trial by jury, or even to regulate the course of descents, or the forms of conveyances, must be very singularly expressed by the terms "to raise money for the general welfare."[20]

On the whole, if the Enumerated, or Delegated Powers do not specifically restrict the interpretations of the Clauses to those unambiguous

Powers in Article 1, Section 8, such liberties like *being armed, freedom of the press, political dissent,* or even *trial by jury,* will eventually be destroyed by the government, in the name of implementing those very Clauses, combined with the power of taxation, whereby law enforcement then legally deviates into the *Color of Law.* In a letter written to Albert Gallatin, Thomas Jefferson makes this point very clear, in response to the House being divided over this issue, that the General Welfare Clause, as with the other Constitutional Clauses, are limited to the Delegated Powers,

> "...that Congress had not unlimited powers to provide for the general welfare, but were restrained to those specifically enumerated; and that, as it was never meant they should provide for that welfare but by the exercise of the enumerated powers, so it could not have been meant they should raise money for purposes which the enumeration did not place under their action; consequently, that the specification of powers is a limitation of the purposes for which they may raise money....For in the phrase, "to lay taxes, to pay the debts and provide for the general welfare," it is a mere question of syntax, whether the two last infinitives are governed by the first or are distinct and co-ordinate powers; a **question unequivocally decided by the exact definition of powers immediately following.**"
> (bold added)

These *spirited debates* and deductions in which the Constitution was actually ratified, eventually lead to the termination of Hamilton's Federalist Party. Thus, limited Federalism, not Nationalism, again, succeeded as the form of American government. So, what is the difference between federalism and nationalism? The simple answer is *power.*

"A national government is a government of
the people of a single state or nation, united as
a community by what is termed the "social
compact,' and possessing complete and
perfect supremacy over persons and things, so
far as they can be made the lawful objects of
civil government. A federal government is
distinguished from a national government by
its being the government of a community of
independent and sovereign states, united by
compact."[21]

A Federal government is limited in power by Law and by the
direct consent of the people within sovereign States. The people then also
limit State power by direct consent, except in circumstances when the will
of the majority seeks to take the rights away from the minority or of others,
thus the Rule of Law prevails and secures the rights of the people. Madison
said during the Convention, "Each State, in ratifying the Constitution, is
considered as a sovereign body, independent of all others, and only to be
bound by its own voluntary act. In this relation, then, the new Constitution
will, if established, be a FEDERAL, and not a NATIONAL constitution."[22]

Law does not necessarily limit a National government's power,
nor are there sovereign States to consent to. National government is a
singular or central power. Comparing a National government to a Federal
government, Jefferson said,

"The several states composing the United
States of America are not united on the
principle of unlimited submission to their
general government; but by a compact under
the style and title of a Constitution for the
United States, and of amendments thereto,
they constituted a general government for
special purposes [and] delegated to that
government certain definite powers. **And,**

> **whensoever the general government assumes undelegated powers, its acts are unauthoritative, void, and of no force.** To this compact each state acceded as a state, and is an integral party, its co-states forming, as to itself, the other party. The government created by this compact was not made the exclusive or final judge of the extent of the powers delegated to itself, since that would have made its discretion, and not the Constitution the measure of its powers."[23] (bold added)

Jefferson is asserting here, in response to the *Alien and Sedition Acts*, that the Constitution is the measure of the government's power and not the government itself. Moreover, the Constitution is established to continue in its limitation upon Federal power, even though the Convention itself originally took place as a means to increase some Federal powers. Recall, again, that it was Jefferson and his later, like-minded colleague, Madison, who eventually won the debates on which type of government the new Constitution would actually establish and how the Constitution specifically related to the new increases in federal power, compared to the Articles. Today, political Parties still debate over the interpretation of such Clauses in the Constitution, rather than actually looking to the Constitution itself, as a whole. Thomas Paine said,

> "It is the nature and intention of a constitution to prevent governing by party, by establishing a common principle that shall limit and control the power and impulse of party, and that says to all parties, thus far shalt thou go and no further. But in the absence of a constitution, men look entirely to party; and instead of principle governing party, party governs principle."[24]

This "common principle" is the freedom philosophy of Locke, which encompasses limited government power, and not isolationism, as the neo-progressives cry out today. In addition, this bickering over power, then, is exactly how American Politics still operates today. "Leaders" do not look to source material or to Constitutional provisions, but still look to Party or legal precedent for a way around fundamental principles. America is perpetually defined as a *Federal Democratic-Republic,* by Constitution and by Compact with sovereign States.

Following the Civil War and the Reconstruction, it would be the rise of the *Progressive Era*, which would then disseminate misinterpretations of the 14th Amendment. This dissemination coupled with the increasingly neo-progressive, reinterpretation of the Constitution, through economically oriented precedent, and/or case law, became the intellectual springboard to "end State Sovereignty." More on this later. The common principle of limited power is still another underlying objective of the federal Constitution today, and the spirit in which it was ratified, and in which it should still be understood and interpreted today.

If the government is not limited by changeless provisions, which are enforced by the people, there can be no liberty. Madison emphasized this, "I entirely concur in the propriety of resorting to the sense in which the Constitution was accepted and ratified by the nation. In that sense *alone* it is the *legitimate* Constitution. And if that is not the guide in expounding it, there may be no security."[25] This *security* Madison speaks of is the security of life, liberty, and property ownership, coupled with other inalienable rights of the people. If the Constitution is not interpreted within the spirit *and* letter in which it was ratified, these freedoms will no longer be secure. Jefferson also conveyed this,

"On every question of construction of our Constitution, let us carry ourselves back to the time when the Constitution was adopted, recollect the spirit manifested in the debates, and instead of trying what meaning may be squeezed out of the text, or invented against it, conform to the probable one in which it was passed."[26]

In this spirit, even Hamilton, who advocated a National government said, "Constitutions should consist only of general provisions; the reason is that they must necessarily be *permanent*, and that they cannot calculate for the *possible* change of things."[27] This infers a reasonable and necessary increase in power, as it relates to government keeping up with the times, not by speculation, however, and provided that the core, or *permanent* provisions of a constitution remain. For example, a Congressional Declaration of War, Separation of Powers or the Bill of Rights, are permanent provisions of the Constitution designed to limit government and to not be violated by government. When secondary laws (statutes) override these permanent provisions, they are deemed color of law and arbitrary. Yet, the fear of Madison and Jefferson was that such power would eventually lead to too much power, and it has. Jefferson particularly feared the battle between the federal government and the states over the use of the Constitution as a justification to increase power over one or the other. This battle between states' rights and the federal government rages on today, and has since the beginning. But, Jefferson concluded that it would be the federal government that would ultimately encroach upon liberty, and that the States are ultimately responsible to stop it. In a letter written to Archibald Stuart in 1791, Jefferson wrote,

"I shall hazard my own ideas to you as hastily as my business obliges me. I wish to preserve the line drawn by the federal constitution between the general & particular governments as it stands at present, and to take every prudent means of preventing either from stepping over it. Tho' the experiment has not yet had a long enough course to show us from which quarter encroachments are most to be feared, yet it is easy to foresee from the nature of things that the encroachments of the state governments will tend to an excess of liberty which will correct itself (as in the late instance) while those of the general government will tend to monarchy, which will fortify itself from day to day, instead of working its own cure, as all experience shows. I would rather be exposed to the inconveniencies attending too much liberty than those attending too small a degree of it. Then it is important to strengthen the state governments: and as this cannot be done by any change in the federal constitution, (for the preservation of that is all we need contend for,) it must be done by the states themselves, erecting such barriers at the constitutional line as cannot be surmounted either by themselves or by the general government."

Still today, "progressives" in general, favor the more nationalistic type of government proposed by Hamilton and others, whereby a more central power governs America, even though the States created and sustain the Federal government. What we have seen during the debates, and what we see today, is a continuation of the underlying dichotomy of Hobbes and Locke within the idea of central vs. limited power. Yet, as Jefferson warned, and from the experience of America thus far, the fear of Madison and Jefferson, of the *silent encroachments* against liberty by a centralized power, through usurpations of State sovereignty, has proven itself to be sound.

The founders of American government adhered to a very different political philosophy than leaders do today. Over the course of American history, great "progressive" efforts have been made to admonish America's founding principles. Madison said that it would be the other two branches of government that would, over the course of time, transform the original meaning of the Constitution, the Rule of Law, into something else, "...the success of the usurpation will depend on the executive and judiciary departments, which are to expound and give effect to the legislative acts; and in a last resort a remedy must be obtained from the people, who can by the elections of more faithful representatives, annul the acts of the usurpers."[28] Over time, these usurpations have become *legal precedent* and a justification for arbitrary laws. And, in time, the "progressive," social engineering of the past, present and future of *faithful representatives* away from these founding principles have also derived from legal precedent. One of these "remedies" against usurpations has potentially become law enforcement, at all levels of American government, which is confined to the Executive Branches, while precedent is confined to the Judicial Branches. Thomas Jefferson, in 1821, wrote in a letter,

> "It has long, however, been my opinion, and I have never shrunk from its expression, ...that the germ of dissolution of our Federal Government is in the Constitution of the Federal Judiciary -- an irresponsible body, (for impeachment is scarcely a scare-crow,) working like gravity by night and by day, gaining a little to-day and a little to-morrow, end advancing its noiseless step, like a thief, over the field of jurisdiction, until all shall be usurped from the States, and the Government of all be consolidated into one."[29]

Like Jefferson said, a little usurpation today and a little tomorrow, will ultimately create a centralized power. Over time, Law and secondary law, throughout America, have digressed from America's founding ideology and have become more arbitrary, designed to secure and protect the interests of the state, as in history. Permanent provisions have become impermanent. It appears now that we have deviated into a National government, rather than being a limited, Federal government. Government is an entity, made up of other people, who are subject to human nature, involuntarily, like all people, and who are no different than you and I. Entities can't think, feel or exploit violence, only people can. When the greed for power, the authoritarian spirit, and the exploitation of violence become dominate again within the entity of government, such progress towards liberty actually digresses back into the *subject and master* plateau of human history. This is what's happening now in America.

The ancients desired individual liberty, but it never came to pass, because of the authoritarian will of the other people who were in government. This ancient idea of liberty, says Benjamin Constant, speaking within the context of the French Revolution, declared that freedom came collectively and was a *privilege* that could always be taken away by the other people in government. He said that liberty "consisted in exercising collectively, but not directly, several parts of the sovereignty" and "with this collective freedom, the complete subjection of the individual to the authority of the community." Under ancient liberty ideology, "all private actions were submitted to a severe surveillance" and "no importance was given to individual independence."[30] The idea of individual liberty as a fundamental and natural right has always had a history, just absent genuine practice, until the birth of America. Yet as it relates to the ancient understanding of liberty, as only a privilege, and not as a fundamental right, this is where America is now headed.

Civilized Society

People today, still, and in general, have learned nothing from history. History simply repeats itself. And, history is repeating itself now. The will of the majority or of a certain class of people do not equate to what a civilized society is, as is the case in what, historically, the ruling classes have determined, by way of forced *social engineering*. This only produces the appearance of "goodness" in the majority's will. During the middle ages, for example, the majority believed in witches, and, state employees, with the power to inflict violence in the name of "morality," burned witches at the stake. Was this a civilized society? The Church made it illegal for individuals to study the scriptures for themselves, and this was enforced by the State. It was "unlawful" to read the scriptures. Was this civilized society? When Galileo was tortured by the Papacy for his beliefs, was that civilized society? Were the destruction of the Native Americans and their culture civilized? When Jackson incited the *Trail of Tears*, was this civilized society? Was the partial genocide of the Native Americans civilized society? Slavery was an accepted and historical practice throughout all of human history, in every religion, government and country. Was the world civilized then? Was the Fugitive Slave Act in America a reflection of civilized society and of sound constitutional law? Today, most people believe that the United States is a Democracy and that *equality* should be forced upon all people. Does this mean America is a civilized society? The ruling classes today and in the past would argue yes, as long as the ruling classes are getting their way. In addition, these few examples of "civilized" societies in history were run by a system of laws that determined that anyone who does not obey them is being "unlawful." So what makes America a civilized society today? Some say one must look at the prison system, for example, "The degree of civilization in a society can be judged by entering its prisons," says Fyodor Dostoevsky.

> "Today, more American men and women struggle to survive in prison than do the citizens of any other country in the world. And here correctional officers, staff, administrators and wardens are virtual royalty, holding unquestioned authority over the lives, circumstances and futures of those entrusted to their care. This is ironic because 'care' is a word ill-used to describe the situations of many who today suffer abuse, discrimination and in some cases torture at the hands of the often ruthless "public officials" who wield power over Secure Housing Units (SHUs) for selected inmates and an Adjustment Center (AC) for the condemned."[31]

Likewise, even Nelson Mandela said of civilized society, "A nation should not be judged by how it treats its highest citizens, but its lowest ones."[32] America has more of its own people in prisons today than any other country. Just the state of Louisiana alone, as of 2014, has five times more people in prison than the entire country of Iran.[33] Moreover, 86 percent of all federal inmates are incarcerated for *victimless* crimes, which costs tax payers nearly 50K per year, per inmate.[33.5] This is something to think about, as it relates to living in a "free" country. People in America today, for the most part, are still very "medieval" in their thinking, because most people take for granted that civilized society is defined by what "authorities" and the ruling classes say it is. Albert Einstein, arguably one of the smartest men in history, said, "A foolish faith in authority is the worst enemy of the truth."[34] This is also called *Group Think.*

So how do the ruling classes, in history and today, always get their way? How does a ruling class always get to determine what civilized society is and then from this rationalize such immoral acts like witch burning, theft, or genocide? The ruling classes, throughout history and today, get their way through their monopoly on violence, and their exploitation of the use and the threat of force. In America, as with authoritarian countries in the past and present, the ruling classes get their way through law enforcement. In government, there are always going to be people who want to use government to force their will on other people, to control other people, to "legally" take property from other people, using arguments that allege the "common good," "public policy," "public safety," and the like. These are all demoralized forms of inequality that the American Rule of Law undermines. Yet, all these excuses for power and control in history and even today are defined by the ruling classes as *civilized society*.

The most basic argument for inequality in history has been class, generally by birth, and by what the ruling class defines as, again, civilized society. Locke was a man, as there were many others, who philosophically sought to change the fabric of society's thinking and fundamentally demoralize the *status quo* that the ruling class, in England at the time, had established. Also, Locke's philosophy of government critically analyzed the conceptual apparatus of what the status quo throughout history has been. The founders used this, not only to challenge the intrusive and abusive history and power of past governments and their ruling classes, but also to make equal, by Law, all people, and to codify fundamental principles that are ethically in contrast to there even being a such thing as a ruling class, which even in the state of nature, is immoral. See the irony?

Alexander Hamilton, who wanted a big, central, aristocratic government, even argued for the continuance of a ruling class,

> "All communities divide themselves into the few and the many. The first are the rich and well born, the other the mass of the people. The voice of the people has been said to be the voice of God; and however generally this maxim has been quoted and believed, it is not true in fact. The people are turbulent and changing; they seldom judge or determine right. Give therefore to the first class a distinct, permanent share in the government. They will check the unsteadiness of the second, and as they cannot receive any advantage by a change, they therefore will ever maintain good government."[35]

Hamilton wanted to continue the history of aristocracy within America. Fortunately, aristocracy, nor Hamilton's idea of national government did not come to pass, or did it? To truly be a *civilized society* and for humanity to truly evolve into a moral, just and free people, means that the responsibility that comes with liberty must be coupled with government's charge to secure such liberty, through education and cultivation, and not by way of containment. Thus, people, especially in government, will not repeat history, whereby the exploitation of the weak, the authoritarian social and financial micromanagement of the people and their property, as a means to secure the wealth of the people in government, and, also to secure the wealth of those people intimately connected to those people in government, will not gain a foothold. But, authoritarian governments tend to suppress such education in practice, because the lack thereof continues to make unequal those people in government to those people not in government. Likewise, and most importantly, society evolves into a moral and just society where the arbitrary threat and use of violence is not exploited by a ruling class to uphold all those historical and contemporary attributes aforementioned. When free people work together with, and are equal to, and are cultivated by the people in government to be responsible for their freedom, when the light of reason and the moral conscious of free individuals collectively work against the autocratic will of a ruling class, with its military industrial complex, its repressive social engineering, its monopoly on force, its corporatism, and its legal plundering of property, this is the beginning of civilized society. Utopia does not come about by government, but by evolution of mind and humanity as a whole. The less free people are, the less they evolve and the less education is necessary. The Dark Ages are an example of this. It is an intellectual and spiritual mistake to assume advances in technology, over and above the moral evolution of human nature, as a premise for concluding society as being civilized.

Public Education

Today, it appears that America is more like Hobbes' Leviathan, than of Lock's principles of liberty. Even many "progressives" today cite Hobbes as a way to accentuate their political ideology. Hobbesian philosophy can play a background into many types of governments around the world. Therefore, perspective, not necessarily statutes, combined with knowledge of the America's Rule of Law, must be government's model to secure liberty combined with education and cultivated responsibility. This appearance of a more Hobbesian society is, in part, a result of the public school systems no longer teaching Locke's principles as a foundation for American government, of what an individual's fundamental rights are or how to defend them, and what the just role of government is, or how to be independent, self-reliant and personally responsible. Instead, state dependency and blind obedience is being socially engineered in schools as what it means to be personally responsible. Thomas Jefferson said to James Madison, in this regard,

> "And say, finally, whether peace is best preserved by giving energy to the government or information to the people. This last is the most certain and the most legitimate engine of government. Educate and inform the whole mass of the people. Enable them to see that it is their interest to preserve peace and order, and they will preserve them. And it requires no very high degree of education to convince them of this. **They are the only sure reliance for the preservation of our liberty.**"[36] (bold added)

Also, Thomas Jefferson said, "I know no safe depositary of the ultimate powers of the society but the people themselves; and if we think them not enlightened enough to exercise their control with a wholesome discretion, the remedy is not to take it from them, but to inform their discretion by education. This is the true corrective of abuses of constitutional power."[37] Moreover, Madison emphasized this in securing the Republic, that public education,

> "ought to be favorite objects with every free people. **They throw that light over the public mind which is the best security against crafty & dangerous encroachments on the public liberty.** They are the nurseries of skilful Teachers for the schools distributed throughout the Community. They are themselves schools for the particular talents required for some of the Public Trusts, on the able execution of which the welfare of the people depends. They multiply the educated individuals from among whom the

people may elect a due portion of their public
Agents of every description; more especially of
those who are to frame the laws; by the
perspicuity, the consistency, and the stability, as
well as by the just & equal spirit of which the
great social purposes are to be answered."[38] (Bold
added)

What are the "great social purposes" that Madison refers to?
Madison continues,

"Throughout the Civilized World, nations are
courting the praise of fostering Science and the
useful Arts, and are opening their eyes to the
principles and the blessings of Representative
Government. The American people owe it to
themselves, and to the cause of free Government,
to prove by their establishments for the
advancement and diffusion of Knowledge, that
their political Institutions, which are attracting
observation from every quarter, and are respected
as Models, by the new-born States in our own
Hemisphere, are as favorable to the intellectual
and moral improvement of Man as they are
conformable to his individual & social Rights.
What spectacle can be more edifying or more
seasonable, than that of Liberty & Learning, each
leaning on the other for their mutual & surest
support?"

Representative government by direct consent, individualism,
liberty, learning, morality, inalienable rights, are all the sound progressive
intentions of public education, as emphasized by the founders. Instead,
public education today is forced, and, generally unbeknownst to the
teachers themselves, to instruct our youth to become "good citizens" and
"good workers." Thus, the end game is that good citizens do not question
authority. Also, public education today socially engineers, again, that

obedience is equal to *responsibility*, which is an intellectual fallacy, because it teaches children what to think rather than how to think. This is contrary to the sound intentions of the founders in establishing publicly funded education, which was to potentially enable all free people to equally participate in government actions, to understand their fundamental rights and how to defend them, to engage in property rights, by holding government officials accountable to the Rule of Law, all through the basics of Math, Reading, Writing and the Sciences, to be a light to the world. This was genuine progress in a world where most people could not read or write and most people had no access to education unless they were of nobility and so on. Public education today is forced upon children as a means to secure economic activity, not liberty.

This new "progressive" intention for public education that arose in the early 20th century, at the rise of the industrial age is evident in a speech by Woodrow Wilson to the 1909 NYC High school Teacher's Association, where he said, "We want one class of persons to have a liberal education, and we want another class of persons, a very much larger class of necessity in every society, to forgo the privilege of a liberal education and fit themselves to perform specific difficult manual tasks." Not only does this subtlety emphasis class and inequality, but this also conveys the intent of socially engineering "good worker" ideology through the public schools. This social engineering also attempts to curb potential *political dissent* by advocating absolute authority in government. John Taylor Gatto, a former NY State teacher of the year, has emphasized over years of study through various books he wrote, that the end game of early 20th century to modern American public education systems is to prepare students to be good, obedient workers who do not question government authority, nor do they understand what genuine liberty and inalienable rights are, or how to defend them. Gatto says,

> "This specific engineering problem confronted this key group of business people and philosophers at the beginning of the 20th century. How could a proud liberty-loving nation of independent families and villages be turned from its historic tradition of self-reliance and independence? Grown ups were unlikely to be tractable. The history, the highly personalized practice of local schooling, offered another possibility. Social thinkers have speculated for millennia, that a political state which successfully seizes control of the young could perform economic miracles."[39]

Self-reliance, independence, knowledgeable defense of one's rights, responsibility through self-education, and the like, are all threats to modern socially engineered society, and are being undermined for the sake of forced economic activity. Moreover, youth today are also taught, subconsciously, to live comfortably within a *police state*, that uniformed authorities with guns will always be there to enforce what a citizen can and cannot do, which is evidenced by metal detectors, armed guards, police and cameras all over public school campuses today. As Josiah Quincy, the Mayor of Boston once said, "Every child should be educated to obey authority."[39.2] It is as though children today are being conditioned to live comfortably within a minimum-security prison. Murray Rothbard says in his book *Education: Free and Compulsory* that, "the effect of progressive education is to destroy independent thought in the child…. Instead, children learn to revere heroic symbols…or to follow the domination of the "group"…. The child has little chance to develop any systematic reasoning powers."[39.4] Furthermore, kids are arrested on campuses and suspended from schools today for simply being kids. Of course, many "progressives" argue that such "enforcement" is necessary to keep our children safe. I seriously question the mental aptitude of an individual, especially a teacher, who calls the cops on a child simply pretending to play with a gun. I also very earnestly question the cop's cerebral and moral fitness, which would then arrest a child for simply pretending to play with a gun. These are serious cognitive deficiencies within authority figures. These mental deficiencies exist within the people who are to be "trusted." They have, as a matter of "policy," become the deliberate sufferers of social engineering and who are "in charge" of our youth. Where does the blame begin? This *new style* of progress, or what I call *neo-progressive,* attempts to socially engineer our children into a very different social compact from what our founding fathers established, by way of public education. Political correctness, for example, has become a debilitating disease on the mind, limiting thinking to a socially engineered grid. Thomas Sowell, a modern political philosopher and economist recently noted in an article, that society is increasingly becoming a non-thinking society; "Some have said that we are living in a post-industrial era, while others have said that we are living in a post-racial era. But growing evidence suggests that we are living in a post-thinking era." He adds, "In an age when scientists are creating artificial intelligence, too many of our educational institutions seem to be creating artificial stupidity.... We have gotten so intimidated by political correctness."[39.5] The most compelling evidence of *forced* political correctness in our public school systems is a child being taught what to think rather than how to think. As Nietzsche the great German philosopher once said, "The surest way to corrupt the youth is to instruct them to hold in higher esteem those who think alike rather than those who think differently."

Social engineering of our youth into "good workers" is also evidenced today by school systems censoring the Internet, for example, by blocking access to websites that emphasize the very educational focus the founders established public education for. To illustrate; a student at a Connecticut High School recently decided to write a paper on *Gun Rights* and *Gun Control* statistics. Upon trying to research the issues, the school had censored his efforts through a program called SonicWALL of any and all pro-gun websites and even GOP and Conservative related websites. Yet, all the websites that emphasized gun control, Planned Parenthood and the Democratic Party were not censored.[40] Why? As it relates to public education today, Ron Paul, the former US Congressman and presidential candidate has said,

> "When government usurps a parent's right to control their child's education, it is inevitable that the child will be taught the values of government officials, rather than of the parents. The result is an education system with a built-in bias toward statism. Over time, government-controlled education can erode the people's knowledge of, and appreciation for, the benefits of a free society."[41]

The censoring of and the controlling of information, as a way to force political correctness and the like, all as a means to thwart political activism, individualism and independent thinking, will eventually become rampant within higher education also, even though students within higher education are adults. This is social engineering, not education.

Cleon Skousen, a former FBI agent and former police chief, wrote a book in the nineteen fifties called *The Naked Communist*, in which he conveys that a Marxist–Leninist philosophy is successfully infiltrating all governments through a series of goals. As it relates to socially engineering the youth in America, Goal #17; "Get control of the schools. Use them as transmission belts for socialism and current Communist propaganda. Soften the curriculum. Get control of teachers' associations. Put the party line in textbooks." The mere absence of teaching children what their rights are and how to defend them, in comparison to the time when American schools did same, is and of itself, subtlety, corroboration of such Marxist philosophy. For example, the Federal Courts have ruled that the 2nd Amendment protects a *fundamental* right to own and carry a gun in public in both *Heller vs. DC* and *Palmer vs. DC*. When a young boy at a public school is suspended and punished for merely pretending to have a gun while playing on the playground, this is itself, socially engineering the boy away from knowing what his *fundamental* rights are and the responsibility that attaches to those rights. This is not a single case, but common. The teaching of such responsibilities that attach to liberty should be one of the essentials of basic education in America. A legitimate government's education system would encourage and legislate the teaching of the responsibility associated with such a right as being armed, speaking one's mind, owning property, and the like. Yet, school officials more often call the police instead and have the children arrested, by school policy. Even in Hitler's book *Mein Kampf*, he says, "The state must declare the child to be the most precious treasure of the people. As long as the government is perceived as working for the benefit of the children, the people will happily endure almost any curtailment of liberty and almost any deprivation."

America may also appear to be more like Hobbes' Leviathan, in part, because more contemporary leaders within American government do not like the idea of being *equal* to the people that they are charged to represent or "rule" over, thus a Hobbesian type of government seems more appealing to them. Otherwise, a Lockean government, whereby the people's liberty, equality, property, fundamental rights and privacy are secure, and equal to everyone else's, would be obvious. And, most importantly, such responsibility associated with the latter attributes of liberty would be taught, encouraged and apparent. To work against this foundation of liberty that Locke and the founding fathers established and thus secured in the US Constitution is not progressive, but neo-progressive.

How many politicians today do you know of that study political philosophy, study history, read the Constitution, hold an original thought, or even exercise thinking outside of their daily political experience, absent a lawyer to articulate their political ideology and/or a lobbyist to fund it? "Leaders" today are self proclaimed demi-gods and demagogues, who are generally sociopathic, cognitively dissonant and who generally operate from the German philosopher Georg Hegel's Dialectic; *problem, reaction, and solution*. This is because the people who want to be in government should not be there, and the ones who should be in government do not want to be there. Government attracts the easily corruptible. Hegel wrote that the state "has supreme right against the individual, whose supreme duty is to be a member of the State... for the right of the world spirit is above all special privileges." Hegel thus inspired Karl Marx, who then wrote the Communist Manifesto. Hegel's Dialectic infers that the ruling classes, or those in real power, can control the masses by deliberately creating division, or conflict, like with republicans vs. democrats, as a *divide and conquer* strategy, which is archaic itself. Of course the masses don't see this, they only see the propaganda indirectly. Once the division, or *chaos*, is established and the masses react, the state steps in with the solution, creating *order* out of chaos, ending in more authority for the state over the people. The populace, then, through social engineering, takes for granted that those people in government, who posses indirect authority, even a little, are almost always right. Where does this come from, the threat of force? Additionally, there are actually Americans today who would prefer to live under a monarchy, or a central power with absolute authority, not only for the simplicity of its decrees, but also for the shadow under its wing. This may be beneficial for a time, however, if, and only if, the era proves to be benevolent. Thus shudders the probability.

Neo-progressives argue that the permanent provisions in the US Constitution are "outdated" and must either be repealed or reinterpreted in a "modern" light. Such pseudo-political ideologies lead to the restructuring of the "real" world. In the case of America, the founding fathers, by way of Locke's political philosophy, created and restructured the "real" world, resulting in the American Rule of Law, which is the US Constitution. The US Constitution not only governs this nation, it also governs the government. In the Declaration, Thomas Jefferson directly opposed the Hobbesian idea that government should have singular and absolute power over the people. Jefferson asserted that, "When a long train of abuses and usurpations, pursuing invariably the same Object evinces a design to reduce them under absolute Despotism, it is their right, it is their duty, to throw off such Government." These "abuses and usurpations" derive from the unrestrained negative aspects of human nature operating in government. Thus, "it becomes necessary for one people to dissolve the political bands which have connected them with another." What is this "despotism" that Jefferson refers to? Despotism is the absolute rule over people by an individual or by a group of individuals, also known as a ruling class. What is the "Object" that Jefferson refers to? Power! This is fundamentally why the US Constitution is not "outdated", as neo-progressives like to argue, because the Constitution is intended as a moral force, codified to restrain the negative aspects of human nature that have historically dominated government power. This new and progressive system of government in America was designed to equalize the people in government to the people not in government, through checks and balances, limited government power and through the Bill of Rights. Today, an Orwellian type of philosophy seeks to take hold of the political landscape. Not necessarily through a genuine progressive view, but by a neo-progressive view. Progressive government is a good thing. Progressive actions deviate into neo-progressive actions when the intent is specific to covertly change our system of government from within, by weakening or circumventing Constitutional restraints upon those people who are in government. Neo-progressives hold a very different view of what American government should be, and their actions go against what America actually is.

Government itself is, again, only a mere entity, made up of other people, no better or smarter than you and I. The *equality* of all people, as asserted in the Declaration, was a radical transition from previous governments in history, where people were born unequal to others and were ruled over by other people who thought that they knew what was best for everyone else. America was intended to be the opposite, where all people are born equal, and are collectively self-governed through this Rule of Law. The emphasis on the equality of all people, in and out of government, was crucial to creating a moral, limited government that is deliberate to secure the fundamental, natural rights and the property ownership of the individual. This collection of free and independent individuals secured an equal opportunity for all, whereby anyone had the chance to be great in their own right, provided the means to become great were coupled with an adherence to, not just a respect of, another's inalienable rights of life, liberty and property.

The mental caliber that the founding fathers possessed no longer exists within American "leadership." Today, for the most part, only imitators and false proponents of Locke's principals of moral and just government have risen up throughout American politics, masquerading only the appearance of the intent to advance liberty within American policy. There is a profound difference between the founding fathers and those who operate in the political system of government today. The difference is that the founders actually existed within and experienced despotism first hand. They knew history, they also knew what overly authoritative governments have been like. "Liberation" from such rule was something longed for deep within their souls, at the risk of death. Yet, people in American government today are actually digressive, in the name of controlling population, in the name of improved technologies, they have actually become more intrusive to individuals than the government was to individuals that our founding fathers fought against. Quintessential, neo-progressive ideology is predicated on this intrusiveness of government into the private life of the individual, for public safety, of course.

The founding fathers also understood directly from Locke's political philosophy that personal freedom was greater than all other aspects of human existence. Thus, they created a system of government by which the disadvantages of too much freedom were far less an inconvenience than those disadvantages of no freedom, or very limited freedom. As Thomas Jefferson once said, "I would rather be exposed to the inconveniences attending too much liberty than to those attending too small a degree of it."[42] This intention to be free and to sustain being free is what was eternalized and codified as the principles of our federal

Constitution. Liberty is the absence of the self-serving restraint of government power. Secondary laws are only sound when they secure, enhance and/or advance our natural rights, and our liberties. This includes necessary regulations to sustain the well being of society, like through reasonable taxation, for example. Ultimately, contrary to mere taxation, liberty is sustained through an individual's ownership of property, because rights originate from property, especially through the ownership of self, and not by way of government. Sound secondary laws, or statutes, for example, designed to regulate the privilege of driving, actually enhance and advance the fundamental right to travel. Today, however, neo-progressive policy makers like to create legislation intended to curb offense, to extinguish the probability of "what if" scenarios, to socially engineer not only our children, but government officials, like law enforcement, away from Locke's principles of liberty, and, most importantly, to secure revenue, power and state dependency within the majority. This ends in people being conditioned to look for solutions to social and financial problems in the government. Nobody has a right to not be offended. Hindsight shows that government intervention into the social fabric of society actually creates more problems, and has created more problems by simply not leaving people alone. The founders argued this from experience. Frederick Bastiat, a French philosopher and economist said that such social problems are not solved by the state, but by liberty,

> "It seems to me that this is theoretically right, for whatever the question under discussion—whether religious, philosophical, political, or economic; whether it concerns prosperity, morality, equality, right, justice, progress, responsibility, cooperation, property, labor, trade, capital, wages, taxes, population,

finance, or government—at whatever point on the scientific horizon I begin my researches, I invariably reach this one conclusion: The solution to the problems of human relationships is to be found in liberty."[43]

The end result of state intervention into all aspects of society is the reduction of the disadvantages of too much freedom, thus securing state dependency in the masses. Our Rule of Law has deviated into the *color of law*, in that nowadays only the appearance of *lawfulness* exists within policy or legislation. Unlawful legislation has actually become "legal" legislation by way of precedent. Thus, there is an underlying difference between what is legal and lawful.

The desire for liberty that the founders had established has been extinguished, due to the usurpation of power. Individual liberty is not only being absent from government restraint, it is also freedom from the will of others who want to use the government to marginalize others who think and believe differently. Recall Locke's freedom from theocracy, for example. American liberty is deliberately secured within the context of our federal Constitution and within many state Constitutions, and this liberty has been greatly threatened by the increase of state dependency and neo-progressive, political ideology that then exploits law enforcement.

Any person who takes a government position of "service" by which they swear a constitutional oath and who then intently does the opposite, is not only guilty of corruption and being authoritarian, they unethically violate the light of reason, which sustains moral and limited government. This is, in part, because these people think that they are above and beyond the reproach of others. This *arbitrary* rule over other people is purely acting on one's own negative human nature. By definition, being despotic is executing power that is unlawful, thus converting the oath into a mere formality. This is why it has become so important for neo-progressives and authoritarians in government to "reinterpret" the Constitution as "living." Law enforcement has become the tool by which these neo-progressives have undermined Locke's principals and have infiltrated more *collectivist* views into the American system of government. Even Alexander Hamilton made the point, as it relates to enforcement at the time, that, "they shall always keep in mind that their countrymen are free and as such are impatient of everything that bears that least mark of a domineering Spirit. They will, therefore, refrain, with the most guarded circumspection, from whatever has the semblance of haughtiness, rudeness, or insult."[44] When people in government feel that they are not equal, but better than the people not in government, a domineering spirit will prevail. The US Supreme Court, in its ruling opinion of *Laird vs. Tatum* (1972), as it relates to the military and law enforcement violating the people's rights, Justice Burger asserts,

"This case involves a cancer in our body politic. It is a measure of the disease which afflicts us. Army surveillance, like Army regimentation, is at war with the principles of the First Amendment. Those who already walk submissively will say there is no cause for alarm. But submissiveness is not our heritage. **The First Amendment was designed to allow rebellion to remain as our heritage.** The Constitution was designed to keep government off the backs of the people. The Bill of Rights was added to keep the precincts of belief and expression, of the press, of political and social activities free from surveillance. The Bill of Rights was designed to keep agents of government and official eavesdroppers away from assemblies of people. The aim was to allow men to be free and independent and to assert their rights against government. There can be no influence more paralyzing of that objective than Army surveillance. When an intelligence officer looks over every nonconformist's shoulder in the library, or walks invisibly by his side in a picket line, or infiltrates his club, the America once extolled as the voice of liberty heard around the world no longer is cast in the image which Jefferson and Madison designed, but more in the Russian image…" (bold added)

Rights

Thomas Jefferson argued that government power in America is to be limited to an individual's rights and not necessarily by law, "Rightful liberty is unobstructed action according to our will, within the limits drawn around us by the equal rights of others. I do not add 'within the limits of the law'; because law is often but the tyrant's will, and always so when it violates the right of an individual."[44.5] Some argue that rights are a fictionary means for people to buy into the great lie of government being an "absolute" necessity for preserving social and economic peace, that no such thing as rights really exist, nor do inalienable rights attach to human beings by nature. Imagine a dark cloud with a silver lining. Is there really a silver lining? It's a nonsensical question. This is true when rights are not understood, nor defended by those who claim to possess them. Does love really exist? If so, how? Like love, if rights are not defended with one's entire person, they are lost. Love is not something that attaches to you like an ear, or a mustache. Neither do rights attach to you like an ear or a mustache. You don't walk around and then literally trip over some love, even though it may feel that way when one *falls* in love. Nor do you walk around and stumble over some rights, like you would if rights were a brick on the ground. Inalienable rights attach to human beings by nature, internally and eternally. And like love, inalienable rights are innate and a quintessential aspect of human existence. Absent love, life is virtually meaningless. Absent rights, life can become meaningless and subjugated. Rights must be defended at all costs if they are to exist as a bond within a consensual relationship, because like love, this defense, coupled with its actualization, is what qualifies and quantifies a right's existence. Moreover, rights, like love, are a sentimental and cognitive driving force that takes hard work and compromise for such a bond to succeed in the best interest of the relationship as a whole. As it relates to government, rights are also a part of the driving force within the relationship that the American people have with their government. The people surrender, in part, their absolute control, and chaos, in exchange for just and morally limited government, who then brings order, while also defending the people's rights. Today, government intrusion is more tolerated because government politicians promise to "respect" the people's rights, rather than adhere to them. Politicians lie and play on the people's sentiments to get elected, especially within a religious context, and then they directly appeal to special interests, which then help create laws that work directly against rights, as a means to secure those special interests. In other words, government is cheating on the American people with special interests. Consequently, the rights that hold the relationship between the people and government together are no longer sincere. Marriage is a contract that secures the relationship between two consenting adults, with love at the center. The Constitution can be viewed as a contract that secures the relationship between two consenting parties, the people not in government and the people in government, and rights are at the center. Recall, there is no real existence of government, only real in the sense of how a silver lining exists. Government is a mere entity only made up of other human beings by contract with the people at large.

Under the law of contract, for example, when an individual *registers* property with a government bureaucracy, they surrender true ownership. They surrender the rights attached to that property, in exchange for *legal possession*. The property itself doesn't have rights painted or written on it. True ownership is absolute control. Likewise, via contract, an individual surrenders their inalienable or natural rights, in exchange for *legal privileges*. This is a corruption of the intent of the right to contract, and the social compact at large, between the people in government with the people not in government. Virtually every time an individual signs a government document, it is a contract that surrenders rights in some way or another. A signature is consent. This is not just and moral compromise, nor is this just and moral reciprocity of the social contract, because, such a compulsory act is predicated upon the ignorance of one party over another, and guess who the ignorant party is?

> "It is the greatest absurdity to suppose it in the power of one, or of any number of men, at the entering into society to renounce their essential natural rights, or the means of preserving those rights, when the grand end of civil government, from the very nature of its institution, is for the support, protection, and defence of those very rights; the principal of which, as is before observed, are life, liberty, and property. If men, through fear, fraud, or mistake, should in terms renounce or give up an essential natural right, the eternal law of reason and the grand end of society would absolutely vacate such renunciation."[45]

Sam Adams is clear here, as it relates to the just and moral role of government, that the *inalienable* or natural rights of the people are not to be merely respected; they are to be adhered to, like love in a relationship. It makes no sense to merely respect your wife and then faithfully abide by your vows when you don't really love her. The neo-progressive reasoning that our Constitution is old-fashioned and no longer realistic is coupled with the effort to redefine what the people's fundamental rights are. Today the "legal" system is actually full of legal and political jargon that tries to relate itself intimately to the concept of *rights*, through language manipulation. The neo-progressive spirit within modern jurisprudence, it appears, has in many ways avoided the foundational conviction of *inalienable* rights for the sake of, and by reiterating concepts such as, *civil rights* and/or legal privilege*s. Inalienable*, which is essentially defined as "unsurrenderable," is the highest of all rights, which are natural and fundamental. These rights can only be surrendered by consent or criminal conviction. Natural/inalienable rights are the most bothersome and restrictive to governmental power, which is why you never hear the term used within modern, political and "legal" jargon. In addition, the neo-progressive legal system today tends to blend "civil rights," "civil liberties," "fundamental rights," "inalienable rights," "natural rights" and "legal privileges," all into the one concept of *rights*. All these terms cannot be legitimately categorized under one term because such an effort undermines the idea that a right limits government power, especially when a *privilege*, for example, is granted by and regulated by government and is thus, also termed a right. It is easier for the people in government to simply manipulate all these terms into one term so that the general population holds no affinity to such a term like *inalienable*, because that would empower them to discern between a right over a privilege. The defense of rights is not a good thing for authoritarians. Thomas Paine, in The *Rights of Man*, makes note of how governments do just that, manipulate and reduce rights to privileges, which in the end, becomes a tool of injustice,

"It is a perversion of terms to say that a charter gives rights. It operates by a contrary effect — that of taking rights away. Rights are inherently in all the inhabitants; but charters, by annulling those rights, in the majority, leave the right, by exclusion, in the hands of a few... They... consequently are instruments of injustice ... The fact, therefore, must be that the individuals, themselves, each, in his own personal and sovereign right, entered into a contract with each other to produce a government: and this is the only mode in which governments have a right to arise, and the only principle on which they have a right to exist."

Paine here is resisting aristocracy and the inequality that comes with it. So, as it relates to *rights*, I want to argue that, in practice, and absent unsound precedent, that civil rights, for example, are not the same thing as inalienable rights. This is the most widespread exercise of government officials reducing inalienable rights into privileges. To blend inalienable rights and civil rights together as just *rights* in the public's thinking is a *manipulation* of the language, which intentionally I believe, thwarts the vivacity of the whole purpose of inalienable rights, which is to limit government power and to empower the individual. Inalienable, or fundamental rights are superior to civil rights by nature and by the Law of the Land. If the "common good" arguments, which are philosophical in nature, whereby inalienable rights are diluted for the collective's sake, and are really what is best for the whole of society, then the individual's inalienable rights would not be jeopardized from the start. Because, the common good is the collection of individuals holding firm to their individual, natural rights. The objective to utilize the argument for the "common good," as a means to undermine natural rights, is historic and despotic, and is an attempt to fundamentally change our system of government from within. Thus Locke argues in the Treatise, "The legislature acts against the trust reposed in them, when they endeavor to invade the property of the subject, and to make themselves, or any part of the community, masters, or arbitrary disposers of the lives, liberties or fortunes of the people." What we are witnessing today is a neo-progressive chess move against inalienable rights and our Rule of Law.

To clarify, inalienable rights are the same as natural or fundamental rights. Civil rights are the same as civil liberties and legal privileges. *Civil* by definition is collective, it relates to the connection of individuals to other individuals in and out of government. *Inalienable* relates to the individual in and of him or her self, absent a connection to other individuals in or out of government. Civil rights are tied to public policy, or statutes, and inalienable rights are tied to the Rule of Law, which is founded upon Locke's *natural law*. Civil rights exist because of government bureaucracy and are intended to promote the collective good, to meet the needs of society in general, to commandeer peace, to protect individuals or groups of individuals from racial or sexual discrimination, for example. Inalienable rights exist within the individual and are beyond and prior to government bureaucracy. Natural rights secure the individual's autonomy from the majority, and from arbitrary government action that attempts to undermine their individualism, their property ownership or their speech, for example. Civil and inalienable rights are not at odds with one another, as neo-progressives assume. Civil rights are created by government through public policy and can be repealed or changed to compliment the will of the majority and/or the technological advances within society. Civil rights are essentially equal to government privileges, and are not rights by nature. Civil rights evolve along side society and can be implemented through taxation, as with the recent implementation of healthcare in *National Federation of Independent Business vs. Sebelius* (2012). Healthcare, for instance, is now evolving into a civil right because of government's taxing power and it's bureaucratic endeavor to remedy a *collective* dilemma that can intimately benefit the individual, at the forced "sharing of financial responsibility," of course. This is also known as forced economic activity. Or, as Matt Drudge calls it, the *Liberty Tax*. Yet, as it relates to the President's handling of the healthcare law (Affordable Care Act), Constitutional Scholar Jonathan Turley says, "The President continues to operate well off the Madisonian map."[46] Moreover, MIT professor Jonathan Gruber, one of the primary designers of 'Obamacare' said, in effect, that the only way to pass the Act was to rely on the stupidity of the American voters. As it relates to being cost affordable, Gruber stated, "The problem is it starts to go hand in hand with the mandate; you can't mandate insurance that's not affordable. This is going to be a major issue…Why should we hold 48 million uninsured people hostage to the fact that we don't yet know how to control costs in a politically acceptable way?"[46.5] My personal opinion is, that the mandate behind the Healthcare Law is a means to capitalize on an industry that the government has yet to capitalize on. Healthcare is not an inalienable right, because healthcare is not attached to the individual apart from government and/or the collective. Nor does Healthcare fall under the inalienable right to life. This is a manipulation, again, of reducing such a right to life into a government privilege. The best predictor of how this new socialized, forced healthcare system will work in America is to closely watch the Veteran's Affairs system and Medicare.

Moreover, inalienable rights are not dependent upon government bureaucracy like civil rights are, because, civil rights cannot be instituted or even managed without tax revenue and paperwork, or *red tape*. Inalienable rights exist prior to and without government bureaucracy and its permission. Civil rights are, again, a creation of government. Inalienable rights are not. Of course many modern, neo-progressive, legal and contemporary thinkers might rebuttal this on the grounds of *modern* jurisprudence, for the sake of the collective and for the sake of government's control over rights. Yet, in disagreement, such discernment between civil and inalienable, as I have simply opened, is true on the grounds of hindsight, and in line with our foundational philosophy and the Rule of Law. In addition, the whole point here is to oversimplify and to show how modern jurisprudence redefines the terms for the sake of jurisprudence itself, which then underscores the modern "legal" system. The neo-progressive consensus today is, that inalienable rights are impractical and are a great stumbling block to government's *progressive* efforts. In 1824 Thomas Jefferson wrote a letter to Major John Cartwright informing him that laws can change to suit the times and people, but that the inalienable rights of the people shall not change,

> "Can one generation bind another, and all others, in succession forever? I think not….To what then are attached the rights and powers they held while in the form of men? A generation may bind itself as long as its majority continues in life; when that has disappeared, another majority is in place, holds all the rights and powers their predecessors once held, and may change their laws and institutions to suit themselves. Nothing then is unchangeable but the inherent and unalienable rights of man."

Unbeknownst to most of the cops themselves, government's redefining of the terms related to *rights* can be seen within the efforts of their enforcement today. To illustrate, driving is a privilege, not a right. Owning a gun is a right, not a privilege. Owning a gun is neither a civil right. Nevertheless, both right and privilege are dealt with in an equivalent manner that is opposite of the *original intent* of what a right and privilege separately exist for. This is by corrupt design, I believe. To restrict or interfere in the exercise of a fundamental right through the enforcement of secondary legislation designed to manage a privilege, absent a crime by way of exercising that right, and the fact that a gun is property first, also protected by the 5th Amendment, not only by the 2nd Amendment, is enforcement working against the Constitution.

Fundamental or inalienable rights, again, are natural and precede government authority. Right to life, speaking one's mind, the right to be left alone, being armed for self-defense, personal privacy, earning a living, traveling and absolute property ownership are examples of fundamental, or inalienable rights. Fundamental rights benefit the individual and cannot be repealed by a legislative body, except temporarily, as a punishment following the conviction of a crime, whereby the rights or property of another have been violated, or *trespassed* against. However, following an individual's paid debt to society, a fundamental right must be completely restored to the individual. Absent this lawful affirmation, the government is circumventing the Rule of Law, again through the Legal System.

As it relates to the fundamental right to earn a living, the US Supreme Court ruled in *Hale vs. Henkel* that,

> "The individual may stand upon his constitutional rights as a citizen. He is entitled to carry on his private business in his own way. His power to contract is unlimited. He owes no duty to the State or to his neighbors to divulge his business, or to open his doors to an investigation, so far as it may tend to criminate him. He owes no such duty to the State,

since he receives nothing there from beyond the protection of his life and property. His rights are such as existed by the law of the land long antecedent to the organization of the State, and can only be taken from him by due process of law, and in accordance with the Constitution. Among his rights are a refusal to incriminate himself and the immunity of himself and his property from arrest or seizure except under a warrant of the law. He owes nothing to the public so long as he does not trespass upon their rights."[47]

This is not to say, however, that reasonable policy, as it relates to the exercise of certain rights, are not necessary as a reciprocal and compromising part of the social compact. For example, when the State establishes secondary laws requiring training prior to carrying a concealed weapon in public, or infers that the soundly, adjudicated mentally ill should not be armed in public, this is good and reasonable policy that does not undermine, but actually enhances the right to bear arms. This is government lawfully legislating education and responsibility associated with a particular freedom, which was emphasized by the founders. To ban the exercise of a right, however, is despotic and unlawful.

Today, the 2nd Amendment makes equal the citizen to the cop, which is, in part, the intent. Prior to the creation of municipal or chartered law enforcement, police, in the 1800s, the 2nd Amendment made equal the citizen to the soldier or to a Sheriff. The 2nd Amendment equalizes the individual with any government official for that matter. The right to keep and bear arms is not inferior to the "job" of carrying a weapon. To underscore this manipulation of the right through policy is unlawful usurpation. Likewise, to legislate the right to own or carry a gun "cosmetically" is also unreasonable and unlawful. There is an ulterior motive here, and generally that motive is authoritarian and neo-progressive. Ironically, George Washington said that government is not *reason*, but *force*, and yet, legal language is laced with the words *reasonable*, or *unreasonable*.

Securing revenue and socially engineering the masses are the building blocks of the modern Legal System, which is intricately designed to protect itself from the actual Rule of Law. The "public safety" argument is an aspect of social engineering, because such an argument seeks to liberate government power from lawful and sound restrictions that are codified within the Constitution. If this were not true, the end result of such policy would not be a permanent increase in government power but the instantiation of the Constitution's objective. Public safety is not argument enough to reiterate this socio-political fact. Sacrificing liberty for safety comes to mind. When the moral compass shifts from a natural law disposition into a system of secondary laws, whereby right and wrong are determined by what is legal and illegal, secondary laws convert into *legislative tyranny*, because such a system of secondary laws take priority over the Rule of Law and its protection of natural rights, for the sake of securing revenue and socially engineering the populace away from such rights. The forced implantation of government privileges over and above the exercise of fundamental rights leads to greater state dependency. American government is not the *Leviathan*.

Equality

Equality between all people is something the world has never seen, until America. Not only were people in government now equal to the people not in government, equal opportunity was also set into place as a guarantee that this equality between all people would be secure under our new Constitution. In a letter to Patrick Henry in 1776, John Adams, said of equality, that the history of inequality was no more,

"The dons, the bashaws, the grandees, the patricians, the sachems, the nabobs, call them by what names you please, sigh and groan and fret, and sometimes stamp and foam and curse, but all in vain. The decree is gone forth, and it cannot be recalled, that a more equal liberty than has prevailed in other parts of the earth must be established in America."

Today, the neo-progressive understanding of equality is "equal" access to wealth and government resources at the control of government bureaucrats, which is fundamentally flawed and different from the founder's understanding of equality. Equal opportunity, on the other hand, is the open path to self-actualization, which includes the acquiring of wealth and resources through innovation and hard work, absent the bureaucratic restraints and supervision of government officials. Rabbi Daniel Lapin of the *American Alliance of Jews and Christians*, recently said, "For those seeking to increase tyranny and totalitarianism, fairness and equality is a great thing to work people up about, because you essentially get a population — particularly a docile population — to agree to almost anything in the name of equality and fairness," that, "Freedom is being eroded steadily … in the name of equality."[48] This manipulation of the contemporary ideology and enforcement of *equality* can be seen within the past despotic regimes of England, Russia, Germany, Cambodia, Italy, the Banana Republics, China, and so on. In nature, as Locke says, all people are equal and the social compact must by Law, sustain this natural equality. It is by way of governments securing the wealth of the ruling classes instead of the people's inalienable rights, historically, that people have become unequal. In history, for example, if an individual or family existed in poverty, then generally such poverty was regurgitated into their offspring, and nothing changed. In the beginning of America, equality and equal opportunity progressively changed this historical and socio-economic fact, because, the Law for government was to leave people alone and let them pursue their happiness, which is no longer the case. If you are born into poverty in America, equal opportunity and being equal to everyone else, including to those in government, was a way out, to become educated and wealthy. Jefferson says in a letter to George Washington in 1784, as it relates to genuine equality in America, compared to the history of inequality and forced equality,

> "The objections of those opposed to the institution shall be briefly sketched; you will readily fill them up. They urge that it is against the Confederation; against the letter of some of our constitutions; against the spirit of them all, that the foundation, on which all these are built, is the natural equality of man, the denial of every preeminence but that annexed to legal office, and particularly the denial of a preeminence by birth."

Neither have governments in history ever provided equal opportunity to all people. In history, people were born unequal to others and surely not equal to the people in government. Government likewise enforced this inequality for its own sake. People were generally born into a class and lived their whole life within that class. Peasants did not become Kings, so to speak. And, those born into the ruling class, likewise, remained within the ruling class their whole life. This is the system past governments protected.

Equality in America today has been "progressively" transformed into something else, a means to an end, an argument, a straw man, a way to frustrate and undermine fundamental rights and property ownership.

Equality today has become *forced fairness*, which is digressing people back into the despotic regimes of the past where an aristocracy rules over common people. The ruling classes do not see themselves as equal to other people. The evidence can be seen in public policy and its enforcement, whereby the outcome is the benefit of some people receiving services at the forced expense of other people. In *Bowers vs. Devito* (1982), the 7th Circuit ruled, in part, "The Constitution is a charter of negative liberties; it tells the state to let the people alone; it does not require the federal government or the state to provide services…" Thus, this new "equality" of forced, equal access to wealth and government resources, and/or services, not only transfers wealth between the ruling classes, it separates those in power from those not in power, simply by the implementation and enforcement of the policy.

People in government now exempt themselves from legislation that they create to control other people. People intimately connected to the people in government use their wealth to create a system of legislation that protects their own interests rather than the fundamental interests of all people. Then they take for granted that law enforcement will be there as the "gun in the room." Mao Tse-tung said that, "Political power grows out of the barrel of the gun." In *Warren vs. DC* (1981), the US Supreme Court ruled,

> "Official police personnel and the government employing them are not generally liable to victims of criminal acts for failure to provide adequate police protection. This uniformly accepted rule rests upon the fundamental principle that a government and its agents are under no general duty to provide public services, such as police protection, to any particular individual citizen. A publicly maintained police force constitutes a basic governmental service provided to benefit the

community at large by promoting public peace, safety and good order."

So where does the authority to force fairness come from since such authority is not authorized in the Constitution? Forced fairness is opposite the Constitutional charge of government officials to secure genuine equality. Genuine equality, again, is established by the Declaration of Independence, secured by the US Constitution, and makes equal the people in government to the people not in government, in the effort to overcome aristocracy. This new "progressive" use of the term *equality* not only separates the people not in government from the people in government, it separates people from their property and it separates people from their natural rights, and it separates people from other people. This new interpretation of equality as *forced fairness* directly opposes genuine fairness, which is secured within genuine equal opportunity, where people are free to become who they truly are because of personal ambition, absent government micromanagement. Yet, equal opportunity has also become transformed and choked by secondary laws designed to, again, force fairness. *Equality* has become the premise on which the federal and state governments have "rationalized" the paths to absolute or centralized power by taking for granted that law enforcement will not object, which they can lawfully do, as their duty. A cop's "job security" is predicated on not thinking for one's self, sadly to say. On a personal note, while on patrol myself, I have heard on many occasions, officers tell me that I am not paid to think. Should superiors, legal updates, training, and the legislative or judicial branches do my thinking for me, as an officer? While it is very true that training does not equal education, self-education is fundamental. What about the separation of powers? Thomas Jefferson argued that, "My construction of the Constitution is... that each department is truly independent of the others and has an equal right to decide for itself what is the meaning of the Constitution in the cases submitted to its action; and especially where it is to act ultimately and without appeal."[49] This *Concurrent Review* likewise stands to reason as Law at the local level, especially upon the incorporation of Bill of Rights as the *supreme* law of the land into the State and local governments, via the 14th Amendment. The inconvenience of this concurrent review, where each branch of government interprets the constitution accordingly, within its own specific power, as noted by Madison, is that,

> "It may happen…that different independent departments, the legislative and executive, for example, may, in the exercise of their functions, interpret the constitution differently, and thence lay claim to the same power. This difference of opinion is an inconvenience not entirely to be avoided. It results from what may be called, if it be thought fit, a concurrent right to expound the constitution. But this species of concurrence is obviously and radically different from that in question. The former supposes the constitution to have given the power to one department only; and the doubt to be, to which it has been given. The latter supposes it to belong to both; and that it may be exercised by either or both, according to the course of exigencies."[50]

The "former" that Madison refers to is the theory that one branch holds a monopoly on interpreting the constitution over the other two branches, which today is the case. It is called *Judicial Review*. Here is what Madison says as it relates to the "former," or of only one branch interpreting the constitution,

> "…an independent exercise of an executive act by the legislature alone, or of a legislative act by the executive alone, one or other of which must happen in every case

where the same act is exerciseable by each, and the latter of which would happen in the case urged by the writer, **is contrary to one of the first and best maxims of a well-organized government, and ought never to be founded in a forced construction**, much less in opposition to a fair one. A concurrent authority in two independent departments, to perform the same function with respect to the same thing, would be as awkward in practice, as it is unnatural in theory."[51] (bold added)

Madison reaffirmed this in 1834, in Federalist 49, by stating that, "The branches of the National Government are coordinate, each must, in the exercise of it's functions, be guided by the text of the Constitution according to its own interpretation of it." Thus, for law enforcement to make reference to either of the other two branches for its own actions, absent its own understanding of the constitution, is complicit to whatever the other two branches have "up their sleeve," and helps usurp central power, which then overrules the power of one branch over the other by way of force. So for example, when a local government creates an ordinance that a home owner cannot grow a garden on their lawn, and they do so anyway, Or a state law directly infringes upon one of the first ten amendments, it is the lawful and ethical role of the law enforcement officer to not enforce such things because not enforcing such legislation checks the executive branch's power against the legislative branch, which is attempting to violate the property rights of the individual. This is what the Oath is taken for. This also works from within the same branch of government. One New Jersey cop, for instance, as it relates to the Executive branch alone, was caught on video specifically saying that "Obama has decimated the freakin' Constitution, so I don't give a damn. If he doesn't follow the Constitution, we don't have to."[51.5]

Today, cops pretty much do just about anything they are asked to do, by any type of authority, whether it is from another cop, a legislator, and judicial official, a councilman, a school official, a board member, a bureaucrat, a federal agent, and even private authorities. Of course this all depends upon the circumstances. One time on patrol, for instance, I received a call to assist an apartment property manager. Upon my arrival, the manager stated that an occupant refused to let her into the apartment for a routine inspection, that a notice was sent out about a week before. The property manager wanted me to *force* my way into the apartment, allowing the manager to inspect the unit against the occupant's will. I nicely told the manager that I would not break and enter into the residence unless it was a life and death situation, or exigent circumstance. I explained that she would have to do it herself, or go through the lawful procedures. She looked at me like I was crazy. And of course I was complained on for "not doing my job." The manager wanted to use me because she knew the resident would not resist if I, a cop, helped her enter the apartment. In truth, I was very much so, doing my job.

As it relates to usurping concurrent review from Madison and Jefferson, who if you recall, actually constructed the Constitution and emphasized its sound interpretation, Chief Justice John Marshall comes along in *Marbury vs. Madison* (1803) and conveys authoritatively through new "progressive" precedent that the judicial branch knows the Constitution best and thus the Court directly establishes *Judicial Review*, as a means to rid the federal government of the "inconveniences" of Concurrent Review. This has created, in part, the legal system that we have today, and this is what the cops enforce today. Jonathan Turley, a Constitutional Law Professor and Scholar has said,

> "James Madison fashioned a government of three
> bodies locked in a synchronous orbit by their

countervailing powers. The system of separation of powers was not created to protect the authority of each branch for its own sake. Rather, it is the primary protection of individual rights because it prevents the concentration of power in any one branch."[52]

When law enforcement, a part of the Executive Branch, *blindly* enforces any and every statute, or ordinance, whether at the local, state or federal level, which comes out of a legislative body, they essentially fail at securing the *Separation of Powers*, and thus nullify concurrent review. Blindly is the key word here. This blind enforcement actually helps blend the three Branches of government into one power, which is contrary to the very purpose of the *Separation of Powers*. Madison asserted in the Federalist #47 that, "The accumulation of all powers, legislative, executive, and judiciary, in the same hands, whether of one, a few, or many, and whether hereditary, self-appointed, or elective, may justly be pronounced the very definition of tyranny." Law Enforcement takes an Oath whereby their individual discretion, or lawful and Constitutional discernment, shall be exercised as a means to *check and balance* the power of the other two branches, and even within its own branch, like against unlawful orders, for example. Neo-progressives will argue that such "checking" of power in another Branch is only meant for its top officials and impractical today for law enforcement. If this were true, then the Oath would have been intentionally established as a formality. But the Oath is not a formality. Thus, *Constitutional Conscientiousness*, contrary to arbitrary orders, should be the driving force behind competent law enforcement officers, which in turn secures genuine equality, property rights, and the Rule of Law. The law enforcement Oath ensures that the Constitution is supreme and that laws not withstanding are enforced accordingly. The Constitution is the Law in Law Enforcement. Yet, law enforcement is trained, not educated, to pass their constitutional responsibilities off to another branch of government when questioned about their actions. A police state cannot take form in America without the complicity of all three branches of government.

Forced "equality," today, rather than genuine *equality* combined with disingenuous *equal opportunity*, through *public policy*, has become the new socio-political paradigm. If the free exercise of the pursuit of happiness, for the individual, becomes limited, while the power of the government expands, for the sake of *equality*, then statutes, in the name of forced "equality," to enforce same, are more than likely unlawful and should not be enforced. This is, again, why reinterpreting the Constitution as "living" becomes so important for neo-progressives. Frederick Bastiat, in his book simply titled, *The Law*, in direct and intentional opposition to Marxism, asserts how the socialist, or collectivist agenda actually separates people not in government from the people in government, in the name of forced equality,

> "Socialism, like the ancient ideas from which it springs, confuses the distinction between government and society. As a result of this, every time we object to a thing being done by government, the socialists conclude that we object to its being done at all. We disapprove of state education. Then the socialists say that we are opposed to any education. We object to a state religion. Then the socialists say that we want no religion at all. We object to a state-enforced equality. Then they say that we are against equality. And so on, and so on. It is as if the socialists were to accuse us of not wanting persons to eat because we do not want the state to raise grain."

The *Declaration of Independence* justly emphasizes that, "All men are created equal." But this term *equal* does not mean that all people are to live equally throughout their life as it relates to earning a living, education, social status, and so on. The term *equal* in the Declaration means that all people are generally born with the same physical and mental capacity, that all people are born with fundamental rights, beyond the reach of arbitrary rule, and that the people in government are now equal to the people not in government. The recent and new idea of *income inequality*, for example, negatively reinforces the neo-progressive use of the term "equality," an equal access to wealth, by way of government bureaucrats, which in and of itself undermines genuine equality. First of all, income inequality would not exist if forced economic activity were not the underlying paradigm of government ambition. As Bastiat once said, "The State is the great fiction through which everyone endeavors to live at the expense of everyone else."[53] It is true and unfortunate today, that the richest one percent of Americans own a third of America's wealth, and one percent owns thirty-five percent. This has happened because of neo-progressive government's marriage to corporations, a reciprocal transferring of wealth between big government bureaucracy and special business interests, whereby public policy, instead of Law, has secured the incomes of big business in exchange for government's financial gain.

> "When under the pretext of fraternity, the legal code imposes mutual sacrifices on the citizens, human nature is not thereby abrogated. Everyone will then direct his efforts toward contributing little to, and taking much from, the common fund of sacrifices. Now, is it the most unfortunate who gains from this struggle? Certainly not, but rather the most influential and calculating."[54]

Bastiat here emphasizes that the ones who create policy to transfer wealth, are the ones who gain the wealth, which is fascist corporatism, and this undermines the sound attempt of Law to restrain negative human nature. Neo-progressives argue that corporatism is a result of capitalism and thus government must force income equality. Corporatism is not a result of capitalism, but a result of *crony-capitalism*. Crony-capitalism is the success of business based upon the close relationship between businessmen and the people in government, and determined by public policy. Recall Hamilton's *implied powers* fiasco. Capitalism is the success of business founded upon the close relationship between individuals or groups of individuals with other individuals, and determined by the Rule of Law and the free market. Crony-capitalism and capitalism is another example of neo-progressives blending together concepts into one, like with rights and privileges, or with forced fairness and equality, or with legal possession and ownership. Equality today represents a forced fairness policy, by way of the exploitation of law enforcement. Freedom is not supposed to be fair.

Give an Inch, a Mile is Taken

Where, when and how did the Declaration's term equality convert into forced fairness? How did the term civil rights and the term inalienable rights melt into the application of the single term privilege? How do permanent provisions in the Constitution become impermanent? How did law enforcement go from standing on the side of the people to standing on the side of the arbitrary will of the government? These subtle changes, or silent encroachments, from America's founding have developed over time and from a combination of historical events: Acts of Congress, State laws, local ordinances, legal precedent, and the like. To oversimplify, these silent encroachments, in the name of social "progress," essentially derive from, or originate from, arguably of course, the *Reconstruction* following the Civil War and the later Progressive Era, in general. Progressive policy during these early times was not inevitably a bad thing. Social and political progress during these times was very good for the country, and necessary, especially in securing the freedom and equality of newly freed blacks, and in securing the right of women to vote, for example.

The Antebellum Period (~1810-1860) was a very brutish and turbulent time in American history. It was a period where the agricultural South and the industrialized North grew apart and great economic friction escalated. The federal government was forced into a very progressive challenge to rectify this violent dichotomy. Yet, such well intended progressive policies that followed have *slippery sloped* into something else, neo-progressive policies. For example, as a means to increase revenue, Americans lost their power over their labor and their income to the 16th amendment, even though the Supreme Court had ruled several times before that income is property and for the government to take a portion of an individual's income by force was a violation of the 5th Amendment dues process clause.[55] Similarly, the 17th Amendment, and to increase federal power over the States, the States no longer directly participated in the construction of federal law, whereby the States held the power to withdrawal senators, immediately, from congress who might vote against the State's sovereignty and to replace them with a new senator. In likeness to the Antebellum Period, today, a new friction is arising. Just as the foreign policy today of *policing the world* has created *blowback*, whereby other countries, now, continually threaten America, leading to invasive anti-terrorism policies, which usurp more federal power at the expense of the fundamental liberties of the people. Likewise, such *anti-*

terror domestic public policy creates domestic blowback, whereby many Americans seek to "take back" their liberties by the threat of force and civil disobedience. This is not a good thing. Yet, there is a cause for all this.

It came to pass that reinterpreting the Constitution as "living" was fundamental to avoid, not only the Amendment process in Article Five of the Constitution, but to "get around" such permanent provisions in the Constitution, quickly, absent State consent, as a matter of policy, and as a way to unshackle the path to "social progress" and "social innovation" within American society. Again, social progress and social innovations are very good for society and such policies help citizens evolve into more mature and responsible people. But when such policies undermine the very intent of organic Law, which is the security of the people's fundamental rights, their liberty and autonomy, then such progression is unsound and in the end, forces people to devolve into subjects. American neo-progressive thinkers argue that the US Constitution is obsolete, impractical and down right ludicrous in today's world. Thus, such archaic, political ideology, does not take into account the innovations of new technology, the rise in criminal and civil disputes, leading to such necessary regulations associated with increased populations. In addition, they argue, for example, that contemporary regulations such as food safety and food distribution, the pharmaceutical industry, environmental Acts, air travel, foreign policy, the internet, cell phones, and the like, are incompatible with the US Constitution today and that it should either be scrapped, revised or *reinterpreted*. How is the Constitution an infringement upon our modern, technological society? It is not. The Constitution is an infringement on power.

The sound reading of the Constitution proved too restrictive for collectivist ideas during the rise of the Progressive Era. Even Woodrow

Wilson said that, "We are in these latter days, apt to be very impatient of literal and dogmatic interpretations of constitutional principle."[56] Lois Brandeis, a "progressive" lawyer and Supreme Court Justice, helped solidify the legal precedent that fundamental rights are inferior to the collective, in direct opposition to the founding principles of what rights are, "All rights are derived from the purposes of society in which they exist; above all rights rises duty to the community." He also stated that, "rights of property and the liberty of the individual must be remolded, from time to time, to meet the changing needs of society."[57] In addition, Justice Oliver Holmes, a "progressive" ally of Brandeis argued, in the dissatisfaction of progressive and social policies being restricted by the Constitution, "Next to amending the constitution, the most feasible means of giving validity to new principles was to change interpretations of provisions."[58] Thus, the permanent provisions the founders established in the Constitution no longer carry the force of permanence because of neo-progressive, political ideology establishing precedent from this new "living" interpretation. The idea of the Constitution being reinterpreted as "living" originates in a book titled *The Living Constitution*, written by Howard Lee McBain, where he wrote that America is "slowly moving from individualism to collectivism, as a move no doubt we must." Judges, politicians and law enforcement officials, representing all three branches, who are sympathetic to socialist reforms, direct this "movement". Thus, the philosophy of a "living" constitution has become the new paradigm for its interpretation and implementation.

Neo-progressive policies sound nice and look pretty on the surface, but the heart of the policies digress society into soft feudalism, or even into soft fascism, whereby the "noble" rulers actually *force the enforcement* of policy, and, the people in government are no longer equal to the people not in government. This digression stems from not only the neo-progressive sources aforementioned, but from the more contemporary uses and interpretations of the historically sound, progressive policies. For example, the 14th Amendment was intended to secure the liberty of freed blacks, to make them equal to everyone else and to protect blacks from states that continue to discriminate and violate their fundamental rights, which includes self-ownership. Yet today, it is *reinterpreted* to empower the judiciary's use of the *Rational Bases Test* and to undermine the individual's liberty it was intended to secure by proclaiming corporations as people too. To implement neo-progressive polices, it takes literally thousands upon thousands of dollars to hire the attorneys to manipulate and construct thousands upon thousands of pages of legal language to circumvent the most basic, or the simplest language within the Constitution. Simple language was the intent. To illustrate, the 4th Amendment reads, in part, "The right of the people to be secure in their persons, houses, papers, and effects, against unreasonable searches and seizures, shall not be violated…" It took three hundred and forty two pages of language within the *Patriot Act* to circumvent this one simple line in the 4th Amendment.

Charles A. Beard, a legal scholar and historian during the early progressive era, was somewhat responsible for the rise of the idea of America as a "business model," whereby the people's rights are actually a smoke screen to promote the economic interests of the big business industrialists, especially in the North. Beard, who was a big fan of Alexander Hamilton by the way, helped shape and inspire the scheme that America's Constitution was ratified upon concealed economic purposes rather than in philosophical principles. In one of his books, *The Supreme Court and the Constitution* (1912), Beard also fundamentally helps structure a neo-progressive consensus against *Concurrent Review* in favor of Judicial Review, which would "progress" the security of the economically wealthy, special interests, over time, into contemporary legislative Acts, which are then upheld by the Court. This is directly contrary to the founders' actual intent behind the creation of the Constitution, and yet, ironically, one of the very premises upon how the Constitution is reinterpreted today. Beard writes,

> "The subsequent action of the Supreme Court in assuming the power to declare acts of Congress unconstitutional was without a line in the Constitution to authorize it, either expressly or by implication. The Constitution recited carefully and fully the matters over which the courts should have jurisdiction, and there is nothing, and after the above vote four times refusing jurisdiction, there could be nothing, indicating any power to declare an act of Congress unconstitutional and void."[60]

The votes Beard refers to were state votes that failed to give the Supreme Court sole discretion over whether legislative acts are unconstitutional and void. Judicial review, or jurisdiction over this power, as it relates to secondary laws, is not necessarily the same as "appellate jurisdiction" over all cases, which are limited to reversing or modifying a lower court's decision, as determined within the Constitution. Article 3, Section 2, reads in part,

> The judicial power shall extend to all cases, in law and equity, arising under this Constitution, the laws of the United States, and treaties made, or which shall be made, under their authority.... In all cases affecting ambassadors, other public ministers and consuls, and those in which a state shall be party, the Supreme Court shall have

> original jurisdiction. In all the other cases before
> mentioned, the Supreme Court shall have
> appellate jurisdiction, both as to law and fact,
> with such exceptions, and under such
> regulations as the Congress shall make.

The *Concurrent Review* of congressional acts as unconstitutional and thus void, is a communal enterprise, shared among all three branches of government, originally. *Judicial review*, then, covertly plays into the exploitation of law enforcement, because absent the constitutional discretion and enforcement powers against legislative acts by way of *non-enforcement*, wealthy special interests take foothold over and above liberty interests. *Kelo vs. New London* comes to mind. This is how neo-progressives think and operate today, still, within both the democratic and republican parties. Moreover, this unshared power is the essence of the American legal system today.

If the government did not legislate the interests of certain groups by way of financial incentives and by way of divergent, political ideology, that is withstanding to the Constitution, and if the people in government lawfully punished those who violate the natural rights of others and who violate sounds statutes, as a matter of Law, and not as a matter of public policy, to avoid the State's burden of proof (plea bargaining), the people in government would remain equal to the people not in government. Thus, those groups who hold that our Constitution is "outdated," would not threaten fundamental rights and property ownership by exploiting the government's monopoly on violence, law enforcement. In addition, such abominations as bias against racial or sexual orientation and religious discrimination, would not be as prominent a social problem because the intent of such groups or individuals to exploit the use of government force could not gain a foothold among free, consciously driven individuals who adhere to the rights of others. Neo-progressives will argue, of course, that it is far more complicated than that. Complicating the issues is another means to separate people from other people. To create entity beyond necessity, or to adhoc the arguments, as a means to usurp power and complicate things even further, at the expense of liberty, people's understanding and for the sake of special interest groups is unsound and circular, only ending in bigger, more intrusive government, which is Hobbesian, not Lockean.

The US Constitution is predicated upon Locke's political philosophy, which concludes that human beings are naturally free and have natural, inalienable rights, and the just role of government is to secure these rights. Our Constitution also makes equal those people in government to those people not in government, even as it relates to force. Negative human nature is the core of the US Constitution's objective, and human nature has not changed in the nearly 6000 years of society. People are the same today as they were during the time of Ancient Egypt, during the Maccabean revolt, during the time of Socrates when he was put to death by the state for "corrupting the youth," actually for just getting the youth to think and ask the right questions to those who thought they knew the answers, but didn't. People are the same now as during the time of ancient Rome and the murder of Jesus by the state. We are the same people today as we were during the Spanish Inquisition, and those who beheaded or burned people who thought independently or differently. Humans are the same today as they were during the middle ages, and during the time of the Renaissance.

Having invented a smart phone, or weapons of mass destruction, or the Internet, does not nullify the supremacy of inalienable rights, and the Constitution's intent to secure them by attempting to thwart negative human nature in government. As American government expands, and it is expanding, it is surely not filling up with intellectuals and angels. We need our Constitution to work. Moreover, public policy, in contrast to Constitutional restrictions, designed for the *prevention* of crime, is not argument enough for such policies to become withstanding to the Constitution. Such legislation then leads to more legislation designed to keep government officials within the Law. It's ridiculous. The argument that the Constitution is "old-fashioned" is primarily a means to weaken the restrictions our Constitution mandates against the active, negative human nature of government officials, which is, but not limited to, the greed for power, the exploitation of the weak, the desire to control other people's lives and their property, the monopoly on violence, the plundering of property, the lust for war, and the exercise of an authoritarian spirit, for example. Have we evolved out of these aspects of human nature? I think not. Once we human beings evolve out of our selfish, brutal and violent natures, then we can rationally conclude that political ideologies like the Constitution to be "outdated." Locke said that, "all men by nature are equal…that every man hath, to his natural freedom, without being subjected to the will or authority of any other man."[59] For Americans in government, at any level, to deviate from this political and fundamentally philosophical reality, by way of *arbitrary* legislation and enforcement, as a covert way to weaken the organic Law designed to restrain them, they are no longer movers of a just and moral government, and the Constitution will have the last word as a moral force against such intentions. As Jefferson asserts, "In questions of power, let no more be heard of confidence in man, but bind him down from mischief by the chains of the constitution."[61]

2

Property

"A right to property is founded in our natural wants, in the means with which we are endowed to satisfy these wants, and the right to what we acquire by those means without violating the similar rights of other sensible beings."

- Thomas Jefferson

When the responsibility that comes with freedom is not a part of the paradigm within public education, or society in general, children grow up to become adults that hold no affinity to their own personal liberty, or to property rights. Property rights are designed to secure property ownership. No longer do Americans truly own their property, or hold absolute control of their property. This is evident, in part, by the fact that people can no longer remain anonymous by choice, nor can people earn an honest living absent the government's forced, financial micromanagement of their right to earn a living, because money is property, and especially by the fact that no American can purchase real property absent the intrusion of government bureaucracy. Guns, money, assets, cars, homes, land, books, clothes, computers, cell phones, documents, art, etc, are all property and our rights ultimately derive from our property,[1] beginning with self-ownership. When you no longer truly own property, you no longer truly have rights. "For not only are there no human rights which are not also property rights, but the former rights [speech, defense, privacy] lose their absoluteness and clarity and become fuzzy and vulnerable when property rights are not used as the standard."[2] Instead, absent true property rights, you only have *legal privileges* and *legal possession*. In essence, we now have a government that takes our property from us to protect us from people who might take our property from us. Property rights have been silently encroached upon by an invasive, neo-progressive philosophy, whereby, in part, one must "register" their valued property, by coercion, thus surrendering principle ownership and the rights attached to that property, to the state. This *legal plundering* then takes for granted that law enforcement will be there to impose the plundering. To register something or someone, has a very diversified history. Generally, to register something or someone means to record it, and/or make whatever is being registered a part of something else, to verify ownership or legal possession. However, *compulsory registration* has become a "legal" means for the state to acquire *jurisdiction* over either a person or their property. Jurisdiction is defined in Black's Law Dictionary, 8th Edition, as "A government's general power to exercise authority over all persons and things within its territory." Think about how much you register something with the government.

The cultivation of existing in a monarchy, made up of royalty, noblemen and commoners, unfortunately made its way into America's founding, minimally at first. The founders did not create the American system of government in a vacuum. Prior legal conditionings like *tort liability*, and the *law of contract*, for example, as it relates to property, were some of the foundations of American policy within the colonies. Why? The 18th century was a time when literally most people were uneducated and could not even read, but merely existed as farmers and of those simply trying to survive through servitude to land owners, and the like. Only the wealthy and educated owned land and participated in government. Thus, the *equal opportunity* for all people to own property was something that had to come about over time and the framers did establish a system, whereby, *absolute* property ownership would become the potential security against poverty and government intrusion for all Americans. Moreover, because property ownership was essential to securing liberty as a fundamental and natural right, Jefferson and Washington, for example, pushed for public education. Education and being able to read was absolutely key to purchasing, owning and defending all natural rights, including property rights, as well as for participating in being self-governed. Otherwise, a person's purchasing power, income, and property rights would be greatly demoralized, not only by those wealthy businessmen in the new free market, but by government officials also. In addition, this is one reason why *pure* democracy was not instituted, but rather a republic was the initial form of government, because, most people simply did not posses the intellectual capacity to participate in government, yet. The Rule of Law would secure the restrictions upon those in government who wanted to exploit the ignorant and poor. Over time, public education has allowed most people to become somewhat educated. And, this sound progression in education has allowed for most people to "own" property. Unfortunately, however, this sound progression towards property ownership in early America has now digressed from a natural right then, into a legal privilege today. Public education no longer teaches the responsibility that is necessary to articulate and defend fundamental rights, which includes owning property. Instead of owning property to secure one against poverty and government intrusion, now one must surrender principal ownership and pay rent to the government to *legally possess* property, all by force, for the sake of collectivist philosophy. This is not to say that sound policy should not be established to regulate commercial property, and some personal property, for example, for public safety, against thieves, and corrupt people in business. I am strictly referring to privately owned, and necessarily basic property, which was designed by the framers too not only keep government away, but to secure people within the basic necessities of their existence. Commercial property is something entirely different.

The founders understood quite clearly that if private property were subject to government oversight or regulations, then property value and its true ownership would decline into *serfdom*. Thus, the founders constructed the Constitution and it's Rule of Law accordingly, which established an array of property rights provisions that are permanent and fixed. James Madison specifically makes this point, which is why education of one's rights is so important to property ownership, and why the fundamental right of property ownership is specifically secured as a way to keep government out of the individual's private life. Madison refers to this government oversight, or secondary laws designed to regulate private property ownership, as *mutable policy*.

> "The internal effects of a mutable policy are still more calamitous. It poisons the blessings of liberty itself. It will be of little avail to the people that the laws are made by men of their choice if the laws be so voluminous that they cannot be read, or so incoherent that they cannot be understood; if they be repealed or revised before they are promulgated, or undergo such incessant changes that no man, who knows what the law is today, can guess what it will be tomorrow. Law is defined to be a rule of action; but how can that be a rule, which is little known, and less fixed?"[3]

Mutable policies are statutes that change over time and are a lawful means to regulate legal privileges, but statutes are not a lawful means to regulate fundamental rights, like basic private property ownership, or the property itself, unless the right is no longer a fundamental right. This is exactly what property law does today, makes regulations on private property ownership "calamitous," whereby such laws "poison liberty," and these laws today are "so voluminous that they cannot be read, or so incoherent that they cannot be understood." This is, in part, and again, why education was so important to the founders. As Jefferson said, "I know no safe depository of the ultimate powers of the society but the people themselves, and if we think them not enlightened enough to exercise their control with a wholesome discretion, **the remedy is not to take it from**

them, but to inform their discretion by education. This is the true corrective of abuses of constitutional power."[4] (bold added)

This is not to say, however, that such permanent provisions in the Law do not allow reflection upon changes over time, like within the increase of technology and social customs. These changes happen through juries and sound precedent, in part, and not directly by centralized power or by unelected bureaucrats. Most importantly however, juries, for example, are restricted also to specificity, as are judges, and are likewise limited by these permanent and fixed provisions within the actual Law. A jury, for instance, cannot convict an individual of a crime where there is a reasonable doubt, for example.

Throughout most of the history of the world, a king or a dictator had always owned all property, absolutely. The people only had *legal possession* of property, and in England, for example, people had to pay rent to the King to simply live on the land and to live in their homes. If the legal possessors did not pay the King his rent, he took their property by force and either jailed or executed them, using his armed minions. This forced monopoly on absolute property ownership by a central power in English history derives from *William the Conqueror* in the 11th Century, who created a "property tax" as a means to increase the power and wealth of the Monarchy. Later on, once the "divine rights of kings" was overruled by an English civil war between the Monarchy and Parliament, the Whig intellectuals, like Locke, expounded upon property rights, which as we have seen, greatly influenced the founders. Thus, America was to be very different, as it related to property ownership. In America, the individual could now truly own property, absent the consent or forced supervision of a monarch or by *mutable policy*. In addition, and again, *absolute* ownership of private property, like a house or land, was something the founders established in America that has been circumvented by neo-progressive policy over time, for the sake of a collectivist philosophy. Absolute ownership means absolute control, and that the owner does not pay the government to keep living on their land or in their home through a property tax, or *quit-rent*. Quit-rent is something that Kings demanded from people who are *subjects* and not free. Non-free people cannot own property in absolute. Jefferson argued that the United States government would not participate in the traditional *rights of kings* over private land and property ownership,

"That we shall at this time also take notice of an error in the nature of our landholdings, which crept in at a very early period of our settlement. The introduction of the feudal tenures into the kingdom of England, though ancient, is well enough understood to set this matter in its proper light. In the earlier ages of the Saxon settlement feudal holdings were certainly altogether unknown, and very few, if any, had been introduced at the time of the Norman conquest. **Our Saxon ancestors held their lands, as they did their personal property, in absolute dominion, disencumbered with any superior. . . . William the Conqueror first introduced that system [feudalism] generally.** The lands which had belonged to those who fell at the battle of Hastings, and in the subsequent insurrections of his reign, formed a considerable proportion of the lands of the whole kingdom. These he granted out, subject to feudal duties, as did he also those of a great number of his new subjects, who by persuasions or threats were induced to surrender then for that purpose. But still much of the land was left in the hands of his Saxon subjects, held of no superior, and not subject to feudal conditions. . . . A general principle indeed was introduced that "all lands in England were held either mediately or immediately of the crown": but thus was borrowed from those holdings which were truly feudal, and applied to others for the purposes of illustration. Feudal holdings were therefore but exceptions out of the Saxon laws of possession, under which all lands were held in absolute right. These therefore still form the basis of the common law, to prevail whenever the exceptions have not taken place. **America was not conquered by William the Norman, nor its lands surrendered to him or any of his successors. Possessions are undoubtedly of the [absolute disencumbered] nature. Our ancestors however, were laborers, not lawyers. The fictitious principle that all lands belong originally to the king, that they were early persuaded to believe real, and accordingly took grants of their own lands from the crown. And while the crown continued to grant for small sums and on reasonable rents, there was no inducement to arrest the error.**"[5] (bold added)

Jefferson here is referring to the King no longer holding such absolute power or ownership over the lands in the Colonies, whereby the colonies had to pay property taxes or *quit-rent* to the King to legally possess and live on the land, or in their homes. Jefferson said that such a government financial scheme, as "feudal duties," would not take place in America.

Under the *Treaty of Paris*, the American lands were given over to the Colonies in *Allodium*. Allodium means absolute ownership, absent and free of any obligations to a higher authority. Black's Law Dictionary 2nd Edition, defines allodium as, "Land held absolutely in one's own right, and not of any lord or superior; land not subject to feudal duties or burdens. An estate held by absolute ownership, without recognizing any superior to whom any duty is due on account thereof." But here is where the government silently encroaches upon period terms to socially engineer the people away from such rights and knowledge of absolute property ownership, as is complimented by such terms. The 2nd Edition of Black's Law Dictionary was written during the 18th Century and reflects the most competent understanding of the legal language at that time. However, when one looks at the more modern legal jargon, as with the newer 8th Edition of Black's Law Dictionary, the term allodium changes very subtly to transition absolute ownership into the limits of *fee simple* title. The 8th addition reads that allodium is, "An estate held in fee simple absolute." Then look up *Fee Simple* in the same 8th Edition, it reads that Fee Simple is, "An interest in land that, being the broadest property interest allowed by law." Isn't "allowed by law" a superior? What does the definition mean by "interest?" What happened to the words, *right* or *feudal duties or burdens* from the earlier definition? *Allodium* doesn't really exist anymore. That is what happened. When a government or entity owns all land and property in absolute and rents that land or property to people for a fee or a tax, these forced payments are called *feudal duties.* Paying such fees on property you "own" is also a type of soft *Feudalism,* absent the middlemen originally called *noblemen.* America was not to be Feudal, at all, as Jefferson asserted above. Well what does *feudal duties* mean today? Feudal duties simply means a fee paid on property under obligation to a higher authority, or as it was called under a King, *quit-rent.* Do you pay your local government annual feudal duties to live on land you "own"? Do you pay your local government annual quit-rent to live in a house you "own?" Do you pay the government an annual property tax to drive in a car you "own?" "Oh," the neo-progressives cry out, "The times have changed. How do we pay to keep you safe and secure? How do we pay to educate our youth?" Just because the government cuts out the *noble classes* today as the *middle-man*, in acquiring property tax revenue as feudal duties, does not change the fact that the government still collects feudal duties, or quit-rent, by force, on property you think you own. The nobles themselves, at the time, and as much as today, paid feudal duties by force to a king also. They simply turned around and took it by force from the peasants (poor people). So what has changed really? Thus, enforcement worked the same then as it does today. On a side note, I recall when closing on my own house, I asked the lawyer what he thought of Allodial title, in comparison to Fee Simple title. He looked at me lost for a sec, and said he didn't know what I was talking about, and that he had never heard of Allodial title. He went back to pointing to where my signatures were needed on the three party contracts.

I want to emphasize here that this absolute, or allodial ownership of property is soundly temporary, "A power to dispose of estates for ever is manifestly absurd. The earth and the fullness of it belongs to every generation, and the preceding one can have no right to bind it up from posterity. Such extension of property is quite unnatural." Here Thomas Jefferson is echoing the mind of Adam Smith, as it relates to sound capitalism and property ownership.[6] Allodium is only *reasonable* during one's own lifetime. Likewise, I am neither advocating an abolishment of property tax. The founders did agree that it was a necessary and a collective, public effort to fund government, in part, and public education through a *limited* property tax. Jefferson made the remark to Madison, for example, that those, "who can find uncultivated land, shall be at liberty to cultivate it, paying a moderate rent."[6.5] Cultivating lands were also generally of a commercial enterprise. Property tax is very necessary for certain areas of government to function. However, there needs to be limits, and the founders did set limits. Limits then are not within the same context of what government redefines limits as today, however.

As it relates to funding education, for example, from property taxes, John Adams said, "The whole people must take upon themselves the education of the whole people and be willing to bear the expenses of it…there should not be a district of one mile square, without a school in it, not founded by a charitable individual, but maintained at the public expense of the people themselves."[7] Thomas Jefferson also emphasized that public tax revenue shall be the funding source for public education,

> "I think by far the most important bill in our whole code is that for the diffusion of knowledge among the people. No other sure foundation can be devised, for the preservation of freedom and happiness…my dear Sir, a crusade against ignorance; establish & improve the law for educating the common people. Let our countrymen know that the people alone can protect us against these evils [tyranny, oppression, etc.] and **that the tax which will be paid for this purpose is not more than the thousandth part of what will be paid to kings, priests and nobles who will rise up among us if we leave the people in ignorance.**"[8] (bold added)

How do we as Americans from the future reconcile this charge of the founders to publicly fund education and other necessary government functions, through property tax revenue, with the equal and sound charge that, "No power on earth has a right to take our property from us without our consent." said John Jay, the first Chief Justice of the United States, who was quoting Locke? Today, neo-progressives will argue the ideology of *implied consent* in the legislatures. This has only undermined protections like *allodium*, however. What do Benjamin Franklin and

Thomas Jefferson both say about a real and private property tax? The framers put a sound and lawful solution into place, to remedy this very squabble, as a way to secure people not only from government intrusion, but to also secure people from extreme poverty and homelessness.

But first, and most importantly, property ownership meant personal liberty. Property ownership meant independence and property ownership meant limited government, which secured personal privacy. Property ownership also meant security from poverty. Today, when an individual wants to purchase real property, for example, some how, someway, government bureaucracy gets involved in the process, thus nullifying from the start, ownership as a way to limit government from being intimately involved in one's personal life. In addition, and sadly so, the individual is actually freer today by not "owning" property, because not owning property keeps government at bay. So what happened to American republicanism? Well, very basically, American Government became a big business, a *corporation*,[9] run by banks, CEOs and big business minded politicians who wanted to capitalize on private property and increase government revenue by controlling and attaching monetary value to any and everything under the sun, which in turn increased government power over any and everything associated with an individual's life. Have you ever met your *strawman*? In 1816, Thomas Jefferson warned his friend George Logan in a letter that what destroys a country morally is when big business becomes a source to create law. From this, government creates and secures aristocracy, that such corporations must be "crushed" before they become powerful enough to determine the workings of government. Today, big American business makes law, contrary to the founders' intent. Making reference to England as the example of this, Jefferson wrote,

"The man who is dishonest as a statesman would be a dishonest man in any station....In this respect England exhibits the most remarkable phaenomenon in the universe in the contrast between the profligacy of its government and the probity of its citizens. And accordingly it is now exhibiting an example of the truth of the maxim that virtue & interest are inseparable. It ends, as might have been expected, in the ruin of it's people, but this ruin will fall heaviest, as it ought to fall on that hereditary aristocracy which has for generations been preparing the catastrophe. I hope we shall take warning from the example and crush in it's birth the aristocracy of our monied corporations which dare already to challenge our government to a trial of strength and bid defiance to the laws of our country."[10]

Corporations here are a bit different than corporations today, but are essentially the same. Corporation in Jefferson's time meant *commercial enterprise*. Combine this business mindedness in government with a collectivist philosophy and corporatism is born. Corporatism is when everything has a price, is regulated by statutes and all property belongs to the government, to everybody in name only, by force, with the dollar at the center. In a recent, well-written article by Jim Sleeper at Salon, he noted that *We the People* in mass are to blame for allowing this, "A liberal capitalist republic has to rely on its citizens to uphold voluntarily certain public virtues and beliefs that neither the liberal state nor markets can nourish or defend." The term "liberal" is not necessarily referring to liberal in the contemporary, political sense, but of the classical "freedom" sense. What we are experiencing now as the failings of our principled republic, are actually symptoms of the laziness and ignorance of the people in general,

"Having miscarried republican self-discipline and conviction so badly, we find ourselves scrambling to monitor, measure and control the consequences, such as the proliferation of mental illness and the glorification and marketing of guns, as if these were causing our implosion.

They aren't. They're symptoms, not causes — reactions to widespread heartbreak at the breakdown of what Tocqueville called republican habits of the heart that we used to cultivate.

Equally symptomatic, not causal, are self-avowedly "deviant" and "transgressive" gyrations by people who imagine that the sunset of civic-republican order heralds a liberating, Dionysian dawn. Sloughing off our bad old repressions, we've been swept up by the swift market currents that turn countercultures into over-the-counter cultures and promote a free-for-all that's a free-for-none as citizens become customers chasing "freedoms" for sale.

Even our war-makers' and -mongers' grand strategies and the growing militarization of our domestic police forces are more symptomatic than causal of the public derangement that's rising all around us."[11]

In the end, the fundamental rights of individual liberty and absolute ownership of basic and necessary property, as established at the founding, and which is still the *Law of the Land*, ironically, proved not to be good for business. Moreover, this *new style* of economic progress, secured in statutes, has digressed society away from the property protections secured in the Law of the Land, back into a type of aristocracy and soft feudalism, as was in England prior to Independence. These statutes that secure this new style of economic progress have now become the law in law enforcement.

What Is Property?

It is important to define property and to define ownership. Unfortunately today, government redefines what property is and redefines what ownership is through property law, or secondary laws, and based upon the property's value and/or the property's purpose. This continually evolves, like with Black's Law Dictionary redefining the term *Allodium*. Similarly, the terms *property* and *ownership* have undergone many "legal" revisions, thus changing the definition of what ownership is for its *reasonable* control and valuation. Recall that property ownership was to be radically different than in past governments, especially and specifically from the English Monarchy. In establishing property rights in America, again, the founders understood how connected such a right is to individual liberty and autonomy, compared to historical views of what property ownership meant and actually was. How can a king, or despot own property absolutely and not a common person? Because, the king had an army that could "legally" commit acts of violence, at the King's will, and simply by the King decreeing that any such violence executed in his name was law. Moreover, common people, all people as a matter of fact, were unequal to the King.

As aforementioned, Jefferson emphasized, by nature, land is not actually attached to an individual beyond that individual's lifetime, therefore absolute ownership is reasonable. Furthermore, part of "progressing" out of a monarchy, where people had to pay a tax to the king, law should secure the individual on their land for that *moment* of their existence, as "stable" ownership. Jefferson reiterates,

> "It is a moot question whether the origin of any kind of property is derived from nature at all... It is agreed by those who have seriously considered the

subject that no individual has, of natural right, a
separate property in an acre of land, for instance. By
an universal law, indeed, whatever, whether fixed or
movable, belongs to all men equally and in common
is the property for the moment of him who occupies
it; but when he relinquishes the occupation, the
property goes with it. Stable ownership is the gift of
social law, and is given late in the progress of
society."[12]

All land, in its natural origin, and until owned by an individual, is
owned by humanity as a whole. And, as it relates to public property, for
example, parks, schools, religious sites, and the like, are always owned in
common, or collectively, by the citizens within a specific jurisdiction.
Private property, however, is not. This is the difference in universal and
social law. The new American government is lawfully charged to secure
the *real* and private property ownership of individuals, again, as the sign of
sound progression out of European aristocracy. Prior to the establishment
of the United States, Jefferson makes reference to this by citing the Native
Americans owning land in common prior to American progress within
society as a whole, whereby individual land ownership is protected by law,

"A right of property in moveable things is
admitted before the establishment of government. A
separate property in lands, not till after that
establishment. The right to moveables is
acknowledged by all the hordes of Indians
surrounding us. Yet by no one of them has a
separate property in lands been yielded to
individuals. He who plants a field keeps possession
till he has gathered the produce, after which one has
as good a right as another to occupy it. Government
must be established and laws provided, before lands
can be separately appropriated, and their owner
protected in his possession. Till then, the property is
in the body of the nation, and they, or their chief as

trustee, must grant them to individuals, and
determine the conditions of the grant."[13]

Today, property law has become unbelievably complicated in an
effort for government to redefine *property, ownership,* and *legal
possession.* Also, this has slippery sloped into the creation of new terms,
all designed to legally connect government intimately to private property,
economically and socially, above and beyond the individual. *Blight* and
zoning are a few terms that come to mind that are heavily abused, but
reasonably necessary. The argument against an individual today truly
owning property is a collectivist argument, which principally reasons that
governments must use quit-rent from any and all real property as a way to
fund public services. Such intended complications within property law are
not only necessary to secure such a system, but have, over time,
transformed the founders' view of property ownership back into the pre-
American philosophy of Hobbes', that all property shall be owned in
common, whereby the people in government hold absolute ownership, just
as the King did before we declared Independence. Try to purchase some
land directly from another individual absent a lawyer and absent
government bureaucracy. It won't happen because the government today
owns all the property. Oh they argue that such bureaucracy is for your
protection one way or another, but is it really? The lawyer is there because
the laws are overly complicated and need to be interpreted and explained.
Bureaucracy is there to make sure that true ownership is secured for the
government and that the individuals are limited to "legal possession" of the
property. I'm pretty sure property laws today are not what Jefferson had in
mind when he talked about laws protecting property rights. If Americans
still truly owned property in principal, there would be far less need for
lawyers and surely less need for bureaucracy, leading to less government,

which in turn would cause great inconveniences for government. And there in lies part of the problem. The irony is, this very thinking sounds absolutely ludicrous today to most people because most people have been slowly, over time, conditioned away from absolute property ownership. Thus the term, "wards of the court."

Neo-progressives argue the need for property co-ownership between government and individuals because most people are incapable of exercising the responsibility associated with principal property ownership. This may be somewhat reasonable, but only because people have not been educated into such responsibility. Big government ideas need big funding, which could not happen if people really owned their property. Property ownership is a fundamental, natural right, and it is because of unsound, secondary laws, derivative of unsound precedent, that such a right is thwarted for the purpose of securing principal ownership for only the government. Recall that government is only an entity, made up of other humans. Government cannot actually own anything, but a human can, within their lifetime. In addition, Jefferson declared it immoral and unjust that government takes property by force for the purpose of *redistribution*, that only true owners may use force to take property stolen by thieves, for example, and not government for its own purposes, "By nature's law, every man has a right to seize and retake by force his own property taken from him by another by force or fraud. Nor is this natural right among the first which is taken into the hands of regular government after it is instituted."[14] So when government is the principal owner of property, it becomes the principal executioner of force in securing that ownership.

On that note, the US Supreme Court in *James vs. The United States* (1992) has ruled that *income* is property. Thus, the *income tax* can actually be viewed as a property tax on one's labor and income, absent due process, but by way of the contract. Some argue that the income tax is an excise tax, or duty, since the Federal Reserve owns the currency, and whereby the Apportionment Clause in the Constitution must apply. Either way, and in the end, this is why the government had to amend the Constitution, for its own sake, to *get around* the Due Process of Law requirement in the 5th and 14th Amendments, and to *get around* or circumvent the permanent and fixed provisions designed originally to secure property rights in absolute, like the right to earn a living.

Are owning socks the same thing as owning a tractor? No. Why not? Because, the people in government can tax the tractor's value, not socks. Plus socks are inside the home, which is still protected by the 4th Amendment, for now. One loophole governments have created to get around the 4th Amendment is to associate property inside the home with economic activity. So if you earn income from within your home, depending on the jurisdiction, the government can tax the property you use to earn that income. As it relates to the outside of the home, you don't truly own the tractor because if you don't pay the tax, the people in government can use their monopoly on violence, law enforcement, to come take it, and resell it for currency, to make up for the tax. They can't do that with socks, because socks hold no value. Frederick Bastiat, in his most famous book simply called *The Law*, where he specifically and intentionally argued against Marxism and the redistribution of wealth by force, calls this act of taxation *legal plundering*:

> "Now, legal plunder can be committed in an infinite number of ways. Thus we have an infinite number of plans for organizing it: tariffs, protection, benefits, subsidies, encouragements, progressive taxation, public schools, guaranteed jobs, guaranteed profits,

minimum wages, a right to relief, a right to the tools
of labor, free credit, and so on, and so on."

Again, what does it mean today to own something? Is owning your car the same thing as owning your shovel? How about land? Is owning land today the same thing as owning your house? Or better yet, is owning land today the same as owning land two hundred years ago? As society advances and populations increase, many people in government argue the need for more revenue by forcefully taxing and redistributing people's property and wealth to fund more social controls and more social programs, and to fund more bureaucracy and enforcement to implement those programs and controls. Such controls are designed not only to control behavior, but also to control the use of property, which is why the government makes itself the principal owner, to make controlling property "legal." Today, secondary laws that are designed to control the use of property are written in such a complicated way as to secure the government's maximum authority. What about maximum liberty for the individual? In *Pennell vs. City of San Jose*, the US Supreme Court explained, as it relates to the city's control of rent, that such controls attract politicians because it imposes costs onto the property owners, which, "permit wealth transfers…to be achieved 'off budget,' with relative invisibility and thus relative immunity from normal democratic processes." In short, this scheme is far easier than asking the people to vote on whether or not the city should use taxpayer money to help pay people's rent.

The whole purpose of property rights, which secures true property ownership, is to also protect the minority from the will of the majority. This was one of the greatest challenges, or prerogatives, of the new American government. This is one reason, in part, why Madison argues for a Bill of Rights, "Another happy effect of this prerogative would be its control on the internal vicissitudes of State policy; and the aggressions of interested majorities on the rights of minorities and of individuals."[15] The will of the majority cannot overrule the property rights of the minority, thus the Bill of Rights protects the minority against what most people want. Our foremost foundational principles, as it relates to property, again, derive from the philosophy of John Locke. It was Locke who paved the way and advanced the building blocks for American property ownership. Not only philosophically, but socially and economically. Locke, again, emphasized three aspects of human freedom that are separate from law, separate from government and separate from other people: life, liberty and property. Locke also argued that, "the individual ownership of goods and property is justified by the labor exerted to produce those goods or utilize property to produce goods beneficial to human society,"[16] that property precedes government and government cannot "dispose of the estates of the subjects arbitrarily."[17] Yet politicians today think that their primary job is to create and sustain government revenue at the expense of property rights.

The later political philosophy of Karl Marx heavily criticized Locke's view of property and plays a profound role in the neo-progressive view of property today. One thing is for sure, it was Locke's view of property that inspired our founding fathers to make property ownership central to liberty in America. It was Thomas Jefferson who took Locke's view of property and absorbed it into what it means to *pursue happiness*, thus changing the foundational liberty premise of Locke in the Declaration of Independence to, "life, liberty and the pursuit of happiness." Private property ownership, according to the founders, was not necessarily about the possessions or goods themselves, but that those possessions are the result of a manifestation of the fundamental right to pursue happiness.[18] "The first principles of association" says Jefferson, is "the guarantee to everyone of a free exercise of his industry, and the fruits acquired by it."[19] Yet this fundamental right to own property, which includes income, as a primary aspect of the pursuit of happiness, has been slowly eroded by *legal plundering*. Without private property ownership, wrote James Wilson, one of the authors of the US Constitution, "the tranquility of society would be perpetually disturbed by fierce and ungovernable competitions for the possession and enjoyment of things, insufficient to satisfy all, and by no rule of adjustment distributed by each."[20] This is what is happening today through *forced fairness*. The government creates more big problems by trying to fix small ones. Property rights are essential to preserving the individual right to pursue happiness as well as the collective right to preserve peace and happiness within society as a whole, thus Madison said, "The personal right to acquire property, which is a natural right, gives to property, when acquired, a right to protection, as a social right."[21]

Over the past century or so, the courts, and law enforcement as well, have continually deviated from their original purpose, which is, in part, to protect individuals from arbitrary legislation. Or, to put it another way, the Judicial Branch should protect people from the Executive and Legislative Branches, or the Executive Branch should protect people from the Legislative and Judicial Branches. Nonetheless, the collectivist effort has undermined individual property rights and has set false precedent in the courts by actually, again, redefining terms. Precedent has redefined the 5th Amendment's *public use* in the *Kelo vs. New London* case, for example, where the Supreme Court ruled that local governments could take private property and give it to private developers. Again, this comes down to philosophy, an ideology adopted by individuals in government who then consciously work against the vivacity of their Oath, for the sake of America as a corporation, a big business. Dissenting in the *Kelo* case,

Justice Sandra Day O'Connor wrote, "Under the banner of economic development, all private property is now vulnerable to being taken and transferred to another private owner.... The founders cannot have intended this perverse result." Specifically and repeatedly, our founders, based upon Locke's philosophy of liberty, designed the American Rule of Law to protect and secure individual property rights from the will of the majority, and especially from the will of those in government. The majority throughout history has had some say in public policy, it still should, to some degree. Yet, not as it relates to undermining fundamental rights like owning property. So if fifty one percent of the population wants to take an individual's land so that a Wal-Mart can be built to create jobs, the majority cannot do it. Why not? Because, in America, property rights are fundamental to personal liberty, which was the whole intention of gaining Independence from an English Monarchy, where all property is feudalistic and owned by the King. Property is the extension of an individual's labor. Labor itself is one's own property. The self is property and what labor creates is property, which is actualizing the "pursuit of happiness" that Jefferson talks about. People today are being conditioned that secondary laws regulate legal possession of property by force, or, even whether or not the individual can own or be in legal possession of property, like a plant. Jefferson makes the point, "He who is permitted by law to have no property of his own can with difficulty conceive that property is founded in anything but force."[22]

The Rule of Law is designed to prevent the people in government and people within a majority of the population from violating the rights of other people. The Constitution only works correctly, as a single power, when the letter and the spirit of the Law are adhered to and enforced. The very idea of the majority agreeing to take one individual's land for the benefit of a private company, to create jobs, is a violation of the landowner's property rights, plain and simple. The *Public Use* clause in the 5th Amendment to the US Constitution is not a means to manipulate an argument to sidestep this protection "legally." Public use is *public use*, not *private use* for public use. Locke emphasized that freedom is not the absence of law, but rather freedom is to be preserved through law,

> "The end of law is not to abolish or restrain, but to preserve and enlarge freedom.... For liberty means, to be free from restraint and violence from others; which cannot be, where there is no law: (for who could be free, when every other man's humour might domineer over him?) but a liberty to dispose, and order as he lists, his person, actions, possessions, and his whole property, within the allowance of those laws under which he is, and there in not to be subject to the arbitrary will of another, but freely follow his own."[23]

Well then how is taking an individual's land for the sake of creating jobs in the community arbitrary, and not for public use? Because public use is predicated upon government sustainability, and, whereby tax revenue is the financial source for such sustainability. A Wal-Mart is privately owned for private profit. Public use property is collectively owned, like a park or a library, which are sustained by tax revenue. In reality, the ulterior motive for such a scheme like *Kelo*, is that the more jobs that are created equals more income tax revenue for the state and the federal government, and an increase in sales tax revenue at the state and local levels. There is always an ulterior motive and it is usually money and power, also known as greed in action. Attached to this greed is a nice benevolent argument. The government didn't support women in the work force, for example, because of *equality*, no. The government encouraged women in the workforce because it literally doubled income tax revenue. That is a fact. Prior to this, women raised children at home and instilled in them life's fundamentals. Now the government gets in there at an early age and instills "fundamentals" like being a good worker and obeying authority, and they do it because women are at work now. This is not a critique of working women at all, but a statement of *a posteriori* fact.[23.5]

James Madison wrote in his essay called *Property*, which sums up Locke's view, "Government is instituted to protect property of every sort; as well that which lies in the various rights of individuals, as that which the term particularly expresses. This being the end of government, that alone is a just government, which *impartially* secures to every man, whatever is his *own*." Where does this transfer of private property to private ownership by force, which benefits public use, and by the courts, come from? *Wickard vs. Filburn*. This case is a prime example of not only how the government transfers private property to private property for public use by force, but this case is a primary example of the manipulation of the language of the *Commerce Clause*, which justified the taking of a man's wheat from his farm, thus creating very bad "legal" precedent and nullifying the farmer's property rights. Moreover, this case has slippery sloped into a war on raw foods and dairy, as a means to disseminate the corporate food system, which of course generates tax revenue. The icing on the cake is the good ol' trusty "public safety" arguments combined with the sweet justification of citing secondary legislation.

Hobbes, contrary to Locke, argued against the idea of individual property rights. Recall that Hobbes was arguing for the *divine right of kings,* specifically rationalizing the rule of King Charles II. Hobbes said that if people owned private property, it would lead to the devastation of civilized society and return the people to a State of Nature, a nature of warfare,

> "A fifth doctrine that tendeth to the dissolution of a Commonwealth is that every private man has an absolute propriety in his goods, such as excludeth the right of the sovereign. Every man has indeed a propriety that excludes the right of every other subject: and he has it only from the sovereign power, without the protection whereof every other man should have right to the same. But the right of the sovereign also be excluded, he cannot perform the office they have put him into, which is to defend them both from foreign enemies and from the injuries of one another; and consequently there is no longer a Commonwealth."[24]

In the end, Hobbes says that if people truly owned private property, it would limit government's ability to protect people from themselves and from foreign invasion. Therefore, Hobbes said, in short, that government should hold absolute, central power over the masses, who are easily manipulated, and who are generally dim-witted and easily subject to violence. Sound familiar? Isn't this America today? Yet historically, governments respond to violence with violence, so what has changed? Like I said before, it comes down to the philosophical views of individuals who either believe or who do not believe in property rights and personal liberty. Sadly, there are many who are employed in government today who simply do not like what the founders stood for. But it is not up to those who do not believe in property rights and personal liberty. The American Rule of Law that secures these fundamentals has already been established. And, those who seek to change it stomp on and spit in the face of those who have died for such principles. These people who seek to undermine our Rule of Law from within are neo-progressive. When these types of government officials undermine property rights through the legal system, they do so because the people not in government let them.

The Law

The US Constitution secures and protects the free individual's property ownership from the will of the majority and from the arbitrary will of the people in government within three of first ten Amendments called the Bill of Rights, as a matter of Law and not as a matter of policy. The Third and Fourth Amendments were designed to protect people's homes from forceful entry and the stationing of military personnel, which was heavily abused in the Colonies by King George the III. The Fourth Amendment reads,

> "The right of the people **to be secure in their persons, houses, papers, and effects, against unreasonable searches and seizures, shall not be violated**, and no Warrants shall issue, but upon probable cause, supported by Oath or affirmation, and particularly describing the place to be searched, and the persons or things to be seized." (bold added)

Notice how strong the 4th Amendment language is, "...shall not be violated?" When law enforcement reasonably suspects a person of having committed a crime, they must find *probable cause* and submit the evidence for review to a judicial official, followed by that judge's/magistrate's approval and signature, in order to secure a warrant. This must be done before a cop can arrest and/or use *force* against the suspect and their property, unless the crime is actually witnessed by the officer. In addition, the warrant must be specific as to the area to be searched and the property to be seized. How certain are we, however, that the magistrate is not being complicit with law enforcement, as to what the lack of probable cause may be within any specific request for a warrant? A magistrate may very well be easily persuaded into issuing a warrant simply by rhetoric within the context of the officer's articulation of what counts as probable cause, for them, or by way of a statute's dictatorial command to issue a warrant in specific circumstances. Officer articulation is extremely important and can be a double-edged sword, depending upon the individual officer's moral compass and constitutional comprehension. Is the judicial official unbiased? Is the cop unbiased? Are the judicial official and the cop's understanding of probable cause founded upon their understanding of the Constitution itself, or is their understanding of what probable cause is based upon their "training?" Or, is their understanding founded upon a combination of both? The latter is more reasonable. Still, one must surrender to one or the other, ultimately. Therefore, conviction of one over the other must derive from knowledge, not necessarily by training. Training and knowledge are not equal. Many times law enforcement officials do not request a search warrant when certain magistrates are on duty. They wait for the one that may easily issue the warrant. This is called *magistrate shopping*.

The 4th Amendment has its origin in the fact that King George III would allow individuals within his enforcement ranks to write their own search and seizure warrants, and then just go into people's homes and take their stuff at will, and on mere suspicion of criminal activity. Moreover, the King would create crime as a means to justify getting into people's homes and to take their stuff. For example, the Stamp Act. How do we, then, define what the term *unreasonable* means in the Amendment? *Unreasonable* is defined within the Amendment itself, which overall, is a search or seizure of an individual, their home or personal property absent a warrant founded upon probable cause. What is probable cause? Probable cause, according to Cornell Law School, is when there is a reasonable basis that a crime may have been committed and that specific evidence of the crime is present in the place to be searched. If evidence can be secured by way of *plain view*, absent a search or a seizure, then generally a warrant is not necessary. In spite of the Law, however, neo-progressive thinking, and even many law enforcement officials, in general, seek to manipulate this lawful process by articulating a mandate to search or seize property as a matter of policy instead of a matter of Law, because the Law itself is too restrictive upon the government's effort in catching the "bad guy." To illustrate, recently Robert S. Litt, general counsel for the Office of the Director of National Intelligence, which runs the NSA, corroborated this fact in counsel with the *Privacy and Civil Liberties Oversight Board*, by actually saying that finding probable cause on individuals to secure search warrants which would allow lawful surveillance of certain individuals is just "too difficult."[25] This "difficulty" then leads to *matters of policy* designed to circumvent the Amendment's provision by articulating, usually through thousands of pages of "legal" and pseudo-rational jargon, ways around the probable cause requirement and thus expanding such enforcement in general. The *Patriot Act*, or *Civil Asset Forfeiture* comes to mind. Secondary laws are created out of a *matter of policy* consensus, which are also ultimately *withstanding* to the Constitution. In the "rationale" of *Civil Asset Forfeiture*, for example, policy redefines and labels such enforcement as "civil," and the property itself as the defendant, thus targeting the actual property as the criminal. Labeling the taking of personal property as *civil* allows cops to "legally" violate or circumvent the Law of the 4th Amendment. Or, as Bastiat called it, *legal plundering*. What about when the Legislative Branch criminalizes the possession of property for the purpose of adhering to specific interest groups? For example, the Brady Campaign's fight against the cosmetic appearance of certain types of guns. Is not a gun property first if not used as a weapon? Is not the Brady Campaign a special interest group? The NRA is not an interest group because it advocates the free exercise of a fundamental right. Rights are not special interests. The Brady Campaign seeks to work against such a right.

To be secure in one's *person* simply means that the cops cannot search or seize an individual without a warrant. A "pat down," however, to search for weapons in the midst of *reasonable suspicion* of a possible crime is not a search.[26] Nor can the cops search a person's residence without a warrant. An individual's "papers and effects" can neither be searched nor seized without a warrant. "Effects" in the 4th Amendment means personal property, such as cell phones, computers, a toolbox, a vehicle, luggage, a purse and the like, unless quantified as a "pat down," which is not a search. None of which can be seized or searched without a warrant. That is the Law. A law enforcement officer generally must ask for permission, or consent, to search any personal property because if they get consent to search, the Constitution becomes null and void, for that moment, unless the individual retracts their consent. Yet, *public policy* can deem otherwise, and especially in the name of "terrorism, a state of emergency or exigent circumstances." which are all later "progressive text manipulations" created as a means to avoid the restrictions of the Law on the people in government, for "public safety," purposes. These "exceptions" are commonly recognized by precedent (Katz v. U.S.). Public policy also incites and socially engineers officers to make reference to the judicial branch as the legal justification for their actions, when questioned by an individual about a search, as opposed to their own right of conscious and by the officer adhering to the simple language of the Constitution itself. A good example of this is the recent case of *Commonwealth of Pennsylvania vs. Shiem* (2014), in which the Pennsylvanian Supreme Court ruled that law enforcement no longer needs a warrant to search vehicles. A competent officer would still seek a warrant when the need to search a vehicle arises. An incompetent officer would readily search a car simply because the court said it was ok, withstanding to what the 4th Amendment actually reads. These are essentially ignorance and character issues in the incompetent officers. A police state can only come about when all three branches of government are complicit to one another. A police state is grossly unlawful and extremely un-American. These legal efforts to control property count as what Madison called, *silent encroachments*, small changes, as a matter of policy (mutable policy), over time, that in the end usurp the Law. The Constitution only allows *Treason*, for example, to be the only crime not completely subject to 4th Amendment protection, adding that testimony itself from two witnesses, or by confession, must be in addition to whatever evidence is secured against the defendant. In short, absent two witnesses or confession, a person cannot be convicted of treason, even though the evidence to the contrary may be overwhelming. However, in the spirit of past despots, to get around this, the definition of Treason merely needs to be expanded on to encompass the controls the government wants. Fortunately, the founder's foresaw such a likely abuse and specifically defined Treason and how it shall commence further. In the Constitution itself, Article 3, Section 3, reads,

> Treason against the United States, shall consist only in levying War against them, or in adhering to their Enemies, giving them Aid and Comfort. **No Person shall be convicted of Treason unless on the Testimony of two Witnesses to the same overt**

Act, or on Confession in open Court. The Congress shall have Power to declare the Punishment of Treason, but no Attainder of Treason shall work Corruption of Blood, or Forfeiture except during the Life of the Person attainted. (bold added)

This is very important because such a specific definition prevents government officials from adhocing the term, or redefining the term treason, as a way to actualize an agenda, or to justify the actions against a specific target. The word "levying" may be another issue. As we have seen throughout American legal history, adhocing is a philosophical process where someone tries to prevent the falsification of an argument that has been created as an attempt to rationalize changes made to the original terms of the argument. For example, the term *ownership* has been adhoced into the term *legal possession* as a means for government to maximize and justify government authority over what it means to own something, while still utilizing the term "ownership."

The next Amendment within the Bill of Rights that protects property ownership is the 5th Amendment, which reads,

"No person shall be held to answer for a capital, or otherwise infamous crime, unless on a presentment or indictment of a Grand Jury, except in cases arising in the land or naval forces, or in the Militia, when in actual service in time of War or public danger; nor shall any person be subject for the same offense to be twice put in jeopardy of life or limb; nor shall be compelled in any criminal case to be a witness against himself, **nor be deprived of life, liberty, or property, without due process of law; nor shall private property be taken for public use, without just compensation.**" (bold added)

"No person shall be...deprived of life, liberty, or property, without due process..." These are the fundamental, *inalienable rights* that Locke, in his political dissertation, said are natural and are beyond the arbitrary rule of government. The founders agreed and made it the *Law of the Land,* whereby such infringement of these rights by government would be subject to very strict rules. *Due Process* of law comes out of the Magna Carta, which declares, "No freeman shall be taken, or imprisoned, or disseised, or outlawed, or exiled, or in any way harmed - nor will we go upon or send him - save by lawful judgment of his peers or by the Law of the Land." *Due Process* basically means that an individual can have their day in court, whereby as the defendant, they can cross-examine their accuser and the accuser's witnesses. As a defendant, they can also submit evidence on their own behalf. And, most importantly, as it relates to due process, the burden of proof falls upon the government, which must be beyond a reasonable doubt. It is here, in the 5th Amendment, that I believe the Supreme Court seriously flawed in its interpretation of *public use* in the *Kelo* case. *Public use* can, arbitrarily, just about substantiate any and all arguments for taking private property. This is another example of adhocing. Madison said, "In framing a government which is to be administered by men over men, the great difficulty lies in this: you must first enable the government to control the governed; and in the next place oblige it to control itself."[27] Thus, the Law, or Constitution was designed, for example, to determine the act of theft equally for the people in government as it is defined for the people not in government. To steal is to steal, period. Assault is assault, period. In chapter three, *The Rule of Law vs. The Legal System,* I'll show how such policies like *Qualified Immunity* have been created as a mean to rationalize, or adhoc, the government's ability to commit crime in the midst of preventing, stopping or solving crime.

Blackstonian Theory

A great dichotomy has slowly arisen in the courts between the intended Constitutional protections of private property ownership and the neo-progressive legal precedent that slowly usurps these "difficult" protections. Similar to the original views that helped establish the principles in the Constitution, this dichotomy also has a history in political philosophy. Let's face it, there are people in and out of government who simply do not believe in private property ownership, or property rights in general. They believe that all property should be owned in common and that any and all property should be allocated and controlled by a centralized power, in such a way that benefits the "common good" as a whole. It sounds nice, but in practice, such a philosophical view would undermine the entire American Revolution, and the Declaration of Independence. Moreover, such a view in practice not only blends modern America into the likeness of other collectivist countries, but it would also return the United States to the historical authoritarianism of 18th Century Britain, where the people in government were unequal to the people not in government, and all property was owned and controlled by one central power, a King.

Locke believed that government should be limited to the natural moral law, as common individuals ought to be. This is, again and again, and in part, why the founders adopted Locke's political philosophy to create the American system of government, which is "centralized" in the US Constitution and the Declaration of Independence. If it is wrong for an individual to murder, steal or violate the fundamental rights of others, then it is also equally wrong for government to murder, steal and violate the rights of others. Government power is limited to a natural, moral law and to the people's fundamental rights. In addition, and again, rights derive from property, first and foremost, and primarily from self-ownership. If natural, moral law is not the foundation of just government, then what is? If this not be the case, then people in government can legitimately rationalize any and all activity within government. In opposition to Locke, there are an array of philosophical views for thinking the contrary of what has become fundamentally the case in America. Hobbes' view was just one example. There is another such view, and many people in American government, in the past and today, consciously and subconsciously, hold to this view, and they hold to this view specifically for the reason of justifying any and all government activity, which has become secured in precedent.

Sir William Blackstone, an English jurist, judge and politician, who published the *Commentaries on the Laws of England* in the 1760s, had a profound effect on legal minds, including many of the founders, helping to establish common law in America. Contrary to Locke and to the founding fathers' views that were victorious in the debates, Blackstone argues in these *Commentaries* that government has "absolute despotic power," that government is an "absolute, uncontrolled authority," and "can do everything that is not naturally impossible." Blackstone rejected Locke's views on natural, moral law as "theoretical," that there are no such moral limitations on government. In Blackstone's view, government can do anything that is not specifically prohibited by its system of laws. Even Thomas Jefferson and James Wilson, two founding fathers, expressed concern over Blackstone's influence on law students and other political thinkers of the time and in the future.[28] In a letter written to James Madison in 1826, Jefferson makes reference to Blackstone's negative influence on pre-revolution, present and future law students. He says that Blackstone's influence had already turned New York and South Carolina away from the US Constitution,

> "In the selection of our Law Professor, we must be rigorously attentive to his political principles. You will recollect that before the revolution, Coke Littleton was the universal elementary book of law students, and a sounder whig never wrote, nor of profounder learning in the orthodox doctrines of the British constitution, or in what were called English liberties. You remember also that our lawyers were then all whigs. But when his black-letter text, and uncouth but cunning learning got out of fashion, and the honied Mansfieldism of Blackstone became the student's hornbook, from that moment, that profession (the nursery of our Congress) began to slide into toryism, and **nearly all the young brood of lawyers now are of that hue.** They suppose themselves, indeed, to be whigs, because they no longer know what whigism or republicanism means. It is in our seminary that that vestal flame is to be kept alive; it is thence it is to spread anew over our own and the sister States. If we are true and vigilant in our trust, within a dozen or twenty years a majority of our own legislature will be from one school, and many disciples will have carried its doctrines home with them to their several States, and will have leavened thus the whole mass. New York has taken strong ground in vindication of the constitution; South Carolina had already done the same. Although I was against our leading, I am equally against omitting to follow in the same line, and backing them firmly; and I hope that yourself or some other will mark out the track to be pursued by us."[29] (bold added)

One of James Madison's appointed judges during his presidency, St. George Tucker, who was a law professor and who published an

American version of Blackstone's *Commentaries*, said in the Appendix that Blackstone's view of government's unlimited sovereignty directly went against "the new lights which the American Revolution has spread over the science of politics." These "new lights" are life, liberty and property. Tucker was also very verbal in his sentiments against slavery and he articulated works in favor of emancipation, which ironically, at the time, went against adherents to Blackstonian theory.

During the early-mid 19th century, Blackstone's political philosophy began to and continues to directly influence law students and lawyers alike. Blackstone's views on absolute *statism* appealed to politicians and lawyers who defended slave owners, for example, and who likewise defended the institution of slavery in general.[30] Upon capture of a runaway slave, lawyers argued that the slave had to prove that he/she had the right to be free. Even James Madison had specifically argued earlier that contrary to Europe, in America, people are free, that no person, absent conviction of a crime, should have to ask permission from government to be free.[31] Also, Thomas Jefferson articulated that, "Under the law of nature, all men are born free," as a premise within *Samuel Howell v. Wade Netherland*, April 1770. Defiantly, Blackstone's views of liberty undermined, or many times even reversed Locke, Jefferson and Madison's views of freedom in the courts. Blackstone's view inspired and allowed lawyers, who also later became judges and politicians, as well as later influential political thinkers, to avoid the principles of natural, moral law, for the sake of *legal precedent*, and the restoration of absolute *statism* that dominated the English Monarchy. Blackstonian theory began structuring modern jurisprudence, thus later paving the way and underlying the "legal" arguments for Reconstruction policy and the Progressive Era. The Oath that is taken by government officials in the past and today, exemplifies the moral and political principles of Locke and of the founders. Yet, when a government official specifically adopts a view like Blackstone's, that is contrary to American principles, whereby their actions are divergent to securing the liberty and natural rights of the people, which includes property ownership, they should be deemed corrupt and a "domestic enemy."

This shift from America's foundational principles to such principles as Blackstone's can be seen creeping into case law since the Antebellum period within American history. Such arbitrary applications of government power have increased greatly, completely changing the way American government interprets fundamental rights, as well as property rights. Thus, over the last one hundred and fifty years or so, we have seen a digression from the founders' embodiment of Lock's political philosophy into Hobbesian and Blackstonian systems of government. And, today, this is still the fundamental question to ask, "What is the just and moral role of government?" The founding fathers say Locke's view is the best view of what the role of government is, and that view is what the Constitution is intended to secure. The neo-progressives and their likenesses in the courts say Blackstone's view is the best view of what the role of government should be. To oversimplify, we have, historically, two competing political *philosophies* working against each other within the American political landscape, and I don't mean democrat vs. republican. One is liberty based (Locke) and one is non-liberty based (Blackstone). Moreover, law enforcement today is predicated on the latter. The courts are riddled with the standards of Blackstonian theory, contrary to the foundational doctrine of property ownership found in Locke.

In *Sharpless vs. Philadelphia*, Blackstonian philosophy, which again is the belief that government can do whatever it wants that is not specifically restricted in its system of laws, was a view held by the Pennsylvania Supreme Court Chief Justice Jeremiah Black. Black allowed government, in 1853, to invest taxpayer money in a private railroad. Justice Black wrote, "If the people of Pennsylvania had given all the authority which they themselves possessed, to a single person, they would have created a despotism as absolute in its control over life, liberty and property, as that of a Russian autocrat." Basically, through *implied consent*, rather than direct consent from the people in their representatives, the lawmakers, and likewise the courts, are only limited by their own judgments or discretions, unless law specifically prohibits same. This directly contradicts not only Locke, but also the founder's intent to limit lawmakers' ability to undermine property rights that are secured in the Constitution. Ironically, this is how most people view American government actions today. This is why the spirit of the law must sync with the letter of the law. Blackstonian theory dominated the courts throughout the Progressive Era and into today. Again, this Blackstonian view is that government can do whatever it wants unless the Law specifically prohibits the act, and, that rights, including property rights, are created by society to serve and protect the interests of society itself, not the individual. Imagine how far you can run with this if you want to undo the Rule of Law. This is also why, in part, reinterpreting the Constitution as "practical" is so very important for neo-progressives. But, not practical in the sense you would think. Practical for government, not practical for the people. This rise of the philosophy of Pragmatism (practical), or Blackstonian Theory, has infected the American system of government like a virus, socially and intellectually engineering the people in government away from the vivacity and lawful adherence to their Oaths, which is designed to hold them accountable to both the wording and spirit of the Constitution. Timothy Sandefur, an adjunct scholar at the Cato

Institute and attorney at the *Pacific Legal Foundation*, writes, as it relates to pragmatism,

> "Morality does not have any necessary connection to the nature of man, these intellectuals argued; rather, it is simply based on social agreement. Now that we had come to understand this fact, older moral and political beliefs – such as the sanctity of individual rights – could be altered in ways that would benefit society. The philosophy of pragmatism gave rise to the Progressive Movement, a cultural and political crusade that sought to liberate society from what were once considered timeless principles of right and wrong, and to scientifically plan the future of humanity."[32]

The legal system today is profoundly based in Blackstonian Theory, which helped give rise to the new "living" interpretation view of the US Constitution. In addition, the legal system today that is *enforced*, unbeknownst to most cops, arose from this collective, social and intellectual endeavor to restructure the American system of government from within the courts, in part, away from the fundamentals that created it, which are natural dispositions of right and wrong, and that human beings have fundamental rights that are *a priori* to society. It is rather satirical that neo-progressives really think, I mean they really believe that their pragmatic views of what America "should be," in likeness to European countries specifically, be primarily collectivist. And, they exploit law enforcement to make this world view as much a reality as possible.

This transition from Lockean to Blackstonian philosophy within case law can be best seen in *Nebbia vs. New York* (1934) where the US Supreme Court established the *Rational Basis Test*, which argues that *any* law is constitutional automatically, if said law "rationally related to legitimate government interest." This then increases government's police powers over a person's property rights, arbitrarily. This also allows government to establish economic policy that promotes the "public welfare," wrote Justice Owen Roberts. He declared it constitutional that the New York law prevented people from selling milk at lower prices than other dairies, thus minimizing competition.[33] This *Rational Basis Test* directly undermines the *Due Process Clause* of the 4th, 5th and 14th Amendments, because it shifts the burden of proof onto the defendant when protecting their property rights from arbitrary legislation. Moreover, this new legal precedent, a pragmatic viewpoint, directly contradicts the Constitution and its mandated Rule of Law. Why? Because, adhering to the Rule of Law is too difficult for government officials who have grandiose ideas for social policy and progress. Thomas Jefferson warned William C. Jarvis, in a letter, of judicial despotism,

> "To consider the judges as the ultimate arbiters of all constitutional questions [is] a very dangerous doctrine indeed, and one which would place us under the despotism of an oligarchy. Our judges are as honest as other men and not more so. They have with others the same passions for party, for power, and the privilege of their corps. Their maxim is *boni judicis est ampliare jurisdictionem* [good justice is broad jurisdiction], and their power the more dangerous as they are in office for life and not responsible, as the other functionaries are, to the elective control. The Constitution has erected no such single tribunal, knowing that to whatever hands confided, with the corruptions of time and party, its members would become despots. It has more wisely made all the departments co-equal and co-sovereign within themselves."

Well how should the separation of powers constitutionally work? Jefferson continues,

> "The judges certainly have more frequent occasion to act on constitutional questions, because the laws of *meum* and *tuum* and of criminal action, forming the great mass of the system of law, constitute their particular department. When the legislative or executive functionaries act unconstitutionally, they are responsible to the people in their elective capacity. The exemption of the judges from that is quite dangerous enough... The people themselves,... [with] their discretion [informed] by education, [are] the true corrective of abuses of constitutional power."

As it relates to law enforcement, when a cop, for example, at any level of government, impulsively takes property from someone by force, like a cell phone, a gun, or land, even by warrant in many cases today, they are not only being exploited by the people who hold to this pragmatic ideology established in the courts, they are actualizing this Blackstonian, political philosophy into society that is directly opposed to the Constitution that they swore to uphold. The Constitution is still the Law of the Land. Therefore, the arguments for such pragmatic enforcement are unsound and are intended as "legal" usurpations. Hugh C. Murray, a California Supreme Court Justice rightly condemns Blackstonian, or pragmatic philosophy within legislation,

> "It has been erroneously supposed, by many, that the Legislature of a State might do any Act, except what was expressly prohibited by the Constitution....To serve the great end which that social compact was designed to secure, and, hence, it cannot be converted into such an unlimited

power….Under our form of government, the legislature is not supreme…it can only exercise such powers as have been delegated to it, and when it steps beyond that boundary, its acts, like those of the most humble magistrate in the state who transcends his jurisdiction, are utterly void."[34]

When a State or the Federal government can create any law it wants simply because the State or Federal Constitution does not specifically prohibit such a law, and the cops then blindly enforce that law, *legislative tyranny* commences. The question to ask now is, how do we stop it? As mentioned before, progress within society is a very good thing. The founders progressively and successfully established personal liberty out of forced, monarchical collectivism. Part of this success came from the fact that genuine property ownership was secured in the Rule of Law as a means to secure individual liberty. To undermine property rights is to undermine liberty and the progression out of a monarchy. To use secondary laws to undermine the progress the founders fought for returns society into the history we progressed out of, where nobody truly owns property, not even their own bodies. The increase in population and the innovation of new technologies soundly and progressively give way to the necessary implementation of government legislation designed to secure and protect the rights of the people. Sanitation laws, new medicines oversight, for example, can enhance an individual's right to life. However, when the argument for progress shifts to undermining the fundamental rights of the people, like property ownership, as defined in the Declaration of Independence, the US Constitution and the State Ratification debates, then such liberty and property rights becomes a stumbling block for government, or rather for those individuals in government, who seek to instantiate a view opposite of the founders', like in the *Nebbia* case. Thus, it becomes imperative for neo-progressives in government to redefine rights, property and to redefine liberty. This is when secondary laws become arbitrary. I have yet to hear a sound argument, whereby modern technology or the legislative controls associated with population increases and/or behavior, can be a rational and justifiable means to rid Americans, in mass, of their fundamental right to own and be secure from poverty and government in their ownership of property. Collectivism, public safety, public policy, Blackstonian theory, Hobbesian and pragmatic philosophy, and the like, are not argument enough to emphasize and rationalize such legislative efforts as "progress." Neo-progressives have predicated this social progress on the "necessary" undermining of property rights, which began by the attempts to redefine what it means to own something. So to illustrate this irrational ideology, now that people have smart phones, for example, privacy must be sacrificed to protect their use of smart phones. Soon enough, even greater privacy will be scarified for the utilization of the US government's public biometric identification systems. It's coming.

Since the rise of the Progressive Era, true property ownership, and property rights in general, have dwindled greatly into more or less renting from a landlord, or near serfdom. The modern argument, propagated as evidence that you still "own" your property, is that you can "legally" possess and *resell* property. This is simple, social engineering. Recall, that absolute property ownership equals absolute control, and was established to secure free individuals from government intrusion and from extreme poverty. Like I've stated previously, it's not simply because of the government that people no longer truly own property, but because of certain people in government who hold a view of property contrary to our founding principles.

Redistribution of Wealth

Personal wealth is property, and its forced redistribution has its history in an array of philosophical ideas, like in *Marxism* or *Market Leninism*, for example. There are many sources for the idea of the redistribution of wealth to choose from, all in direct opposition of what America is really about, originally. Forced redistribution of wealth has always historically failed because of the corruption and greed attached to its implementation. History shows this. Recall, human nature has not changed. Corruption creates the *economy of exclusion*. These philosophical dreams of economic utopia are implemented at the expense of the actual intended beneficiaries and the health of a sound financial culture, all in the name of fighting wealth inequality. When these grandiose ideas are implemented into free and open societies by force, it incites the need to intellectually and legally redefine initial terms like *liberty*, *property*, and *rights*, at the expense of actual liberty, property and rights, because the actualization of the original terms are great hindrances to such grandiose ideas. Now new terms are created to actualize the redefining of the original terms, like *legal possession* and *registration*, as mentioned earlier. Recently, even Pope Frances said that the way to justifiably undermine the economy of exclusion is, "the legitimate redistribution of economic benefits by the state, as well as indispensable cooperation between the private sector and civil society."[35] This "legitimate redistribution of economic benefits by the state" is the source of financial inequality and the source of the *economy of exclusion* to begin with. Moreover, the forced redistribution of wealth actually creates more poverty because the corrupt and greedy people, who hold the power of oversight, dip their fingers into the pie, somehow, someway. Redistribution of wealth by forcefully extracting wealth from other people is not the answer because not only is it immoral, it is stealing. If an action is wrong, it's wrong. America is a nation built upon natural law and the genuine equality of all people, remember? Government people cannot steal from non-government people ethically. But they do, they do it by socially engineering cops to believe it's the law, and that it's for the good of the people. Retired Philadelphia Police Captain Ray Lewis said in a televised interview recently, of law enforcement, that, "It's an oppressive organization now controlled by the one percent of corporate America. Corporate America is using police forces as their mercenaries." This statement of Lewis' is the essence of what this book is about.

The financial world today is unbelievably complicated because the original terms aforementioned, which are the underpinning of the country, are not upheld and enforced anymore. Why? Because humans in government want to control humans not in government, which includes all of their personal and business finances, as a means to curb the probability that individuals or businesses may commit a financial crime, or not be successful. That is *theoretical* politics in action. Secondary laws designed on the probability of criminal activity are virtually always against the Constitution. So, what happens if the state self-referentially applies its own logic? Exactly, it fails. It fails because human nature is still the dominant, negative force in government. Today and in the past, greed in government, for example, can be when a judge seeks to attach their name to precedent. Greed can be when the legislator seeks to attach their name to a piece of legislation. Greed can be when the cop seeks to execute their will simply because they are a cop. All these arbitrary attributes of greed within government are the direct result of the individuals ignorantly nullifying their oath and forgetting who their maker is, the US Constitution. Yes, a document. Recall that is was a document, the Magna Carta, that initially undermined the absolute sovereign power of Kings.

The original financial system is a free and open market founded upon capitalist principles. Sound Law is in place to go after those who commit financial crimes or financial fraud. Within this sound financial system, forced redistribution of wealth cannot exist, just as forced fairness cannot exist in our original Constitutional Republic. Silent encroachments must take place first. The rebuttal against this original capitalist system goes like this; technology and the increase in financial diversification within the financial system today, coupled with increases in population, demand more intrusive regulations, at the expense of financial privacy, for the well being of society as a whole. Regulations can be a necessary and good thing. Yet, greed and the security of special interest income create intrusive regulations, as its own source of revenue, thus creating a completely different financial system that excludes the non-wealthy, and thus extracts wealth from the people in mass, all by force. This works when the legislators criminalize any and all financial innovations related to free market principles, at the whim of appeasing special interests, simply on the probability of coming in second to the wealth of the people. This also happens when any and everything has a price, especially those things necessary to simply exist. A recent study done at Princeton and Northwestern University has declared that America is no longer a democracy, nor a republic, that America is an actual oligarchy, run by a powerful elite.[35.5]

Just recently, Senator Bernie Sanders touched upon this by asking the new Federal Reserve Chair Janet Yellen, "Are we still a capitalist democracy or have we gone over into an oligarchic form of society in which incredible economic and political power now rests with the billionaire class?"[36] Yellen responded and admitted that she no longer knows what type of financial system America has, "I don't know what to call our system....I prefer not to give labels, but there's no question we've had the trend toward growing inequality, and I personally find it a very worrisome trend that deserves the attention of policy makers."[37] The most intrusive and ultimately destructive aspect of the forced redistribution of wealth, furthermore, is designed to undermine genuine property ownership in the name of "wealth equality," which is actually moving backwards and is blatantly counter-constitutional. The question to ask is, is the contemporary process of the redistribution of wealth actually making average Americans poorer?

The Russell Sage Foundation published an economic study in the summer of 2014 entitled *Wealth Levels, Wealth Inequality, and the Great Recession*, showing that the typical household in 2003 held a net-worth of about $87,992. In 2013, the typical household held a net-worth of only about $56,335. That is a drop of nearly thirty-six percent. This was, in part, due to the housing bubble, and the Great Recession. There is something deeper that is causing inflation and the drop of household wealth. Fabian T. Pfeffer, the University of Michigan professor who led the study said, "The housing bubble basically hid a trend of declining financial wealth at the median that began in 2001."[37.5] What hidden trend? The study concluded,

> "While large absolute amounts of wealth were destroyed at the top of the wealth distribution, households at the bottom of the wealth distribution lost the largest share of their total wealth. As a result, wealth inequality increased significantly from 2003 through 2013. The American economy has experienced rising income and wealth inequality for several decades, and there is little evidence that these trends are likely to reverse in

the near term. It is possible that the very slow recovery from the Great Recession will continue to generate increased wealth inequality in the coming years as those hardest hit may still be drawing down the few assets they have left to cover current consumption and the housing market continues to grow at a modest pace."

Wealth redistribution has always been an *unsound* and an unethical process within an oligarchy because financial elitists run it at the expense of the wealth of society as a whole. And, they do it in the name of the "common good." Displacement of blame within such a financial system is always pointed away from the actual system itself, covertly, which is the real source of wealth inequality. Such a stealthy government financial system is based upon many controversial and necessary factors: debt based currency, any and everything having a price, an easily manipulatable monetary policy, non-allodial or non-absolute ownership of real property by private individuals, property and financial laws designed to maximize government and corporate interests, tricky "legal" trading practices within the stock market, devaluation of the dollar through inflation, the conversion of property and financial rights into privileges, credit based government spending while forcing a tax on labor to pay the interest on such use of credit, government pensions funded by future generations, and the list goes on. What did President Franklin D. Roosevelt mean when he wrote in a private letter to Colonel Edward House in 1933 that, "a financial element in the large centers has owned the government ever since the days of Andrew Jackson?" What did Vice President John Calhoun mean when he said in a speech in 1836 that, "A power has risen up in the government greater than the people themselves, consisting of many and various powerful interests, combined in one mass, and held together by the cohesive power of the vast surplus in banks?" What did President

Woodrow Wilson mean when he wrote in 1913, after signing the Federal Reserve Act and the Income Tax Amendment, that,

" A great industrial nation is controlled by its system of credit. Our system of credit is privately concentrated. The growth of the nation, therefore, and all our activities are in the hands of a few men...[W]e have come to be one of the worst ruled, one of the most completely controlled and dominated, governments in the civilized world - no longer a government by free opinion, no longer a government by conviction and the vote of the majority, but a government by the opinion and the duress of small groups of dominant men. Since I entered politics, I have chiefly had men's views confided to me privately. Some of the biggest men in the United States, in the field of commerce and manufacture, are afraid of something. They know that there is a power somewhere so organized, so subtle, so watchful, so interlocked, so complete, so pervasive, that they had better not speak above their breath when they speak in condemnation of it?"

What did Congressman Louis T. McFadden mean when he said in a speech to Congress in 1932,

"Mr. Chairman, we have in this country one of the most corrupt institutions the world has ever known. I refer to the Federal Reserve Board and the Federal Reserve Banks. The Federal Reserve Board, a Government board, has cheated the Government of the United States and the people of the United States out of enough money to pay the national debt. Mr. Chairman, when the Federal Reserve act was passed, the people of the United States did not perceive that a world system was being set up here...and that this country was to supply financial power to an international super-state, a super-state controlled by international bankers and international industrialists acting together to enslave the world for their own pleasure?"

What did Senator William Jenner mean when he said in a 1954 speech that,

> "Today the path to total dictatorship in the U.S. can be laid by strictly legal means... We have a well-organized political-action group in this country, determined to destroy our Constitution and establish a one-party state...It operates secretly, silently, continuously to transform our Government... This ruthless power-seeking elite is a disease of our century... This group... is answerable neither to the President, the Congress, nor the courts. It is practically irremovable?"

What did New York City Mayor John F. Hylan mean in 1922 when he said in the NY Times that,

> "The real menace of our Republic is the invisible government, which like a giant octopus sprawls its slimy legs over our cities, states and nation... The little coterie of powerful international bankers virtually run the United States government for their own selfish purposes. They practically control both parties... and control the majority of the newspapers and magazines in this country. They use the columns of these papers to club into submission or drive out of office public officials who refuse to do the bidding of the powerful corrupt cliques which compose the invisible government. It operates under cover of a self-created screen [and] seizes our executive officers, legislative bodies, schools, courts, newspapers and every agency created for the public protection?"

What did J. Edgar Hoover mean when he wrote in the Elks Magazine in 1956 that, "The individual is handicapped by coming face-to-face with a conspiracy so monstrous he cannot believe it exists. The American mind simply has not come to a realization of the evil which has been introduced into our midst. It rejects even the assumption that human creatures could espouse a philosophy which must ultimately destroy all that is good and decent?" This financial system, this oligarchy, has become the norm in America. Moreover, the sustaining of this financial system is also the foundation of law enforcement. Such an oligarchic system can't work without force, or at the least the exploitation of force, especially in light of our republic's foundational principle's being fundamentally contrary.

During the mid 19th Century, a new philosophy arose in North America that directly affected genuine property ownership and the rise of this oligarchy within the United States; the *Georgist Philosophy*, or *Georgism*. Contrary to the founder's emphasis on absolute ownership of property within the realm of necessary existence, or property that was essentially basic, which included land, a home and tools of the trade, Henry George (1839-1897), an economist and philosopher, whole-heartedly in his own mind, developed a philosophy intended to minimize poverty and a means for all people to acquire *legal possession* of property through the *Land Value Tax*, or property tax. We touched on this earlier. Many people in government liked this ideology because it increased the wealth and power of the local government. The problem with this political philosophy is, that it not only directly flies into the face of Locke, the American Revolution, the Constitution and individual liberty, it has easily been *taken for granted*, thus allowing a "legal" system to slippery slope into the forced taxation of virtually all property having any taxable value whatsoever, outside of the actual contents of a home. And, being that rights derive from property, when property rights are thwarted by way of a tax, so are all rights. This is another example of Blackstonian theory, which allows the government to do what it wants as long as what it wants is not directly prohibited within its system of laws. In addition, this redefining of property ownership creates forced *co-ownership* of property between government as principal owner and the citizen as co-owner, or legal possessor. Government, again, is a mere entity, only made up of other people and cannot actually own anything. Therefore, it is the other people in government, collectively, who by the exploitation of force, come to own and control the use of an individual's property, not "society." Such a pro-collectivist statement, as it relates to the state owning property, is nonsense. Moreover, and most intrusively, this forced redistribution of property, directly *secures* a "legal" path for local, state and federal government officials to intimately dive into the private and personal life of the individual, through the barrel of a cop's gun. What about the security of the individual from poverty or from government intrusion, as the intended purpose of property rights? Just recently the Bureau of Labor Statistics for May of 2014 reported that the poorest American families spend upwards to forty percent of their income on housing alone.[38] Can we actually restore financial equality, or at minimum, secure people against the most devastating effects of being poor, which is hunger and homelessness?

Georgist philosophy is one intentionally developed to redistribute wealth, George says that, "What has destroyed every previous civilization has been the tendency to the unequal distribution of wealth and power."[39] Yes, this is true, which is why, in part, the founders acknowledged the need to secure individual property ownership, opposite of "previous civilizations," by establishing absolute or true ownership of the very basics, like a plot of land and a home. Redistribution of wealth today, as originating in Georgism, has actually deviated open societies back into the likeness of "previous civilizations" by legally thwarting true property ownership through this land value tax, allowing government to become richer and more powerful. In many countries, for example, some governments actually tax the value of property *inside* a family's home, like Germany. Local governments have tried this in America, but the 4th Amendment stops them, thankfully. In "previous civilizations," extracting wealth from the populace always funded and secured the aristocracy's separation from commoners, who were deemed unequal. The destruction of governments in the past was of moral consequences, masked as economic issues, as will happen here. Recall, that the American founders ended the immoral practices of feudalism and serfdom. Henry George comes along and resurrects both; because, people are again, as in feudalism, forced to work as a means to pay *quit-rent* to government in order to simply live on the land they "own". Again, Georgism sounds nice, but Georgism is the history of the world, as it relates to property rights, repeating itself.

A recent article on WshingtonsBlog.com, written by Charles Smith, touched upon how not only neo-progressives control property through credit creation, manipulation, and the "reduction of selfhood," but that the process is a *new style* of feudalism in America, also know as neo-feudalism. Smith describes neo-feudalism as necessarily dependant upon neo-progressives, "those with access to the low-interest unlimited credit spigot of the Federal Reserve become more equal than others – the perfect Orwellian description of a Neofeudal arrangement in which financial leverage buys not just rentier assets but political power and control." Thus, to summarize the endgame of neo-feudalism, Smith cites correspondent Bart D,

>"What if financial elites enter the market with their 'free' Federal Reserve cash and buy up a lions' share of accommodation to keep home ownership unaffordable and force the majority to live as renters? If, in a dwindling economy, the Power Elite can't hold power over the masses by keeping their jobs or other income streams under threat, maybe they will switch to wanting everyone to owe them rent and use the threat of homelessness as another tool to keep people under control.
>It's an extension of the food stamps concept. The system is moving towards making sure most people don't have future access to the resources that enable them to survive and create wealth outside of the system.
>I think the economy is now about controlling people. We are headed for a societal structure in which opportunities to rise economically will be increasingly stifled by those at the top. The money is irrelevant now, the real game is being played is in controlling tangible and 'essential for life' assets: housing, water delivery, food, clothing, energy. Those at the top want power to control everyone below them, particularly to keep them from revolting."[40]

Even NASA suggested that societies have collapsed in the past because it did not redistribute wealth.[41] I see this as a bit over simplistic and ironic. Past societies collapsed because of corruption, the greed for power, and the forced extraction of wealth from the masses. Governments failed by not creating a path of equal opportunity for all people to acquire wealth and to keep it. In addition, past governments failed by not securing a way to own property in absolute, as the founders originally did for Americans. The past arguments for such inequality has been a collectivist effort, evidenced in the extraction of more wealth from all people by way of quit-rent. Quit-rent, especially from one's own income, in and of itself, is still forced collectivism through the exploitation of law enforcement. This is the direct result of American government becoming more business oriented rather than liberty oriented. Individualism and absolute property ownership are what real progression out of history is, because, it secures the individual from poverty by allowing them to have a place to live, which is a basic necessity of existence, and they can think for themselves, absent the threat of death by the state. Failed governments happen because of the want of more power. Modern governments set themselves up for future failure by creating fiat currencies, as a means to get around the finiteness of real money. Thus, modern governments rely upon borrowing at the expense of the people's labor and the future labor of the unborn, creating massive debt that future generations must pay by force. This is grossly unethical. This is what will primarily lead to the fall of a nation today, the failure of fiat currency. Not the lack of redistributing wealth, but the failure of allowing people to keep their wealth, which is their property. Governments would not have to borrow as much at the expense of future generations to help secure the poor from being poorer if the people were allowed to own their basic property in allodium, as intended.

Stanley Druckenmiller, a hedge fund manager and philanthropist, recently said of the Federal Reserve's continued *quantitative easing* and it's decision to delay the tightening of monetary policy, "This is fantastic for every rich person... this is the biggest redistribution of wealth from the middle class and the poor to the rich ever."[42] *Redistributing wealth* is more of a modern *tongue in cheek* move for governments in bed with corporate interests to amass more wealth for themselves and power, while appearing to appeal to set standards of benevolence. When an individual must spend all their time acquiring income to be forcefully *redistributed* and to forcefully pay taxes on property they only "legally possess," such private charity efforts become impractical because the average person has virtually no income left, thus the need arises for government to forcefully extract more wealth and to borrow more currency to turn around and subsidize those very people. It is a vicious circle that ends horribly. The end result of bad government economic policy and the forced transfer of wealth is *income inequality*. Nobel economist Joseph Stiglitz said,

> "Inequality is not inevitable. It is not ... like the weather, something that just happens to us. It is not the result of the laws of nature or the laws of economics. Rather, it is something that we create, by our policies, by what we do.... We created this inequality—chose it, really— with [bad] laws ..."[43]

Stiglitz also said that the government's toxic asset plan, a scheme to inflate the value of assets held by banks, basically "amounts to robbery of the American people". Economics professor Randall Wray writes, "Thieves...took over the whole economy and the political system lock, stock, and barrel. They didn't just blow up finance, they oversaw the swiftest transfer of wealth to the very top the world has ever seen."[44] In this same spirit, highly regarded economist Michael Hudson, Distinguished Research Professor at the University of Missouri, Kansas City, said,

> "You have to realize that what they're trying to do is to roll back the Enlightenment, roll back the moral philosophy and social values of classical political economy and its culmination in Progressive Era legislation, as well as the New Deal institutions. They're not trying to make the economy more equal, and

> they're not trying to share power. Their greed
> is (as Aristotle noted) infinite. So what you
> find to be a violation of traditional values is a
> re-assertion of pre-industrial, **feudal values.**
> The economy is being set back on the road to
> debt peonage. The Road to Serfdom is not
> government sponsorship of economic progress
> and rising living standards, it's the
> dismantling of government, the dissolution of
> regulatory agencies, to create a new feudal-
> type elite."[45] (bold added)

Harry Dent, of Dent Research, an economic think tank that predicts economic waves, stated that the U.S. and Europe are headed in the same direction as Japan, a country still in a "coma economy precisely because it never let its debt bubble deleverage." Dent argues, "The only way we will not follow in Japan's footsteps is if the Federal Reserve stops printing new money."[46]

Like I've mentioned earlier, society, as it relates to human nature, is actually digressing back into history, and history tells all. Government's intent to force fairness and redistribute wealth by controlling and owning property is actually leading all of us back into a soft, feudal type of culture. This can be stopped in America when and if people truly own their essentially basic property, as intended by our founders. Many neo-progressives will come along and reinterpret the founders into a contemporary view that says no such arrangement had been established at the founding, as it relates to absolute property ownership. This is completely in effort to maintain the status quo. Study it out for yourself. We all know that most tax revenue created to fund social programs goes directly to the bureaucracy and enforcement attached to its implementation. The neo-progressives also argue that private charities would not be enough to sustain the amount of help people need. In other words, private charities are not enough to also fund the government's control of property and to secure its financial incentive.

On the other hand, I also want to assert the genuine and necessary balance of progress in American society that also entails economic compromise within the social contract. Such economic compromise does allow limited property taxation, or redistribution of property to benefit the collective, which does include helping the poor and to fund some social programs designed to temporarily help people who may need it. This is a good thing and most Americans support these sound progressive policies founded in reasonable taxation. The founders understood this, yet tried to minimize its abuses through the balance of property rights and limited taxation of property. John Locke says that,

> "Every one, as he is bound to preserve himself, and not to quit his station wilfully, so by the like reason, when his own preservation comes not in competition, ought he, as much as he can, to preserve the rest of mankind, and may not, unless it be to do justice on an offender, take away, or impair the life, or what tends to the preservation of the life, the liberty, health, limb, or goods of another."[47]

Society as a whole has a duty to care for the handicapped, or indigent, for example. But the *forced* redistribution of wealth at the expense of basic property rights and the basic necessities of life is unethical, because it actually creates poverty. How is attaching monetary value to the basic necessities of human existence, like water, food, land, tools to cultivate land, a home, any more ethical than a woman attaching monetary value to her own vagina? Such efforts of government to capitalize on the essentials of human existence for profit, through bedding down with corporations and special interests, are unethical and are neo-progressive, because they adhere to a political philosophy that accentuates the power of government rather than the genuine, natural property rights of free individuals. This is pragmatism at work. Why not capitalize on air then? Oh wait, the Carbon Tax. I am not referring to essentials like water, food, a home and land that are valued beyond what is necessary to exist. The social contract employs compromise, not dominance. Yet crony-capitalism dominates. Maybe if income tax revenue were rechanneled into securing the basic property ownership for people rather than funding an empire abroad, poverty would be a lot less a social problem in America. Actually poverty is a money problem. If the homeless, for example, were spending money, then there would probably be *homeless special interest groups*, with bureaucracy attached. But since homelessness is not about actual homelessness, local governments make it illegal to feed the homeless because they don't actually buy the food. Pacifying human hunger now takes a back seat to liability. The neo-progressive sentiment is, that homelessness is not good for business. The National Law Center on Homelessness and Poverty, and MSNBC, reported in July 2014, that about 187 cities across America are banning homelessness, which, "prohibit sleeping in public, begging in public, loitering, sitting or lying down in public spaces, food sharing, and sleeping in vehicles, among other behaviors." The report states that, "Many cities have chosen to criminally punish people living on the street for doing what any human being must do to survive." The report further asserts, "Despite a lack of any available alternatives, more cities are choosing to turn the necessary conduct of homeless people into criminal activity.... Such laws threaten the human and constitutional rights of homeless people, impose unnecessary costs on cities, and do nothing to solve the problems they purport to address."[47.5]

So, when a cop arrests someone for feeding a homeless person, is the cop doing his or her job ethically? Are they upholding the rule of law or are they upholding an elitist agenda? There is a relatively simple "alternative" that puts a significant dent into poverty and homelessness. The founders came up with such a solution. But like I also mentioned earlier, the founder' solutions for poverty and homelessness are, sadly, not good for America as a business model. Because, its all really about money, or currency actually, and homeless people not having a *strawman.*

Neo-progressive policy increases the power of government for its own sake, and, it surrenders by force the privacy and property of the individual to the bureaucratic endeavor of *forced charity* in the name of helping the poor. Even Benjamin Franklin acknowledged, "In different countries...the more public provisions were made for the poor, the less they provided for themselves, and of course became poorer. And, on the contrary, the less was done for them, the more they did for themselves, and became richer."[48] The proper role of government is to secure the citizen's capability, with very little help from the government, to take care of themselves first and then the poor, to the best of their financial ability. There must be a balance that secures government revenue and secures people from poverty, absent a welfare state. Sound poise is not the case today, however. Most peace loving people don't have a problem with limited property taxation to fund social programs, to help pay for police and fire, or to help secure services that care for those who cannot otherwise care for themselves. This is a good thing, and again, a sound aspect of Locke's social contract coupled with the founders' limited role of government. Even George Washington emphasized *proportion* in a letter to Alexander Hamilton in 1783, "It may be laid down, as a primary position, and the basis of our system, that every citizen who enjoys the protection of a free government, owes not only a proportion of his property, but even of his personal services to the defense of it…" Fundamentally, it takes most of us, some through defensive capabilities, and a proportion of our property, or a property tax, and other avenues of reasonable taxation to help keep the peace. Today, a proportion of the value of all property, which is the land, the house and all other property outside the home, like a car, a boat, a trailer, etc. are all taxed, which is a slight corruption of what the founders had in mind, but more consistent with Georgism. Taxing the value of basic and essential property does not secure one from poverty, nor from government intrusion, as intended, thus Georgism prevails because such taxation is intended to secure government revenue first.

So how can American governments, today, put a significant dent into poverty and homelessness? A sound taxation scheme on private and real property should only be applied beyond a certain valuation, securing the basic necessities that it takes to live freely and securely. Today, the federal government, county governments, state governments, municipal governments and the like, tax any and all property of any value whatsoever, including income. Ben Franklin commented on a sound principle for taxing property in a letter,

> "All the Property that is necessary to a Man, for the Conservation of the Individual and the Propagation of the Species, is his natural Right, which none can justly deprive him of: **But all Property superfluous to such purposes is the Property of the Publick, who, by their Laws, have created it, and who may therefore by other Laws dispose of it, whenever the Welfare of the Publick shall demand such Disposition**. He that does not like civil Society on these Terms, let him retire and live among Savages. He can have no

right to the benefits of Society, who will not
pay his Club towards the Support of it."[49]
(bold added)

It would make more economic and lawful sense today, to concur with Franklin, that non-commercial, real property, for example, is only taxed above a certain value, which secures lower income people on their land and in their homes. Even in their tools of their trade, like a tractor. Taxes would only be extracted from property that was not essential to existence and not commercial in nature, or as Franklin says, taxes should only apply to property that is *superfluous*, or beyond essential. A small plot of land to cultivate and a home to live in and raise a family are essentially basic to existence and should not be taxed. This is what the founders agreed upon. This would not only better secure general equality between all people, it would also secure natural rights. Most importantly, the non-taxation of essentially basic real property secures those who have less from homelessness. Because, as Franklin says, "All the Property that is necessary to a Man, for the Conservation of the Individual and the Propagation of the Species, is his natural Right, which **none can justly deprive him of.**" Thus, taxation of all property at any valuation, like a family's basic necessity of a home and land to grow food, or their basic income, is "unjustly" depriving the individual of their natural right, which is exactly what Georgism advocates.

Thomas Jefferson also asserted this very same thing; that property tax should only apply to real property above a certain value, as a way to sustain genuine equality, and to protect people from deviating into extreme poverty and homelessness. Such property laws are a sound protection of one's natural property rights. Property laws that allow no limitation on property tax below a certain value violate the natural rights of property ownership. Thus Jefferson writes to James Madison,

> "But after all these comes the most numerous of all the classes, that is, the poor who cannot find work. I asked myself what could be the reason that so many should be permitted to beg who are willing to work, in a country where there is a very considerable proportion of uncultivated lands? These lands are kept idle mostly for the aske of game. It should seem then that it must be because of the enormous wealth of the proprietors which places them above attention to the increase of their revenues by permitting these lands to be laboured. I am conscious that an equal division of property is impracticable. But the consequences of this enormous inequality producing so much misery to the bulk of mankind, legislators cannot invent too many devices for subdividing property, only taking care to let their subdivisions go hand in hand with the natural affections of the human mind. The descent of property of every kind therefore to all the children, or to all the brothers and sisters, or other relations in equal degree is a politic measure, and a practicable one. Another means of silently lessening the inequality of property **is to exempt all from taxation below a certain point**, and to tax the higher portions of property in geometrical progression as they rise. Whenever there is in any country, uncultivated lands and unemployed poor, it is clear that the laws of property have been so far extended as to violate natural right. The earth is given as a common stock for man to labour and live on. If, for the encouragement of industry we allow it to be appropriated, we must take care that other employment be furnished to those excluded from the appropriation.[50] (bold added)

Property taxes on any and all property of value, especially land and houses, and on any and all income, today, are secured through property law because the intent of such laws are *business oriented* to sustain special interests, rather than being liberty oriented, as Jefferson notes. Recall that the income tax was intended for the top one percent of income earners, not for poor people who had very little income. But now virtually all people are taxed at all levels of income, "from whatever source derived." The natural rights to own basic property, to secure one's basic existence from homelessness, is violated when one must, by force, pay a government a tax to exercise that natural right. Imagine how such a limited tax valuation policy would help the poor. The option to acquire Allodial Title (absolute ownership) on non-commercial, privately owned, real property, under a certain value, when a mortgage is paid in full, is sound property law. This also frees one up to pursue further passions and ambitions without worrying about the need to constantly come up with payments to simply live in their home that they have spent years paying a bank for. They are secure in the "Property that is necessary to a Man, for the Conservation of the Individual and the Propagation of the Species," as Franklin asserted. They don't ever have to worry about becoming homeless in their lifetime. In addition, owning property in allodium allows room for younger people to work the jobs that older people must work in order to pay rent/tax to local governments to stay in their homes after retirement. Yet, contrary to sound compromise, it is the basic and essential property that modern government bureaucracy arbitrarily thrives upon, which works directly against what Franklin, Jefferson and Washington emphasized above. We all know what happens when this sort of tax-all is created and enforced. Most goes to government itself, which ultimately inflates the currency and, again, also increases the intrusion of government into the private life of the individual, because they want more. It then also increases the debt, whereby the government must dream up more ways to tax property and extract wealth, to pay the interest on that debt and to fund more bureaucracy and its enforcement. This is not what the founders had in mind.

If I were a state or even a federal representative who, to the best of my ability, tried to adhere to the founder's view on property, I would specifically write a Bill, at the state level, that authorized limited taxation on the people's non-commercial, essentially basic, real property, only beyond a certain valuation, consistent with the increase of the cost of living and inflation. At the federal level, I would limit the income tax to only a certain amount of income, as originally intended. This is what helps the poor, not redistribution of wealth. Oh my, can you imagine the corporate lobbyists, lawyers, special interest groups, and the like, that would target my office and other possible sponsors of my Bill? All parties would be hell-bent to kill such a Bill, because actually helping the poor is not in the best interest of government "business." Even if such a Bill were to become law, however, the Bill's provisions would be manipulated by amendments, as a means to maximize tax revenue for private pockets. One-roomed cabins would become palaces on paper, for example.

In 1794, when the 3rd Congress appropriated $15,000 to assist some French refugees, James Madison, in a speech, objected to this redistribution of wealth by saying, "I cannot undertake to lay my finger on that article of the Constitution which granted a right to Congress of expending, on objects of benevolence, the money of their constituents." However, Madison was not necessarily against monies allocated to help the poor, or the French in this case. He was afraid of such allocation of funds establishing a dangerous precedent. The *Annals of Congress*, therefore, put his point into context:

> "Mr. Madison wished to relieve the sufferers, but
> was afraid of establishing a dangerous precedent,

which might hereafter be perverted to the countenance of purposes very different from those of charity. He acknowledged, for his own part, that he could not undertake to lay his finger on that article in the Federal Constitution which granted a right of Congress of expending, on objects of benevolence, the money of their constituents."

The redistribution of wealth is not the same thing as helping the poor. Government officials get no moral credit for helping the poor through the barrel of a gun. Forced charity has created bad precedent that has paved the road to redistribution. Madison later added, "The government of the United States is a definite government, confined to specified objects. It is not like the state governments, whose powers are more general. Charity is no part of the legislative duty of this government."[51] Legislative duty refers to *sound* precedent. The irony is, that neo-progressives will argue, again, that this ideology of Madison's is "outdated." The US Constitution is still the Law of the Land because human nature has not changed, only technology and knowledge have increased. In addition, the present abuse of the welfare state in America has grown to become unsustainable and unbelievably costly because the federal and state governments have, contrary to Madison's and the other founders' views, like Franklin and Jefferson, made charity a monstrous part of the "legislative duty" of government, by force. Since America is now a corporation under Title 28 of the US Code, whereby everything under the sun has a price, the welfare state has become a means to keep the poor economically active. This is the redistribution of wealth. It is now impossible to go back. To financially trim, significantly, the welfare state today would create panic and chaos in the streets, because, for statism, state dependency has become a paramount incentive to social engineering and control, which leads to the need to exploit law enforcement to keep it working as smoothly as possible. A reasonable question to ask now is, would there be such a concept as "illegal immigration" had the American welfare state not gotten out of control? Another question to ask is, how did this all begin? I want to cite, in part, an "elitist" document published by William Cooper in his book *Behold A Pale Horse*. Cooper, a former Navy Intelligence Officer, advises that the document is a "top secret" programming/technical manual for acquiring mass control over property, social and economic activity. The title of the document is called, *Silent Weapons for Quiet Wars*. Cooper also articulates that this neo-progressive "agenda" was written and set in motion during the mid fifties, whereby aristocracy must replace genuine American equality,

> "Consequently, in the interest of future world order, peace, and tranquility, it was decided to privately wage a quiet war against the American public with an ultimate objective of permanently shifting the natural and social energy (wealth) of the undisciplined and irresponsible many into the hands of the self-disciplined, responsible, and worthy few.... In order to achieve a totally predictable economy, the low-class elements of society must be brought under total control, i.e., must be housebroken, trained, and assigned a **yoke** and long-term social duties from a very early age, before they have an opportunity to question the propriety of the matter. In order to achieve such conformity, the lower-class family unit must be disintegrated by a process of increasing preoccupation of the parents and the establishment of government-operated day-care centers for the occupationally orphaned children. The quality of education given to the lower class must be of the poorest sort, so that the moat of ignorance isolating the inferior class from the superior class is and remains incomprehensible to the inferior class. With such an initial handicap, even bright lower class individuals have little if any hope of extricating

themselves from their assigned lot in life. This form of slavery is essential to maintain some measure of social order, peace, and tranquility for the ruling upper class." (bold added)

This agenda is, in part, the underpinning of the modern legal system. As it relates to welfare again, Cooper also cites from *Silent Wars* that,

> "The social welfare program is nothing more than an open-ended credit balance system which creates a false capital industry to give nonproductive people a roof over their heads and food in their stomachs. This can be useful, however, because the recipients become state property in return for the "gift," a standing army for the elite. For he who pays the piper picks the tune. Those who get hooked on the economic drug, must go to the elite for a fix. In this, the method of introducing large amounts of stabilizing capacitance is by borrowing on the future "credit" of the world."

Now ask, what might the "yoke" be that this document is referring to? "In this structure, credit, presented as a pure element called "currency," has the appearance of capital, but is in effect negative capital. Hence, it has the appearance of service, but is in fact, indebtedness or debt."[51.2]

Another example of this compulsory redistribution of wealth is the forced *registration* of property, like with a vehicle, for example. Around 2005-06 I was a bit shaken by some information I had read in Michael Badnarik's book: *Good to be King*. He had talked about how the title to a vehicle was not the actual title, but a certificate that conveyed co-ownership of the vehicle with the State. I was a cop and I wanted to know how this stuff really worked, so I began to dig. At first, I was only limited to NC Motor Vehicle Law books, but as I dug further, into other State and Federal Law books and their apparatus, Badnarik was right. *The*

Manufacturers Certificate of Origin (MCO), also know at the actual *Title*, is taken into possession by the State upon the purchase of a new vehicle, and in its place, a *Certificate of Title* (CT), is given to the new "owner" of the vehicle, with the name of the State and the new buyer information printed on the CT. What this does is surrender principal or absolute ownership and control of the vehicle and the rights attached, to the State. This allows *legal possession* of the vehicle by the purchaser, and thus converts those rights attached into *legal privileges*. This is the same process with boats, trailers, land, etc., depending on the jurisdiction and the property. Why? There are several reasons. One is because when the state is the principal owner of property, and the individual is the co-owner, or holds only legal possession of property, the state can then "legally" tax the property and control its use, as it wants to, by funding the implementation of secondary laws, or regulations. Also, and most importantly, such a scheme that transfers true ownership of property, or wealth, from the buyer to the state allows the state to avoid Constitutional restrictions that protect an individual's ownership of the property and their free use of it. This is where lots of "what if" scenarios come into play, as it relates to articulating the need for such policy; "The founders didn't foresee cars." Right? Also, the fact that the State owns the roads is another reason for such a scheme.

The question to ask now is, why is absolute ownership of property, like a vehicle, a bad thing? Because, this kind of liberty is not good for business and it is not good for "public safety." Being the principal owner of your property limits the power the ruling class and of government officials who want to tax it for revenue to help fund local services, and, being the principal owner of the vehicle limits the power of government officials to regulate the use of the vehicle. Moreover, principal ownership hinders the *conveniences* of the state owning the vehicle. Think of all the corporate income that is secured through this kind of *co-ownership* policy, as it relates to property. Absolute ownership of property threatens crony-capitalism. True ownership of property empowers individuals and limits government. Again, this is not good for government as a "business," especially when the government can increase its own income tax revenue by securing a corporation's income by law. Insurance companies come to mind. Civil law, for instance, is in place to deal with accidents and mishaps between two parties, for the most part, as it relates to property. The "what if" scenarios made up by insurance lobbyists only rationalize the desire for their corporations to woo government into securing their income, and, thus minimizing the inconveniences of civil suits being the traditional discourse for dealing with property damage in response to accidents. Unfortunately, for government, such civil process would be too costly, thus the need to mandate insurance. Which can be more reasonable if more options were unavailable. In addition, absolute ownership of basic property by non-government individuals does not secure a government's budget prospective, which then can shrink the workload of bureaucrats and law enforcement. Absolute property ownership also *forces* government to cut spending. Is this a bad thing? The forced taxing and registration of property has its history in governments, ultimately deriving from Monarchs, or Kings, who, arguably, created the process to forcefully extract wealth from their subjects and then redistribute that wealth primarily among consorts and ultimately to fund the King's will and lifestyle, all for the people's benefit, of course. Recall William the Conqueror. And, like the King's soldiers who enforced such a scheme, law enforcement today in America mimics the same enforcement efforts.

Again, taxing and registering property, coupled with the forced redistribution of wealth, have a history in political philosophy and in past authoritarian governments. The founders, like Franklin and Jefferson, tried to establish a system of government that works against this history. The cops today enforce a modern legal system, which is specifically designed to work against the founders' effort to undo this authoritarian history. In addition, cops are socially engineered to secure this legal and *oligarchic* financial system through the breakdown of the separation of powers, training and legal updates.

Governments traditionally adopt and use various political and philosophical views as a means to create their own policies and systems of government. Russia uses the views of Karl Marx and Lenin, for example, while America uses, or used, the views of John Locke and Adam Smith. But it appears today that America wants more and more to rid itself of Lockean philosophy, for a more Market Leninist philosophy. Why? Because today, any property that has any value becomes a means to increase and sustain government revenue and power. Politicians today seek election on promises from the treasury, and once they are elected, their energy is spent trying to generate more revenue for themselves and government through special interests. The bubble will burst.

Again, I'm not arguing here for an abolishment of property taxes or the end of reasonable regulations. I'm simply trying to point out how it works today and why. A reasonable taxation on property, above the essential, helps to pay for local law enforcement. We all know this. Without this, residents would need to stay at home all the time, armed, protecting their property from criminals. Law enforcement patrols help free up people's ability to spend time away from their home, to work and travel. If the government's intent, however, were truly about securing individual liberty, the natural rights that are attached to the individual, and their general economic welfare, as it is charged to do, and as it swore to do, then not taxing property up to a certain value would be the most reasonable means to secure people from extreme poverty. This can help avoid the forced redistribution of *essentially basic* property. The Institute on Taxation and Economic Policy concluded in a study titled, *Who Pays: A Distributional Analysis of the Tax Systems in All Fifty States*, that the lower one's income, the higher their local tax burden, "Combining all state and local income, property, sales and excise taxes that Americans pay, the nationwide average effective state and local tax rates by income group are 10.9 percent for the poorest 20 percent of individuals and families, 9.4 percent for the middle 20 percent and 5.4 percent for the top 1 percent."[51.5]

Another example of the benefits of Allodial Title on real property would help limit the IRS from taking a lien out on newly purchased homes and land automatically, which it actually does, at closing, under the *Federal Reserve Act*, which plays heavily into the Tax Code, Title 26. The US Treasury itself has "first lien," not necessarily the local Bank itself. This is because the property was purchased in Federal Reserve notes, or dollars, which has "debt labor" attached to each note. It's like being born and automatically owing money to the National Debt, which you do actually, instead currency is Fed's property. The National Debt, in part, is actually made up of the interest that the government owes to the Federal Reserve for borrowing currency to help it function beyond what it takes in tax revenues. It's credit, and your labor pays the interest. This Debt attaches to all newborn US Citizens. The income tax is a type of property tax on the labor you think you own.

This same kind of thing happens to real and private property. You gotta eat right? But, instead of absolute ownership, and like the Kings and many despots before, all property of value shall continually be taxed, especially labor, and for as long as there is a National Debt. In addition, and very importantly, owning property in allodium would not undo the lawful police powers the government has when crimes are committed against others. And, even if one did truly own their house, for example, allodium does not make one immune from reasonable search and seizure.

What can Americans do today to limit government intrusion into their private life and to avoid excessive taxation on their property? The simple answer to this question today is, sadly, don't own property. Avoiding the "ownership" of property today is the *new* and practical way to limit government intrusion. I write this as Jefferson and Madison role over in their graves.

Guns

We can all agree that gun safety and gun responsibility should be equivalent to gun ownership. Also, we can all pretty much agree that there are people who should not have access to firearms, the mentally ill that are easily prone to violence, for example. But at the same time, as it relates to the mentally ill, we don't want people in government determining who may be mentally ill, we want educated doctors doing that, absent any political bias. Once we allow people in government to determine who is mentally ill, simple political dissent will become a mental illness, over night. Neither can we infer that all mentally ill people are prone to violence any more than the non-mentally ill. Besides, there is no such thing as a perfect brain. So there is a necessary effort to find balance and common ground that, under our social compact, legitimately and lawfully prevents the wrong people from possessing guns. In addition, such an effort must not simply respect, but adhere to the 2nd Amendment, which is the Law of the Land. The issue needs to be approached philosophically and lawfully, not necessarily politically. Ethical dilemmas should never be approached from a political perspective.

Gun ownership and gun carrying, as the exercise of a fundamental, natural right, absent personal responsibility, is ludicrous and dangerous to other people. Thus, education and training, as it relates to such a right, and as a means to acquire and sustain such responsibility, is paramount and must become a collective effort. This section will not be a glorification of guns or gun culture. Such glorification tends to emphasize a lack of the education and responsibility associated with the right to keep and bear arms.

The fact is, a free individual is not truly free if the individual cannot, without government restraint, *a priori*, choose to be armed. Being armed makes the non-government individual equal to the armed government official. This is equality. Is the duty to carry a gun, as part of one's government job description, superior to a free person's fundamental right to carry a gun? Yes, if government is operating in Hobbesian or Blackstonian theory. No, if government is operating from a Lockean perspective. Thomas Jefferson said that, "No free man shall ever be debarred the use of arms."[52] Let's face it, there are many people in America who simply do not like guns, for whatever reason, and that's ok, people are free to not like guns. There are people who want to use government force to stop other people in mass from owning and carrying guns. This is special interests in action. There are also many people who do not like guns who get into government and then try to use their "power" to undermine gun ownership, which is unlawful and corrupt, because they swore an Oath to uphold the Second Amendment. The 2nd Amendment reads, "A well regulated militia, being necessary to the security of a free state, the right of the people to keep and bear arms, shall not be infringed."

Notice the strong language, "shall not be infringed?" Black's Law Dictionary, 2nd edition, which in the late 18th, early 19th century, defines infringement as, "A breaking into; a trespass or encroachment upon; a violation of a law, regulation, contract, or right." *Encroachment* here is a strong word, used by the founders often. The same edition of Black's Law Dictionary defines *encroach* as, "To gain unlawfully upon the lands, property, or authority of another; as If one man presses upon the grounds of another too far." This changes the sentiment a bit doesn't it, from today's definitions of encroach and infringe? Trespass is a crime. Another good resource for understanding the terms of the period is the *Dictionary of the English language*, by Samuel Johnson, 1792. Here also the word *infringe* is defined as, "To violate; to break law or contract; to hinder." Now here is the odd thing about the word infringe today, as it is defined in the modern Black's Law Dictionary, 8th Edition, for example. The term *infringe*, as in the contexts cited above, does not exist anymore. The term today, in the later editions of Black's Law Dictionary, is only defined in the context of intellectual property. Why is that?

The 2nd Amendment is the *Law of the Land*, and this Law was incorporated into the States as the Supreme Law of the State under the 14th Amendment, whereby State and local governments must also *obey* this Law. This was originally done to give the federal government authority over a State when the State violated a fundamental right. How has that been working out so far? Moreover, a gun is *property* first, principally when the gun has not been used as a weapon in a crime or by threat.

Gun violence is the primary argument used by many anti-gun people to make a case for gun control in the United States, and, gun violence is a reasonable argument. But there is a huge difference between gun violence and gun crime. Cops are lawfully charged to deal with gun crimes, which do entail some gun violence. But gun violence, by itself, absent crime, statistically entails self injuries, deaths, gun mishaps, accidental shootings, suicides, and the like, that are not necessarily linked to crimes. These are also not necessarily acts of violence. These statistics are taken out of context for reasons of manipulating the perspective on guns. As it relates to genuine or actual gun violence, which is equal to gun crimes, similarly, banning all medicines that can cause possible death, which accounts for far more deaths than guns, is also reasonable. The US Food and Drug Administration estimates that nearly 100,000 people die each year from adverse prescription drug reactions.[53] Where is the outrage? Gun related deaths and injuries don't even come close. In addition, according to the Center for Disease Control, nearly 61% of gun related deaths are suicide.[54] Where is the outrage? These suicide numbers are also then linked in with gun violence, which is purposely misleading. Neither statistical facts, nor all the founding father quotes in the world, are a match for anti-gun sentiment, however. The *gun violence* argument holds weak ground logically because the sound premises of *gun crimes* are not in conjunction with the unsound premises of non gun crimes, like injury and/or suicide, especially in light of the statistical deaths and injuries also related to gun mishaps by law enforcement and military personnel. The second leading cause of death amongst law enforcement officers is being shot with their own weapon. The first is heart disease. The latter premise of non gun crimes arguing itself into the context of gun violence as a whole, and as a way to establish gun control, is unsound. This is especially true in light of the constitutional charge that government officials not *infringe* on the right to own and carry guns. Going after someone who commits a gun crime is lawful and sound. Only one unsound premise, however, in the gun violence argument, weakens the whole argument itself. Moreover, in this case, the gun violence argument becomes another premise in an even bigger argument, gun control, which then, in the end, weakens the even bigger argument.

In political truth, the fundamental right to bear arms is simply a potential and theoretical threat to authoritarian government. In other words, people who are armed and not in government are a threat to the people who are armed and in government. This is classic *us vs. them*. These people in government, in all probability, hold an affinity, naturally or by conditioning, to the historical inequality of the common people not being armed, which has historically, in turn, allowed the authoritarian and brutal rule of dictatorships and despots. *Public safety* arguments are basically all that pro gun control people have, which is not argument enough to establish gun control measures in America. Such legislative efforts are silent *encroachments*, especially when the "legal" measures are aimed at the people in mass. Sound objectivity would infer that if guns are really bad, then cops should not carry them either. What does "shall not be infringed" mean? Jefferson said,

> "Laws that forbid the carrying of arms are laws of such a nature, that they disarm only those who are neither inclined nor determined to commit crimes. Such laws make things worse for the assaulted and better for the assailants; they serve rather to encourage than prevent homicides, for an unarmed man may be attacked with greater confidence than an armed one."[55]

In light of the increases in population, and the present day ownership of guns being more then there have ever been in America, gun violence as a whole, which encompasses gun crimes, is still the lowest it has ever been and it is still decreasing, according to FBI Crimes Statistics of 2012. This is why neo-progressives need to manipulate the statistics of gun crime in with gun violence. In addition, in a recent study done by the Pew Research Center in May, 2013, it stated that gun homicides are down by forty-nine percent from 1993, which puts gun related violence back to the levels during the sixties, all in spite of more people having guns now then *ever* before. Also, the study concluded that such decrease in crime might be related to more people being armed, thus, "Despite national attention to the issue of firearm violence, most Americans are unaware that gun crime is lower today then it was two decades ago."[56] If the FBI, the CDC and think tank studies like Pew have all concluded that gun "violence" is down significantly, why the continual push for gun control? With record low crime rates today, why continue the push to militarize police? Even Chicago's new concealed carry law, which was ordered by a federal court that ruled the lack of such a policy was unconstitutional, has helped drop the city's gun crimes to a fifty year low in about a year. Law enforcement leaders in Chicago think differently, however. I wonder why? Gun violence, excluding gun crime, which includes accidental shootings, suicide, and the like, has been around since the beginning of gun existence. Only now is it common knowledge, because of media outlets reporting on the matters, generally by coercion, and in line with the neo-progressive effort to socially engineer people away from their inalienable right to personal defense with a weapon, and to undo the genuine equality between the armed government official and the armed non-government individual. Where are the media reports on the positive use of guns as self-defense? Even the Chief of the Detroit Police Department said he believes drops in crime are because more people are arming themselves. Chief James Craig said that, "Criminals are getting the message that good Detroiters are armed and will use that weapon. I don't want to take away from the good work our investigators are doing, but I think part of the drop in crime, and robberies in particular, is because criminals are thinking twice that citizens could be armed."[57]

The accidental deaths and injuries from guns themselves, again, are not argument enough to undermine our Rule of Law or individual liberty. What is the difference in gun deaths and deaths associated with alcohol, for example, or by prescription drugs? All are heavily regulated already. The lawful difference is, primarily, there is no *codified* fundamental right that individuals take prescription drugs and/or drink alcohol, even though both of these lead to more violence and deaths in America today then guns ever have. This comparison seems a bit ridiculous because people are contemporarily conditioned that legal privileges are equal to inalienable rights. They are not equal. Drinking alcohol and taking prescription drugs are regulated, legal privileges. Owning a gun and carrying it is an inalienable right. All three sources of death are not the same. All death is the same, however. Therefore lets end the consumption of alcohol and medicines. Exactly, the latter is not superior to the former. A legal privilege and a right cannot lawfully be dealt with in the same manner, which is why this comparison is rather dim-witted.

The similar line of reasoning that compares the United States with other countries, as it relates to guns, is itself nonsensical because such comparisons tend to "umbrella" America and other countries into some *unionized* legislative scheme, which, intently I believe, subtlety weakens American sovereignty and America's identity. James Madison argued in Federalist 46 that,

> "Besides the advantage of being armed, which the Americans possess over the people of almost every

other nation, the existence of subordinate Governments, to which the people are attached, and by which the militia officers are appointed, forms a barrier against the enterprises of ambition, more insurmountable than any which a simple Government of any form can admit of. Notwithstanding the military establishments in the several kingdoms of Europe, which are carried as far as the public resources will bear, the Governments are afraid to trust the people with arms."

Recently, for example, President Obama praised Australia's very severe 1996 anti-gun *National Firearms Agreement*; "Couple of decades ago, Australia had a mass shooting, similar to Columbine or Newtown. And Australia just said, well, that's it, we're not doing, we're not seeing that again, and basically imposed very severe, tough gun laws, and they haven't had a mass shooting since. Our levels of gun violence are off the charts. There's no advanced, developed country that would put up with this."[58] This Act literally eviscerated gun rights. Even the library of Congress made note of Australia's Law as "successful" legislation,

"In 1996, following the Port Arthur massacre, the federal government and the states and territories agreed to a uniform approach to firearms regulation, including a ban on certain semiautomatic and self-loading rifles and shotguns, standard licensing and permit criteria, storage requirements and inspections, and greater restrictions on the sale of firearms and ammunition. Firearms license applicants would be required to take a safety course and show a "genuine reason" for owning a firearm, which could not include self-defense. The reasons for refusing a license would include "reliable evidence of a mental or physical condition which would render the applicant unsuitable for owning, possessing or using a firearm." A waiting period of twenty-eight days would apply to the issuing of both firearms licenses and permits to acquire each weapon."[59]

In my mind, the government officials in Australia do not see their citizens as equal, but as subjects, who are not equal. The United States today is still a Constitutional Republic, intended to be different than other governments in history and around the globe today. America was designed to be a force against the history of authoritarian aristocracy, and an armed citizenry does just that, in addition to personal self-defense. Madison continued in Federalist 46, "A government resting on the minority is an aristocracy, not a Republic, and could not be safe with a numerical and physical force against it, without a standing army, an enslaved press and a disarmed populace." So, compared to the citizens of Australia, the armed government officials are a minority, thus corroborating Madison's point.

As a way to curb gun injuries and accidental deaths associated with guns, Constitutionally accountable States should, of sound intent, create incentives and motives for individuals to seek out more training and education on the responsibility attached to the right of gun ownership, maybe even a *tax credit* or a *write-off* of the costs associated with education expenses related to gun safety and gun storage, for example. Responsibility that is connected to the Right to Bear Arms, as with the responsibility connected to any fundamental right, or civil right for that matter, should be a primary objective within early public education, especially upon the charge of *just* government being created to protect those rights. Public education is government. Also, those who exercise sound responsibility associated with bearing arms, like taking courses on gun safety and who train regularly, thus acquiring a Carry Conceal license, should posses greater liberty within society, as it relates to bearing their arms. Thomas Jefferson, in a letter written to Giovanni Fabbroni, in June 8,

1778, in recognizing the importance of early edification coupled with the right to bear arms at a young age, was a primary factor in the victory of the Revolutionary War against Britain. He said, "I think that upon the whole it has been about one half the number lost by them, in some instances more, but in others less. This difference is ascribed to our superiority in taking aim when we fire; every soldier in our army having been intimate with his gun from his infancy." Technological innovations can also be a legitimate source for establishing greater gun safety. I personally like the idea of the smart gun. Unfortunately, this is also a technology that could, or would, be hugely exploited by people in government.

It is cognitively deficient that the idea of despotism will never again happen in modern America, and therefore, the general people should not be armed. Again, have we evolved out of human nature enough where people can be confident that government officials will never again commit mass murders, democide, and/or force the arbitrary imprisonment of those who politically dissent? So history will never again repeat itself, because now we have trustworthy, smart and benevolent people in government who love and care for the well being of the masses above personal interests, and, such Laws as the Bill of Rights no longer carry force against the government officials, because humans are different now and technology makes the modern people and the Bill of Rights incompatible? Sounds stupid right? Like George Mason said, "To disarm the people is the most effectual way to enslave them."

The people in government who do not like guns, foolishly like to throw the baby out with the bath water, and it appears that this neo-progressive reasoning has become a matter of policy contrary to being armed as a matter of Law, for some time now. Rights that are non-threatening to government are the ones government seeks to secure and protect. But, when it comes to rights that may pose a threat, even theoretically, to others or to the people in government, than such rights should at least be reduced to *legal privileges*, which to do so would be criminal in and of itself. Our Rule of Law protects the minority from the majority, even if the sentiments of most Americans are to get rid of guns. This is also why, in part, the founders steered away from pure democracy and established America as a republic. Pure democracies can be easily subjugated to the whims of leaders and special interest groups, who then incite the people. Therefore, and this is why, in part, that the Reconstruction transforms the American form of government into a democracy, because now America can be easily subjugated to the whims of leaders and special interest groups. Campaigns on and legislation to edify people on gun safety and personal responsibility should be the response to non-crime gun violence and gun mishaps. The enforcement of Law, the Courts and jail time are the lawful responses to gun crimes. Yet this won't happen because keeping and bearing arms advocates the exercise of a fundamental right that the government sees as theoretically and potentially threatening.

Regardless of the numbers published to encourage gun control, whether by the FBI or the CDC, or whoever, the numbers are still not argument enough to undermine the Rule of Law, which is that Americans hold an individual, fundamental right to be armed with a gun (*Heller / Palmer vs. DC*). Sound, progressive efforts in our society are made when public policy regulations not only secure the well being, equal opportunity and the technological innovations of the collective, but equally secures and protects the fundamental rights of the individual. Such policy is not withstanding to the Constitution. Public policy and public safety are subservient to individual liberty and natural rights, not above them. The effort to progressively advance the common good is to equally advance the fundamental rights of the individual. To do the opposite is unlawful, yet these policies have become "legal," and such policies undermine the collective's well being. The collective is made up of individuals, who have individual rights and individual minds.

On the whole, what we have here, again, as it relates to our Constitution, are other individuals who hold to a different philosophical view of what American government should be, and how Americans should be, rather than what we have and who we are. Yet, the Constitution, and the Second Amendment specifically, is still the Law of the Land. And, even if the Constitution is scrapped and done away with, under a lawful Convention, the inalienable right to bear arms still stands and shall not be infringed. "Constitution be never construed to authorize Congress to infringe the just liberty of the press, or the rights of conscience; or to prevent the people of the United States, who are peaceable citizens, from keeping their own arms." said Samuel Adams. Oh but today the Constitution is *construed* to authorize government to do what it wants, especially as it relates to guns, which is private property first. A general example of this *construing* is the possession of a firearm by felon. Again, this is an area where the purposeful, over-complication of statutes, leading to hundreds of pages of legal jargon, is written as a way to rationalize, or interpret a way around the Second Amendment. In addition, many legislators who dislike guns attempt to elevate misdemeanors to felonies as a way to curb gun ownership even more. The right to bear arms shall exist whether government is charged to secure that right or not. American government is charged to secure that right, period.

Again, if most of the US population wanted to take guns away from the people who own them, the Law would prevent it because the Law is designed to protect the minority from the majority. Once more, the United States is a Constitutional Republic, not a *pure* Democracy. Article 4, Section 4 of the US Constitution reads, "The United States shall guarantee to every State in this Union a Republican form of government...." This has nothing to do with political parties but has everything to do with a guaranteed *form* of government, which is the protection of individual rights against the will of the majority and Law Enforcement swears an Oath to do just that. Yet, neo-progressive thinkers try to thwart such an Oath through statutes, and/or public policy. Again, and again, our Constitution is essentially designed, in response to the history of governments on this planet earth, to thwart negative human nature both in and out of government, and to equalize people in and out of government. The Second Amendment, therefore, makes equal the Law Enforcement Officer to the Citizen, as it relates to being armed. The 2nd Amendment should also protect gun owners from people in government who want to make mean looking and ugly guns illegal. Unfortunately, and again, scary "what if" and cosmetic arguments have been successful in legislation designed to ban many types of weapons today. It is unsound reasoning to argue that government officials are above and beyond reproach, when it comes to bearing arms. And, at the same time argue "service" and "protection" of the people's liberty. Liberty is defined, in part, by the fact that an individual can be armed. It is also unreasonable and unlawful for an officer to approach an individual exercising a fundamental right, like carrying a gun, equally to that of one exercising a privilege, like driving, unless there is reasonable suspicion, at minimum, that the gun has been used in a crime. Mere possession of a gun cannot reasonably be itself a crime, *a priori*, in light of possession being a fundamental right. Such reasoning is ludicrous and arbitrary. The US Constitution, again, on purpose, goes against the history of authoritarian governments and aristocracy. And, for a law enforcement officer to negatively respond to an individual exercising their right to keep and bear arms, to own and carry a gun in public, absent suspicion of a crime, as though the individual is exercising a legal privilege, the cop then, on purpose, sides with the history of authoritarian governments and goes against the Constitution.

Yet again, government is an entity, only made up of other people, who are no smarter or better than you and I. Until we as a species evolve enough, whereby the greed for money and power, authoritarian rule, the desire to control other people, the exploitation of the weak, and the use of violence to get what we want, are no more, then, and only then, have we no more need of a moral, codified force to restrict negative human nature within government. In fact, we probably wouldn't even need government anymore. This is what separates America from other countries in the world today, and what separates America from the governments in history. On the contrary, we humans have not evolved out of our natures. We must, therefore, for the time being, do our best to hold firm to the efforts our founders made to undermine the history of what governments have been like. Thus, public policy that is withstanding to our Constitution, today, only prevents us from truly progressing, and actually moves society backwards, towards the days of authoritarian regimes and the inequality of people in and out of government. The inconveniences of too much liberty are not argument enough to make policy whereby those inconveniences are weakened, for the sake of greater control over society, or for more convenience in exercising same. There will always and forever be stupid and morally corrupt people who seek to do harm to others and their property. Our Rule of Law is sound enough in dealing with genuine criminals. Criminalizing any and all human activities and especially criminalizing the exercise of fundamental rights like bearing arms, and then enforcing such regulations by letter of the law only, will not fix the moral problems of society, but will only make them worse. On the House Floor in 1789, Rep. Elbridge Gerry of Massachusetts voiced this concern over the 2nd Amendment, "Whenever Governments mean to invade the rights and liberties of the people, they always attempt to destroy the militia, in order to raise an army upon their ruins."[60]

In addition, to address the arguments for gun control again, there underlies the controlled conflict of, "us vs. them," which is an ancient political ideology that has nothing to do with actual reality, but is creating political reality in America today. The *divide and conquer* perspective is doing very well so far, in socially engineering not only the people away from their rights, like possessing guns, but away from other people who think differently from those who do not like guns. Thus, the whole left/right paradigm, a form of mental slavery itself, has gained a foothold as a limited and narrow way of thinking, for most people, sadly so. The argument of our political reality being based in a left/right paradigm obviously has its source in this limited and narrow way of thinking, combined with restoring the subconscious historicity of authoritarianism.

Recently the District Attorney of Los Angeles refused to charge officers of the LAPD who shot over one hundred rounds into a vehicle carrying two unarmed women. Is this not gun violence? One woman, 71, was shot in the back. This decision not to charge the officers was a matter of policy and not a matter of Law, whereby the Commission *articulated* that officers were in fear of their lives. The car was not being used as a weapon. Thus, accountability is reciprocal of both people in government and people not in government, which is reflective of genuine equality. If the judicial branch, who also swears an oath, upheld the equality that the

Constitution is intended to secure among those people in government with those people not in government, as it relates to gun violence and gun mishaps that cause death and/or injury, then District Attorneys, as a matter of Law and not of policy, would likewise charge law enforcement officers *equally* for the same "use" or "misuse" of a firearm, as they do with individuals who are not in government, and, DAs should even be more aggressive because officers are well trained and held accountable to the Constitution. Yet, the record shows that this is not the case, overwhelmingly. District Attorneys, for the most part, grossly abuse *qualified immunity* more often by refusing to charge cops who have "mishaps," or are overly aggressive with their weapons, like the firing of over 100 rounds because they were scared. These are character and educational issues that apply to all people. *Officer safety* is not paramount to the citizen's exercise of the right to carry a gun because such an argument would nullify the *honor* in swearing to uphold same, especially in light of the risk chosen by the officer. Where is the dignity and honor in law enforcement, if public policy prefers and enforces officer safety over the security of a citizen's fundamental rights? This is backwards logic that underscores the cop's carrying of a weapon, which is not a right, over the citizen, who clearly has the right to be armed above and beyond the officer's job description. Cops, in the modern sense, were created long after the right to bear arms was codified as the Law of the Land. Neo-progressive thinking will determine that this affirmation is ludicrous, and rightly so, when their reasoning is founded upon the unequal separation of the people in government with the people not in government. The latter reinforces the false notion that such actions are "heroic." A real hero, in my mind, was the Tank Man at Tiananmen Square.

Nobody here is suggesting a return to the Wild West. As a part of the social compact, reasonable firearm regulations are necessary to actually secure the right to bear arms. Problems arise when regulations either ban or prevent most people from exercising the right to own or carry a gun. Again, the Second Amendment makes equal the citizen to the government official. Gun laws that restrict or criminalize simple possession absent just and adjudicated cause related to that individual, or simply because of a gun's cosmetic appearance, is not only plain stupid, but reveals the intent on which the people in government who create such legislation are limited in their thinking to their own political ideology, rather than the ideology they swore to uphold. For an officer to enforce such secondary laws designed to thwart the right to bear arms via cosmetic squabble, is more than likely an authoritarian in their nature and does not have the people's rights in mind, but rather his or her desire to control other people. Public safety is not argument enough to disarm an individual in public when the individual has posed no threat. There are valid secondary laws in place for such threats, like *going to the terror of the public*. In addition, simply responding to a call, whereby an individual has a gun is not argument enough to disarm an individual either. Absent even the mere reasonable suspicion of a crime, the seizure of an individual for exercising the right to bear arms becomes unreasonable and is against the Constitution. The gun is property first. Nor does answering a call qualify as reasonable suspicion or especially probable cause, and a competent officer knows this, no matter what policy may dictate. All the "what if" arguments and fear propaganda cannot get around this lawful fact. All are bad neo-progressive arguments and such arguments are only a means to *articulate* the disarmament of the individual, simply because of the theoretical threat, which only has an effect on those government officials who desire power over others and who do not see themselves as equal to those people not in government.

The Ninth Circuit Court of Appeals recently struck down California's gun law in, *Peruta v. San Diego* (2014), which mandated that a citizen must prove good cause to police as to why they needed to carry a concealed weapon. The "good cause" clause in the statute is unlawful, the court ruled. Such a clause creates an *infringement* for most people. The court ruled the law is unconstitutional, stating that citizens had the right to carry handguns for lawful protection in public. *Palmer vs. DC* also ruled that banning the carrying of handguns in public, even by non-residents, was unconstitutional. These rulings are in conjunction with the US Supreme Court's *Heller vs. DC*, and *McDonald vs. Chicago*, in which both rulings asserted that when the lower courts interpreted the Second Amendment to be limited to militias only, they were incorrect, based upon the historical context of the Amendment's purpose, which is to equalize the force of the people to their government. Thus, the US Supreme Court, DC Federal District Court and the Ninth Circuit Court of Appeals have all concluded that the Second Amendment protects the right of the individual to be armed with a gun in the home *and* in public, which is what is meant by to keep (own) and bear (carry) arms. Yet, even after such rulings, people in government continue to thwart the right of people to be armed, even law enforcement. They should know better and focus on actual gun crimes, or crimes that use a gun. Citing statutes and ordinances, again, do not justify the interrogation and/or seizure of citizens and their weapons (property) absent probable cause or even reasonable suspicion that a crime has been committed, period. Such actions are unlawful and are only regurgitations of socially engineered fear propaganda, "what if" scenarios, threats of force and the threat of being caged. Such threats are illegitimate and reflect negative human nature on the part of government, which the Constitution attempts to protect the people not in government from.

True story: suppose you are a gun owner who carries concealed, with your state's "permission." You want to drive three states away to visit family. As you pass through one of the states, you are pulled over and asked to exit the vehicle. The officer asks you "Where is the gun? You are a gun owner, correct?" But you decided to leave the gun at home, because you understand that some states and their minions are unlawfully hostile to the Second Amendment. You explain to the officer that you left your gun at home. The officer then proceeds to force you and your family out of the vehicle and calls for back-up. Other officers arrive and one has a K9. A search of you and your family take place. Then a search of your luggage and of your vehicle takes place, while you and your family sit on the side of the road, handcuffed (policy). One of the officers explains, while securing you and your family, that they have *probable cause* to search you, your family, your belongings and your vehicle because you hold a concealed carry permit in another state. Wow!! Right? How do they know this? Well because in most states that allow concealed carry, such information is attached to your drivers' license information and tags when pulled up on a cop's computer. The information shows you are a 'carry and conceal' gun owner. Nothing is found during the search and after two hours the cops let you go. What do you do? Most people would do nothing. What you should do is sue the cops and the agency for violation of your 2nd, 4th, 5th and 14th Amendment Rights, in Federal Court. You are not a subject, but a free individual. This was clearly *unreasonable* search and seizure. I would even go so far as false imprisonment. "Legally" owning and carrying a gun cannot lawfully be considered probable cause by itself, at all. Unless there is a fundamental difference in what is legal and what is lawful. The irony of this fiasco is, this particular state's constitution specifically reads in its declaration of rights,

> "The Constitution of the United States, and the Laws made, or which shall be made, in pursuance thereof, and all Treaties made, or which shall be made, under the authority of the United States, are, and shall be the Supreme Law of the State; and the Judges of this State, and all the People of this State, are, and shall be bound thereby; anything in the Constitution or Law of this State to the contrary notwithstanding."

In other words, the 2nd Amendment is the supreme law of the state, and lawfully so. However, similar to *Peruta v. San Diego*, this state is a "may issue" state, which means that a free individual must show "good cause" as to why they want to exercise their fundamental right to bear arms, thus contradicting, by force, that the Constitution is the supreme law of the state. This "may issue" statute was also declared unconstitutional in federal court. The state's attorney general appealed the ruling and in March of 2013 the Fourth Circuit Court of Appeals overturned the District Court's ruling in *Woollard vs. Gallagher*. This particular state is Maryland. In my mind, this is a state that rationalizes inequality for the sake of public safety. True equality, again, in the historical and philosophical sense, not in a political sense, comes down to force. When force is not equal between a free individual and a government official, in a free country, then genuine inequality commences. Patrick Henry said, "Guard with jealous attention the public liberty. Suspect everyone who approaches that jewel. Unfortunately, nothing will preserve it but downright force. Whenever you give up that force, you are inevitably ruined."[60.5]

These cops clearly and *consciously* acted against the 2nd Amendment, which is the Supreme Law of the State, and clearly violated the fundamental rights of this family's privacy, who committed no crime. The cops' argument is that the Law is different in their state and that they were acting in accordance to their lawful power. No! This is highly unintelligent. These officers were acting on training, not education. Ignorance is blissful when such ignorance is secured within "training" alone, absent actual knowledge that comes through mere education. Like I said before, a police state can only happen when each branch of government is complicit to the other. A lot of times, training secures injustice, and it is unlawful power. Recall *Concurrent Review*. This is another example of where law enforcement is exploited and then socially engineered by legislation designed to undermine fundamental rights through the regulation of privileges. Driving is a privilege. Bearing Arms and traveling are fundamental rights. In this case, the 2nd amendment became inferior to secondary law or statute, a possession crime, which is color of law. Thus the officers went against the Constitution.

First of all, and yet again, the 14th Amendment incorporates the Bill of Rights into the States whereby the Law of the Land supercedes State and local statutes. This means that in each State of the Union, the Bill of Rights is the highest Law in that State, next to the State's own Constitution. Second, absent a real crime, a gun is property first and the owner of the gun is also protected by the 4th and the 5th Amendments, which say that probable cause and due process must attach to the confiscation of property. Once a gun is unlawfully used as a weapon, then enforcement action against the individual being armed is lawful. Third, it is morally absurd and despotic to falsely imprison innocent people who are merely exercising their fundamental rights. Even before the Bill of Rights became the Supreme Law in the States, Thomas Jefferson said, "The Constitution of most of our states (and of the United States) assert that all power is inherent in the people; that they may exercise it by themselves; that it is their right and duty to be at all times armed."[61]

Neo-progressive legislators and their attorneys like to manipulate legal language and thus structure "what if" arguments as a way to prop-up secondary legislation, which then stifles fundamental rights. Then they "train" cops to enforce such intention. Secondary legislation is statute, or public policy designed to regulate privileges and is inferior to primary legislation, which is the 2nd Amendment, designed to secure a fundamental right. Why is this so hard to grasp? This does not take into account the lawful legislation designed to regulate in general, however. So, individuals in government who are in positions of power and who hold a view of government that differs from the founding principles, which are adopted from Locke, will create legislation to inconveniently regulate the fundamental rights of the people through mere public policy regulations. This is what gives birth to the monstrous *legal system,* also known as the Leviathan. The lawful taking of property from individuals, by government officials, is only just as punishment for a convicted crime that is directly connected to that property. The due process of law is the Law of the Land in America and again derives from the Magna Carte, "No freeman shall be taken, or imprisoned, or disseised, or outlawed, or exiled, or in any way harmed - nor will we go upon or send him - save by lawful judgment of his peers or by the Law of the Land."

If the cops in this actual case were constitutionally minded and conscious of their Oath to protect and secure the fundamental rights of the people, then such a road fiasco would not take place. In fact, the whole gun issue would not have come up at all during the stop. The whole experience would have been associated with the privilege of driving, whereby the officer had witnessed a driving violation, instead of the officer randomly running a tag to learn information on a driver and using that information as *reasonable suspicion* for the stop, then taking it further by violating the driver's right to unreasonable search and seizure for being suspected of exercising their right to bear arms, all because the tags were *out of state*. These actions are the direct result of the *neo-progressive exploitation of law enforcement* that comes through "training." It is unreasonable to decrease the risks involved in law enforcement by creating policy that undermines the very reason such a profession is honorable. If the government exists for the preservation of property, then for an officer to take a driver's gun, absent a crime, is stealing, pure and simple. And, such an act is immoral and a violation of the proper role of government that is confined to the US Constitution.

The United States is saturated with this type of enforcement. There is no room here to cover the vast amount of court cases that make up violations of the 2nd Amendment by government officials. Again, the 2nd Amendment is the Law of the Land and is to be enforced equally as with other Amendments. Imagine if Law Enforcement, at all levels, enforced the Second Amendment, as it should do, equally as much as it enforces the Thirteenth or especially the Sixteenth Amendments. Why is this not the case? Because, the 2nd Amendment empowers the people. The 16th Amendment empowers the government. One case I will mention, below, however, should be understood well.

In the United States Supreme Court Case *Printz vs. United States*, 1997, the High Court ruled in favor of two Sheriffs who refused to enforce the federal government's *Brady Handgun Violence Prevention Act* in their Counties, saying they believed the Act was unconstitutional. Again, recall *Concurrent Review*. The Supreme Court agreed. Within the ruling opinion, the Court concluded, as it relates to States' Rights:

"The great innovation of this design was that-our citizens would have two political capacities, one state and one federal, each protected from incursion by the other"--"a legal system unprecedented in form and design, establishing two orders of government, each with its own direct relationship, its own privity, its own set of mutual rights and obligations to the people who sustain it and are governed by it."

Then, quoting James Madison, the Court's Ruling continues, "The local or municipal authorities form distinct and independent portions of the supremacy, are no more subject, within their respective spheres, to the general authority than the general authority is subject to them, within its own sphere. - The Federalist Papers No. 39." The Court basically ruled that there are, in concert with the founders established Rule of Law, sovereignty in the States and that the States are not subject to the Federal Government, nor are local municipalities, in this case, Counties, except by way of those *delegated powers* in the Article 1, Section 8 of the Federal Constitution and its Bill of Rights. How is that for precedent? The Sheriffs in this case were doing exactly as they swore to do, be a lawful check and balance against the arbitrary Act of the federal government. This check against legislation by law enforcement also applies to state law. When an officer blindly enforces any and all laws on the books, the intended separation of powers blends into one. First of all, society cannot pay an officer enough money to enforce every law on the books. Thus, officer discretion, as it relates to enforcement, is imperative. Blind public policy enforcement is not an act of valor, but an unconscious subservience to exploitation. The most important thing to remember about the 2nd Amendment is that it equalizes force between the people and their government, securing genuine equality against the history of inequality.

Self-Ownership

It stands to reason that if you do not own your own life, your own body, you do not own the products of your life. If someone controls what you can and cannot put into your own body, within your own home, you do not own your self. Like I've stated before, and I will again many times later, the Constitution was established as a moral force, codified to restrain the negative aspects of human nature in government. Forgive my brevity, but there are people who have existed in history who never should have, and people who exist today that should not. Specifically, but who are not limited to, those people in the past who have enslaved, by way of violence, other human beings to exploit their existence for personal or collective gain. These people are a scar upon human evolution and are the furthest from the most divine aspects of human benevolence. And yes, enslavement of human beings still happens today, especially within the context of economic debt and debt labor.[62]

The most fundamental of all the inalienable rights, self-ownership, has become the most damaged and the most subjugated by those in and out of power, in all of human history. And we are all guilty in some way or another. I am not going to attempt to rectify the fact that our founders owned slaves and personally benefited from them. I want to show how the Constitution, as a moral force, was arguably a hope for the Framers to end slavery, and why it took so long to do so and the difficulties in ending it right away. Thus, I want to dive into slavery, quite briefly, as it is the most abhorrent aspect of American history because of its blatant violation of human rights. All laws that pertained to the protection of property rights, as it relates to another human being as property, were, are and forever will be null and void. It was pure violence that made the laws work for those who owned slaves. Quite frankly, the Constitutional protections of property do not hold weight when it comes to people being property, period. In fact, such laws are ludicrous, non-sensical and were not even laws at all.

When Frederick Douglas was no longer a slave, he discovered the spirit of self-ownership and the fruits of his own labor. He writes,

> "On my way down Union Street I saw a large pile of coal in the front of the house of Rev. Ephraim Peabody, the Unitarian minister. I went to the kitchen door and asked the privilege of bringing in and putting away this coal. "What will you charge?" said the lady. "I will leave it to you madam." "You may put it away," she said. I was not long in accomplishing the job, when the dear lady put into my hand *two silver half dollars*. To understand the emotion that swelled my heart as I clasped this money, realizing that I had no master who could take it from me – *that it was mine – that my hands were my own*, and could earn more of the precious coin – one must have been in some sense himself a slave."[63]

Slaves were property, property of their owners. Slavery was a violation of not only natural, moral law, but of one's natural rights, which, again, was self-ownership. James Madison makes reference to the idea that laws are null and void as protections of property rights when it comes to other people being property, that it is mere violence that sustains people as slaves and as property, not law,

> "We must deny the fact, that slaves are considered merely as property, and in no respect whatever as persons. The true state of the case is, that they partake of both these qualities: being considered by our laws, in some respects, as persons, and in other respects as property. In being compelled to labor, not for himself, but for a master; in being vendible by one master to another master; and in being subject at all times to be restrained in his liberty and chastised in his body, by

the capricious will of another, the slave may appear to be degraded from the human rank, and classed with those irrational animals which fall under the legal denomination of property. In being protected, on the other hand, in his life and in his limbs, against the violence of all others, even the master of his labor and his liberty; and in being punishable himself for all violence committed against others, the slave is no less evidently regarded by the law as a member of the society, not as a part of the irrational creation; as a moral person, not as a mere article of property."[64]

Stephan Molyneux, a contemporary philosopher, who writes extensively on politics and ethics, put together a thorough synopsis on the history of slavery into what he called, *The Truth about Slavery*. I want to vastly trim his presentation down and paraphrase his research into the next few paragraphs: Slavery has grossly been a common and accepted practice throughout all of human history by virtually every government, every religion and every country that has ever existed. Even the Bible conveys advise on keeping slaves. Slavery was generally a result of a family's debt, by selling a child into slavery, or by being captured, either in war or by slave traders. In fact, the term "slave" derives from the Eastern European term "slavs."[65] Plato in his Republic said that owning fifty or more slaves signified wealth. During the time of Christ, literally half of all the Roman population was slaves. And, significantly, more than half of all the arrivals to the new American colonies were actually white slaves. At the height of the slavery of blacks in America, only six percent of the South owned slaves and 1.4 percent of the North owned slaves. This ownership of slaves was comprised of the very wealthy. And, twenty-eight percent of free blacks owned black and white slaves. People who were not wealthy generally hated slavery. Historically, the reason for there being a rise in black slaves in the Colonies was because of warring tribes in Africa. They would enslave others blacks during violent conflicts and then sell them to Europeans at the ports, and to Arabs inland. Black slaves were basically cheaper than European slaves because there were so many. During the years between 1530 and 1780, for example, North Africans, primarily Muslims, abducted and enslaved millions of Europeans, including many American colonists. Essentially, slavery was not a race issue, at first, but a state power and economic issue. And, because of the increase of black slaves in America, due to their cheap purchase by the wealthy in the Colonies, slavery evolved also into a race issue. Missionary explorer David Livingstone said that in slavery, "truly Satan has his seat."[66]

During the height of black slavery in America, in both the North and the South, the wealthy would lobby individuals in the government to author statutes, or secondary laws, that would establish forced "patrolling" in the streets by white males, to monitor blacks and to look for escaped slaves, thus resulting in a "legal" use of violence against blacks, including blacks who were free. These white "enforcers" received pay by either returning slaves to their masters, and/or by reselling them, which was more common. And, for many of these enforcers, the legal use of violence against blacks was pay enough. The use of violence was a matter of public policy, and not of Law, whereby local governments legalized the use of *necessary* violence as a means to *enforce* the statutes, which attracted and gratified the authoritarian spirit within many of the white men in these patrols. Basically patrolling the streets and monitoring blacks was a way for many authoritarian men to satisfy their desire to control other people and be violent towards others, thus feeding into their own racism, and racism in general. In addition, these men who were forced to *patrol* the streets were heavily exploited by the special interests of the wealthy that economically benefited from domestic slavery, which was, again, a blatant violation of the most fundamental of human, inalienable rights, self-ownership.[67] Two really great books to read for further in depth history on this subject is *Christian Slaves, Muslim Masters: White Slavery in the Mediterranean, the Barbary Coast and Italy, 1500-1800*, written by Robert Davis, a professor of History at Ohio State University. Another book is: *Race and Slavery in the Middle East: An Historical Enquiry*, written by Bernard Lewis, a professor of Near Eastern Studies at Princeton University. So now I ask the question, why did the Constitution not work to protect such a fundamental right like self-ownership?

The abominations of slavery and the rise of racism itself, for the most part, derive from the founding of America, which, ironically, sought to abolish slavery along side of establishing Independence. Thus, being allowed to carry on as it did, slavery scarred the country. Here James Madison, as President, makes reference to slavery being a violation of natural, moral law, which, ironically is also the underpinning of the Constitution,

> "American citizens are instrumental in carrying on a traffic in enslaved Africans, equally in violation of the laws of humanity and in defiance of those of their own country. The same just and benevolent motives which produced interdiction in force against this criminal conduct will doubtless be felt by Congress in devising further means of suppressing the evil."[68]

Slavery was not a result of the free market, but by those who were immoral and who held economic special interests, thus exploiting the use of force in government with their wealth. In fact, it was the people in government who were bought and paid for by these special interests who actually banned and made illegal the freeing of slaves as a way to sustain government revenue, as it related to domestic slavery. If these people in government who profited from slavery had allowed the increase of slaves buying their freedom and the manumission by owners, slavery may have naturally been abolished in shorter time, absent a civil war. Later, it was the sound progression through the Amendment process that ultimately undid slavery. *Sound* because the 13th Amendment enhanced and secured the liberty and fundamental right of self-ownership, individual autonomy, while also keeping government limited to its delegated powers.

During the Debates, James Madison infers that such an abolishment of slavery could happen, absent the postponement of the abolishment of the slave trade in 1808, which was twenty years in the future, and as a natural course, if it were not for particular state governments that economically benefited from the slave trade.

> "It were doubtless to be wished, that the power of prohibiting the importation of slaves had not been postponed until the year 1808, or rather that it had been suffered to have immediate operation. But it is not difficult to account, either for this restriction on the general government, or for the manner in which the whole clause is expressed. It ought to be considered as a great point gained in favor of humanity, that a period of twenty years may terminate forever, within these States, a traffic which has so long and so loudly upbraided the **barbarism of modern policy**; that within that period, it will receive a considerable discouragement from the federal government, and may be totally abolished, by a concurrence of the few States which continue the unnatural traffic, in the prohibitory example which has been given by so great a majority of the Union. Happy would it be for the unfortunate Africans, if an equal prospect lay before them of being redeemed from the oppressions of their European brethren!"[69] (bold added)

But the States did not terminate the practice; therefore the federal government rightly ended it. The founders did early on hold the consensus that the Rule of Law would eventually abolish slavery if all people were free and equal, as the Constitution intended. "It is much to be wished that slavery may be abolished. The honour of the States, as well as justice and humanity, in my opinion, loudly call upon them to emancipate these unhappy people. To contend for our own liberty, and to deny that blessing to others, involves an inconsistency not to be excused."[70] On that note, and very importantly, emancipation could not have taken place in the Colonies without first establishing Independence from the Monarchy. Benjamin Franklin emphasized this by asserting, that whenever the Colonies had attempted to end slavery under the Monarchy, the King had indeed thwarted those attempts,

> ". . . a disposition to abolish slavery prevails in North America, that many of Pennsylvanians have set their slaves at liberty, and that even the Virginia Assembly have petitioned the King for permission to make a law for preventing the importation of more into that colony. This request, however, will probably not be granted as their former laws of that kind have always been repealed."[71]

Such Independence of the Colonies, I believe, would have never been actualized if the Founders attempted to first abolish slavery under a King, whose kingdom benefited from slavery. Thomas Jefferson noted that,

> "He [King George III] has waged cruel war against human nature itself, violating its most sacred rights of life and liberty in the persons of a distant people who never offended him, captivating and carrying them

into slavery in another hemisphere or to incur miserable death in their transportation thither. . . . Determined to keep open a market where men should be bought and sold, he has prostituted his negative for suppressing every legislative attempt to prohibit or to restrain this execrable commerce [that is, he has opposed efforts to prohibit the slave trade]."[72]

John Quincy Adams argued that the Colonies were not initially responsible for slavery, that slavery in the Colonies was because of the King. The Colonies originally sought to end the practice, as cited above. Thus, it was of the utmost importance, before abolishing slavery, to first free the Colonies from the King by way of Independence,

"The inconsistency of the institution of domestic slavery with the principles of the Declaration of Independence was seen and lamented by all the southern patriots of the Revolution; by no one with deeper and more unalterable conviction than by the author of the Declaration himself [Jefferson]. No charge of insincerity or hypocrisy can be fairly laid to their charge. Never from their lips was heard one syllable of attempt to justify the institution of slavery. They universally considered it as a reproach fastened upon them by the unnatural step-mother country [Great Britain] and they saw that before the principles of the Declaration of Independence, slavery, in common with every other mode of oppression, was destined sooner or later to be banished from the earth. **Such was the undoubting conviction of Jefferson to his dying day**. In the Memoir of His Life, written at the age of seventy-seven, he gave to his countrymen the solemn and emphatic warning that the day was not distant when they must hear and adopt the general emancipation of their slaves."[73] (bold added)

John Quincy Adams notably argues that Jefferson himself, who had slaves, was not a hypocrite, that such a practice had been cultivated from the Monarchy. This no way justifies the fact, however. To put this into context today, imagine believing something is wrong and immoral, but doing it anyway, simply because it is so common a practice amongst your class of people. Wall Street tactics come to mind, or charging people for water.

Freedom from such a Monarchical government was primary before attempting to end slavery in the colonies. Once Independence happened, then, the abolishment of slavery would naturally follow, in time. "Every measure of prudence, therefore, ought to be assumed for the eventual total extirpation of slavery from the United States."[74] The point I want to drive here is that the founders, most of them, were against slavery from the beginning, but could do nothing about it in the Colonies while subject to the King. And, after Independence, slavery continued as the result of the King's cultivation and State Sovereignty. Thus, it was the attempt of the founders, among many of the Sovereign States to abolish the practice over time. In addition, if the Southern States, primarily, would have not continued the horrible violation of the most sacred of human inalienable rights, self-ownership, through its enforced cultivation by wealthy land owners and their minions in government, combined with federal and state laws to protect slaves as property, recall Blackstonian Theory, the Civil War may have never happened. The Federal Government had to do what it had to do to end the Southern States' violation of the most basic of human rights, self-ownership.

Following the Civil War, the federal government, during the Reconstruction, rightly took it upon itself to amend the constitution, thus increasing federal power in two ways. First, the 14th Amendment incorporates the Bill of Rights into the States as the supreme law of a State, so that the federal government may have just authority and jurisdiction over a State that violates an individual's *Bill of Rights*. During the 39th Congress, Senator Jacob Howard, who helped guide the 14th Amendment to passage, declared that, "the States could no longer infringe upon the liberties that the Bill of Rights had secured against the federal government. Henceforth, they must respect the 'personal rights guaranteed and secured by the first eight amendments.'"[75] Second, the 14th Amendment created a Federal or US Citizenship, primarily as a way to protect newly freed slaves from State abuse. "It is a singular fact," declared Wendell Phillips, as Congress deliberated, "that, unlike all other nations, this nation has yet a question as to what makes or constitutes a citizen."[75] As a result of the 14th Amendment becoming the Law of the Land, John Bingham stated that, "the powers of the States have been limited and the powers of Congress extended."[75] He also said, as it relates to the Amendment, that, "It takes from no State any right…but it imposes a limitation upon the States to correct their abuses of power."[76] Therefore, and from then on, if a particular state violates the fundamental rights of American Citizens, whose rights are secured in the Bill of Rights, as the southern states did within the context of slavery, the federal government can lawfully intercede by force. The 14th Amendment was well intended. However, as with most government legislation that is "well intended," such intention becomes exploited over time and deviates into something else. The 14th Amendment is now the source for the federal government to usurp and exploit state's rights as well as to regulate the individual's finances, relationships, education, travel, etc. After a bit of hindsight, maybe, in 1871, Edward Godkin wrote that, "The government must get out of the 'protective' business and the 'subsidy' business and the 'improvement' and 'development' business…. It cannot touch them without breeding corruption."[77]

Slavery can be roughly defined as the ownership and force of human production, whereby an individual human or group of humans is property of another human or group of humans, and the one or ones owned has no liberty to do as they please with their own body and their own life, nor with whatever it is they produce with their own labor. Freedom can also be defined as being absent the subjective and physical restraint on one's property, body and mind. Thus, the most fundamental ownership in your existence is yourself. If you do not absolutely own yourself, then you cannot possibly truly own anything else, ever. Absolute ownership must exist somewhere. Right? Otherwise, how are individuals told what they can and can't put into their own bodies? Government cannot be the absolute owner of an individual, because government is an entity, incapable of the ownership of anything. So it must mean that the individuals within the entity of government own the people not in government. They establish and enforce the absolute ownership of other individuals for themselves, collectively, utilizing a vast array of arguments designed to protect an individual from him or herself.

> "If the natural tendencies of mankind are so bad that it is not safe to permit people to be free, how is it that the tendencies of these organizers are always good? Do not the legislators and their appointed agents also belong to the human race? Or do they believe that they themselves are made of a finer clay than the rest of mankind?" – Frederick Bastiat, *The Law*

Once you accept the fact that government is made up of individuals who then call themselves government, the more it becomes clear that the people in government think they absolutely own other people, who may or may not be in government. All the people in government really have on their side is the monopoly of violence, no more. Violence is what allows government to get its way. To illustrate, resist an officer and threats of bodily harm on you are regurgitated. With violence on their side, the people in government can tell other people what they can and cannot put into their own bodies. What they can and can't do with their own property. What they can and can't do with their own life. What they can and can't do with their own labor. This is why equality through force is so important. So the question to ask is, who absolutely owns whom? Would there have been slavery if slaves were equally armed? Doesn't take much thought huh? Just because slavery of the body no longer exists, doe not mean slavery of the mind does not exist. The arguments related to these simple questions are vast and extensive, and are generally neo-progressively answered, contrary to Locke's view of property, especially of self-ownership. "Every man has a property in his own person. This *nobody* has a right to, but himself."[78] The highest of all property ownership is your own self. Neo-progressives feel differently. So another question to ask yourself, "If someone can tell me what I can and cannot put in my own body, within my own home, do I own myself?" Locke would answer "no." Thomas Jefferson made the point, as it relates to people being owned by other people, "The mass of mankind has not been born with saddles on their backs, nor a favored few booted and spurred, ready to ride them legitimately..."[79] But have they not?

Self-ownership does not exist today. Has it ever really existed at all? Maybe, for a King. Slavery still exists of the mind, and of one's labor, which can be worse actually. Because, the threat of violence keeps the mind in servitude. This is evinced not only by the *forced* tax and control upon one's labor, but also by the *forced* tax and control upon the fruits of one's labor, their property. Slavery also exists today by way of socially engineering the masses into the left/right paradigm of the political landscape. Such mental slavery *divides and conquers* the population, as in ancient Rome. As it relates to law enforcement, the non-ownership of self is likewise evinced by the exploitation of the enforcement of the statutes that are designed to secure all the aforementioned, all as a matter of policy and not as a matter of Law, which in the end, secures the interests of the state, which in its very essence is contrary to the US Constitution.

Postbellum America, the time following the Civil War and its Reconstruction, was a time when many state and federal statutes came into existence, as a "legal" way to regulate and control newly freed blacks and their property. Many such statutes were designed out of fear of a black rebellion, or uprising, because of slavery. So to try and prevent this, and to control newly freed blacks who were now freely armed, for example, governments created marriage licenses, property zoning, gun permits, property registration and certain property taxes, and the like. People in government, white people specifically, did anything and everything legally feasible to establish ultimate power over anything and everything blacks did and owned. Over time, these statutes encompassed everyone. Most of these statutes today, however, are still only "directive" in nature, which are unenforceable.

Civil Asset Forfeiture

In the 16th century, King Charles VIII of France said that his soldiers do not invade other countries and engage in warfare because of their pay, or for moral reasons. They invade other countries and fight in wars because of the plunder, or booty, also know as property. Do you actually think that when a cop today takes property from an individual under civil forfeiture statutes, that such action is of moral or constitutional approbation? The fact is, just as in history, plunder is the sweet reward for fighting in a war. In the case of civil asset forfeiture, personal property like cash, cars, computers, homes, real-estate, and so on, is the sweet reward for fighting in the *War on Drugs*. In Tarrant County Texas alone, cops seized more than 3.5 million dollars in property from citizens. Of this amount, $845,000 went to county employees' salaries within the District Attorney's Office while only $53,000 went to various nonprofits. More than $426,000 went to law enforcement salaries.[80] On top of this, *equitable sharing* of seized property with the feds actually encourages local law enforcement to circumvent state law for the sake of enforcing federal law. This is blatant corruption of and abuse of the Supremacy Clause in the Constitution, all for the lust of plunder. In fact, in 2012, Columbia, Missouri Police Chief Ken Burton, was testifying before the city's Citizen Police Review Board, where he stated that civil asset forfeiture cash was "pennies from heaven," to help buy law enforcement "toys." Think about that.

The modern War on Drugs was created by an *imperial wanna be president* who was nearly impeached for vast corruption, but resigned quickly prior, and the War on Drugs reflects that corruption that encompasses a greed for power and money. Drug laws are shaped more by politics than by medical or social concerns. In fact, such drug prohibitions began within the context of political racism and the greed for power, whereby minority factions were to blame for the "injustices" of whites. Minorities were seen as an economic threat to the "white" status quo. To quickly illustrate, opium was first made illegal in the 19th century because the Chinese, it was believed, were taking white jobs away, and they legally smoked opium. Later during the early 20th Century cocaine was then made illegal because Blacks used cocaine and were taking the whites' jobs away. Then it was the Mexicans who were smoking marijuana and taking the whites' jobs away. Basically these minorities moved into America to pursue their own happiness and brought their cultures and recreational activities with them. Their banding together and working hard to acquire wealth and property threatened white populations, and, such recreational substances were made illegal as a means to suppress those minorities, imprison them and advance the whites' economic standing as favorable. This doesn't take into account the demonizing of such substances through false propaganda coupled with securing re-elections.[80.5] How is that for securing equal opportunity? These socio-economic facts are still reflected upon within contemporary prison population statistics today.

Such statutes and tactics generally only attract the politically corruptible. Civil asset forfeiture is a modern "legal" means of specifically increasing the funding of a government agenda and/or the wealth of a law enforcement agency and all agencies involved, because basic tax revenue is unfit to acquire such desired wealth. In other words, civil asset forfeiture statutes validate the legal plundering of property, nullifying the chains of constitutional protections, because such restrictions are just too "difficult" to abide by when trying to get the "bad guy." Civil asset forfeiture varies from state to state. Generally, civil asset forfeiture, as intimated by the Justice Institute,

> "Civil forfeiture laws represent one of the most serious assaults on private property rights in the nation today. Under civil forfeiture, police and prosecutors can seize your car or other property, sell it and use the proceeds to fund agency budgets — all without so much as charging you with a crime. Unlike criminal forfeiture, where property is taken after its owner has been found guilty in a court of law, with civil forfeiture, owners need not be charged with or convicted of a crime to lose homes, cars, cash or other property. Americans are

supposed to be innocent until proven guilty, but civil forfeiture turns that principle on its head. With civil forfeiture, your property is guilty until you prove it innocent.'[81]

EndForieture.com elaborates on the history of Civil Forfeiture, in part, by articulating what it actually is,

"Civil forfeiture is a legal fiction that pretends to try inanimate objects for their involvement with criminal activity. Civil forfeiture actions are *in rem* proceedings, which means "against a thing." That is why civil forfeiture proceedings have bizarre titles, such as *United States v. $35,651.11 in U.S. Currency* or *State of Texas v. One 2004 Chevrolet Silverado*. Of course, cash, cars and homes do not break laws. The legal fiction arose out of the medieval idea of "deodand," which superstitiously held that objects acted independently to cause death."[82]

Another term for civil asset forfeiture is *policing for profit*. It was recently reported in the Wall Street Journal,[83] for example, that police departments in Colorado and Washington States have lost significant financial incentive to the legalization of marijuana. Primarily, because pot is legal now in those two states, the cops lose a lot of the power and legal access to plundering the people of property. This is where *equitable sharing* with the Feds comes in as a loophole. Double agents, agents sworn into local and federal jurisdiction, can simply enforce the Federal Statutes instead. Crime pays, especially when criminalizing human activity is designed to not only secure revenue, but to increase revenue. Imagine if the United States, like Portugal, decriminalized all drugs, which has been very successful by the way, in combating addiction and the criminal activity attached to addiction. We can only really and legitimately deal with one, reasonably, not both crime and addiction forcefully. If decriminalization happened in the US, civil asset forfeiture would either die, unlikely, or be purposely linked to other new crimes, simply because the plunder is too good to lose. Cops would have to go back to enforcing actual Law designed to secure liberties and property ownership. I'm not saying they don't do that now, but to lose such financial incentive and legal power over other people's property, kind of takes the *zing* out of being on the streets, especially for corruptible authoritarians who signed up for the *zing*. New gadgets like computers, guns, military gear, LED lights and so on, must now become more of a budget issue for local agencies within States that legalize pot, now and in the future. In addition, outside of Washington and Colorado, probable cause has been increasingly abused within civil asset forfeiture patrolling, as it relates to pot. For example, at a vehicle stop, if no evidence of a crime can be visible within the *lundgable area* of a vehicle, and no consent to search is given, it is very easy for a corrupt cop to say they smell marijuana, or an individual in the vehicle appears to look like someone they have a warrant on. Boom there's PC. Cops can now scan a vehicle with an x-ray device, or call in a K9 to do a "sniff." The idea that implements are designed to increase the natural senses of an officer, as a means to get inside a vehicle, is in and of itself usurpation of the Law, because the intent of such apparatus is to weaken the restriction of the Law on the officer who wants to look inside property without probable cause. How does the 4th amendment protect the individual's reasonable expectation of privacy if privacy is no longer reasonable, but subject to technology that extends the natural limitations of the officer as a means to specifically chip away at such privacy? Then, the government gets mad when people get innovative as a means to "outsmart" the cops. Reciprocity my friend. More importantly, equality. Again, as a matter of policy and not of law, hypothetical scenarios become the primary arguments for such usurpation. If such ideas like civil asset forfeiture are that good and moral for society, the manipulation and exploitation of violence, by way of the barrel of a gun, would not logically be the means to employ such good and moral ideas. Fortunately the courts are ruling more and more against civil asset forfeiture. In addition, no such case to date, involving civil asset forfeiture has made its way to the Supreme Court, and for good reason. Like the Patriot Act, civil asset forfeiture would surely be ruled unconstitutional, if it went before the US Supreme Court, which is why policy is in place like plea-bargaining and deals to drop charges in exchange for entrapment schemes. These are made before such a case climbs that high in the courts.

United States vs. The Motel Caswell (2012), Russ Caswell and his wife spent their life savings to build a hotel as retirement income in Tewksbury, Massachusetts. The property is valued at around one million dollars. During the course of daily business, various drug dealers and such rented rooms with the intent to deal drugs, absent the knowledge of the Caswells. Following a number of convictions involving the hotel, the Tewksbury Police Department teamed up with the US Department of Justice to seize the hotel under civil asset forfeiture statutes. The plan was to sell the property and split the proceeds. WHOOHOO!!! The judge in the case ruled in favor of the Caswells, however, saying that Law Enforcement "grossly exaggerated the evidence and that the cops did not have the authority to forfeit the property." The DOJ "wisely" stated no appeals would take place. This is a victory against civil asset forfeiture, again. It is a very sad case indeed, that free people cannot travel the highways without worrying about their hard earned money and property being stolen by the government, who is supposed to protect their property from theft. The justice system is littered with cases of cops taking cash and other property from people simply because they articulate that they reasonably believe such cash and property will be or has been commissioned in a crime. More often than not, it is far less expensive to let the property go rather than hire an attorney to sue the agency, which is the only way victims of civil asset forfeiture can get their property back. Thus, "successful" litigation of the agency is the only way the property can be returned to the owner. People and primarily their property are essentially guilty unless they can prove their property innocent. Its ridiculous. Incompetent cops know this and exploit it, which only reinforces the legal plundering. I don't even have room here to go into the IRS's "legal" exploitation of Civil Asset Forfeiture, as it relates to people's property, which includes currency.

Let me share a story about a similar case I was involved in while a supervisor on patrol. This is not a civil asset forfeiture case, but one that involves taking property. First of all, I did not personally participate in civil asset forfeiture, and I never did, simply because, in part, my right of conscious would not allow me, no matter the kicking and screaming of superiors. I simply wouldn't do it. I was mistakenly perceived often as "not doing my job." In reality, I really was. There were a lot of things I would not do as an officer, that I could do. Anyway, one day I received a call to assist some state tax agents who had come down from the capital to take property from a home. The residents, I was told, had failed to pay state income tax. Following a brief few minutes of small talk, an agent handed me a sheet of paper that listed handwritten items on it, such as a large flat screen TV, a computer, some jewelry, DVD player, and so on. They asked if I would assist them in taking the property, listed on the paper, out of the house and transfer it to the office for later pick up. I said, "Sure, no problem. Let me see the seizure order." It was silent. They looked at me dazed for a moment and like I was crazy. They didn't have the order on them and appeared disturbed, because I would not take their word for it. So I left, without assisting them. Later that day I was called into the Lieutenant's office because the Department of Revenue had called to complain on me, and asked who do I think I am? They said the agents were very embarrassed and that I should not be an officer. I said "whatever, they should have had the order on them." I explained to the Lieutenant that I would not assist them in taking property out of the house without seeing the order, because for me, it would be breaking and entering, committing larceny, and I'd be in possession of stolen goods. The next day I was called back into the Lieutenant's office and he basically told me that I was correct in not assisting the tax agents because, if the home owner turned around and sued, I and the department would also be liable. I was pleased. Yet, not because I potentially avoided a lawsuit, but because to assist the agents on their word alone, to go into someone's home and literally take their personal property from them, without an order, in my mind anyway, was wrong and unlawful. For the record, I did learn later that an order was in place. My actions at the time, however, were sound and ethical.

The questionable competency of government officials created Civil Asset Forfeiture as a means to circumvent the Law, as it specifically relates to people's property. Similarly, through the exploitation of the term *civil*, another way for people in government to acquire jurisdiction over personal property is marriage. The First Amendment reads in part, "Congress shall make no law respecting the establishment of religion...." Recall, the 14th Amendment incorporated the Bill of Rights into the States, whereby state and local governments are lawfully accountable to the Bill of Rights as the supreme law of the State. Fact: marriage is an establishment of religion.

Marriage is a covenant between two people, and /or two families, who exchange vows within the context of their faith and cultural traditions. Government did not create marriage. There is no way around this, or is there? What authority does American government have, state or federal, over who can marry whom, and why? There is no authority. In America, government officials must reinterpret marriage as a *civil or domestic union*. This way, in opposition to common law marriage, for example, government can establish itself as a third party within the union, thus giving itself jurisdiction *over* the relationship, via contract, or the marriage license. Otherwise, why would government even need to be involved in people's committed sexual relationships? The answer is, their property. This usurped power gives the government jurisdiction over all the fruits of the marriage, including children. Have a baby naturally, without a hospital or government involvement. Watch what happens.

The marriage license is a contract between a couple and the government that derives from *miscegenation*. In the mid 19th century, following the Civil War, when interracial couples wanted to marry, they had to get permission and pay for it, as a means to be accepted by society. This also gave jurisdiction of the interracial couple's property to the government because such regulations had already been established for newly freed blacks. If one party of the union was black, then such regulations became justified. Black's Law Dictionary, 3rd Edition, defines a marriage license as, "a license or permission granted by public authority to persons who intend to intermarry." Over time, this proved financially beneficial for government officials, thus the practice of paying a fee for permission to marry spread to all people over time, as did the jurisdiction over their property, like income. The federal government then passed into law in 1923 the *Uniform Marriage and Marriage License Act*. But, being that marriage is a religious institution, such regulation on sexual unions between two consenting adults was constitutionally questionable. In fact, the US Supreme Court ruled in *Meister v. Moore* (1877), which has not been reversed, that state statutes requiring permission to marry are, "as before remarked, the statutes are held merely directory; because marriage is a thing of common right..." *Directory* simply means a secondary law or statute that cannot be enforced. One good example of this is in August of 2014 in *Brown vs. Buhman*, also known as the *Sister Wives* case, the federal court struck down Utah's law against polygamy as unconstitutional. Thus the ruling asserted,

> IT IS HEREBY ORDERED, ADJUDGED, AND DECREED that Utah Code Ann. § 76-7-101 (2013) is facially unconstitutional in that the phrase "or cohabits with another person" is a violation of the Free Exercise Clause of the First Amendment to the United States Constitution and is without a rational basis under the Due Process Clause of the Fourteenth Amendment; to preserve the integrity of the Statute, as enacted by the Utah State Legislature, the Court hereby severs the phrase "or cohabits with another person" from Utah Code § 76-7-101(1)[84]

The government does not have the lawful authority to tell individuals whom they can and can't marry, nor whom they can and cannot consensually live and have sex with. Marriage is an establishment of religion, and is subject to 1st Amendment protections from government intrusion. Special interest groups, in this case, those special interests of a religious nature, in particular, who want to control behavior that they don't like, generally concoct these intrusions and then lobby legislators to officially establish these types of regulations, as they originally did, in part, over newly freed blacks. Such authority is usurped. To get around non-enforceable statutes, governments then like to deny access to certain benefits and the like, which is a way the government, in the end, forces couples into contracts. Just leave people alone, right?

There are many such statutes related to regulating rights, which are enforced, yet unlawful. So today, by secondary laws, all people need to pay for permission to marry through the exploitation of a "civil" marriage or union, on paper. The ceremony doesn't really matter. This is illegitimate because such a law requiring people to pay for permission to marry is respecting the establishment of religion. Common law marriage has been done away with by the legal system because under common law marriage, people who have lived together for so long were considered married anyway. The problem with this is, there is no contract in place giving government jurisdiction over the relationship and over their property. Thus, common law marriage has been eradicated in most states. In addition, common law marriage has not been financially beneficial to government. Civil marriage, or domestic unions, depending on the state, are mere legal mechanisms to get around the fact that government has no real authority over who can marry whom, unless they attach the word *civil* via contract. Such secondary laws that criminalize cohabitation or even sexual relations, for example, between consenting adults, are all the more examples of usurped authority. These are usurped, predominantly, because the language within the statutes themselves, distinctively the elements, make reference to such a statute being null and void within the confinements of marriage. This in and of itself is making law respecting the establishment of religion because it limits the sexual behavior to marriage itself, which government does not have the authority to do, in America. Many argue that such statutes are necessary especially within the context of plea-bargaining and within circumstances such as rape, or sexual assault. These can be reasonable to a degree. But is reasonableness actually reasonable when the Law of the Land says NO? This is another example of Blackstonian theory in action for government gain. Since the Constitution does not specifically restrict the government from involving itself within marriage by using the word *marriage*, the government can take it upon itself to regulate marriage. Sheesh!! Again, marriage is an establishment of religion and the first amendment restricts laws related to same. Therefore, this leads to the need for government officials to create lots and lots of legal jargon to get around it. The people in government should simply leave people and their property alone. Government should also stay out of the religious institution of marriage and let people marry whom they want, and moreover, stay out of people's bedroom. In addition, people and/or interests groups should not lobby the government's monopoly on violence as a means to force other people who think differently about marriage, politics, or religion in general, to be forced to comply with their beliefs, especially if such beliefs are contrary to personal freedom. It's wrong.

The fact is this, that through the excessive manipulation of legal language, whereby terms such as *civil* are exploited to criminalize behavior anyway, and circumvent the Law, the government can now take and control property without you having even committed or having been convicted of a crime. And, the government can now tell you whom you can and can't marry or whom you can and can't have consensual adult sex with. These pseudo-rationalized and "what if" scenarios that allows such circumventions of the Law are all aspects of the modern, new style of progression (neo-progressive) in the legal system, as it directly relates to property.

The legal system today is specifically designed to work against, and to protect itself from the Rule of Law. The founders created a path to individual security against poverty and government intrusion, for free people, through property rights, which included absolute ownership of the essentially basic. The Rule of Law protects and secures this ownership through very specific and fixed Laws, not statutes. Rights and liberty itself derive from property. The inconveniences of too much liberty, in contrast to the history of the world avoiding these inconveniences, are, on purpose, and progressively the design of the United States Constitution. However, the legal system today is redesigned to subtlety reverse this, and digress society back into history, by re-establishing and *enforcing* the intended conveniences of less liberty, which necessarily must happen first through property rights. Guns are property. A home and land is property. Your self is property. One's sexual relationship is property. Income and financial assets are property. The fruit of one's labor is property. The more American governance happens through the barrel of a gun, the more corrupt and desperate such efforts have to become to get around the Law. This is a sure sign that the legal system is failing, and it's just a matter of time before all hell breaks lose.

I can't help but fear that another civil war will happen in America. This has happened once before, obviously. The Civil War was the catalyst to transition our original republic into a democracy. The question is, if and when another civil war happens, who will the victors be and what type of government will they set up? Will the victors establish socialism, communism, a dictatorship, another democracy? My hope would be that the victors restore our original constitutional republic, whereby individual liberty and true property ownership are the paradigms of law and order.

3

The Rule of Law vs. The Legal System

"When all government, domestic and foreign, in little as in great things, shall be drawn to Washington as the center of all power, it will render powerless the checks provided of one government on another, and will become as venal and oppressive as the government from which we separated."

- Thomas Jefferson

Over the past century or so, since the rise of the progressive era, there has been a "taking for grantedness" of our law enforcement by politicians, bureaucrats, lawyers, corpcrate lobbyists, and special interest groups alike, who then create the modern legal system. Operating from within this legal system, the cop's Oath to uphold the Constitution and to enforce its mandated Rule of Law has become virtually impossible. Instead, what we have is the enforcement of a neo-progressive legal system, which undermines the very foundational principles of our Democratic Republic. Thus, contrary to the security of the fundamental rights and liberty of the individual, collectivism, social engineering and the legal plundering of property are being forced onto the American people through the exploitation of our law enforcement, at all levels of American government, while systematically advocating the necessity of such *public policy* for *public safety* and for *national security*. The legal system has created for itself a tradition where the law is interpreted to side with what is legally right, rather than what is lawfully right. This interpretation is a fallacy, because lawful does not equal legal. Thus, bad laws die when their enforcement is denied, which is *concurrent review* in action by competent law enforcement.

Law Enforcement efforts, as a whole, have become a matter of policy enforcement rather than a matter of Law enforcement, whereby today, the primary objective of a law enforcement officer is to enforce the legal system, rather than the actual Law itself. The legal system is separate from the Rule of Law. The legal system ideally derives from the legitimate intent to enhance the Rule of Law. But does it do that, today? Instead, the exploitation of law enforcement secures and protects the legal system from the Rule of Law, by exaggeratedly enforcing the regulations of personal finances, property use, relationships, social interactions, behaviors and the like, above and beyond the inalienable rights of individuals. All these "legal" aspects of enforcement are tied into legal privileges, which on a lawful basis do have their place for maintaining genuine law and order. The enforcement of the legal system over inalienable rights and property ownership, however, tend to be a necessary means to secure special interests related to business, corporate financial interests, and the money trail that secures elections and power, instead. The enforcement of inalienable rights gets in the way of this. As mentioned before, a police state can only come about when all three branches of government are complicit to one another. The legal system blends the three branches of government into one power. The Rule of Law keeps them separate. The Legal System should primarily be a means to enhance individual liberty and property rights through constitutional law and order, while the regulation of business and legal privileges come in as second. This is backwards, however. Legal privileges are civil in nature and are *alienable*, not *inalienable*. Only natural rights are *inalienable*. But this is not how most individuals in government think of the legal system, especially those who write policy. Generally a legislator will construct policy that is based upon some personal conviction, belief, special interest and/or some grandiose ideology. Lawyers are then hired to make the idea work "legally," through hundreds of pages of manipulated legal language. Public policy, then, and generally on purpose, undermines fundamental rights for the sake of these special interests, because, fundamental rights limit the implementation of special interests and the powers associated with them.

The increase in the power and exploitation of law enforcement, in part, can also be traced to the increased size and power of the executive branch as a whole, for example. Many Constitutional scholars argue that such an increase of power in the executive branch has been slowly growing over time, thus nullifying the Madisonian system of the *Separation of Powers*. To illustrate, Jonathan Turley, a Constitutional scholar and Professor of Law at George Washington University, recently wrote in a article that, "There has been a dramatic shift of authority toward presidential powers and the emergence of what is essentially a fourth branch of government — a vast network of federal agencies with expanded legislative and judicial power." He then argues that, "The growing authority invested in federal agencies comes from a diminished Congress, which seems to have a dramatically reduced ability to actively monitor, let alone influence, agency actions." This diminished Congress, or the public consensus of the incompetent legislative branch, "…is due to the fact that courts routinely refuse to review constitutional disputes.'" Like I mentioned before, a police state only happens when all three branches of government are complicit to one another, whereby each Branch works in sync with the other. The Courts have routinely, but not always, ruled in favor of special interests and public policy rather than actual Law, which is predicated on the Constitutional *Separation of Powers*. Thus, Turley concludes,

> "The framers believed that members of each branch of government would transcend individual political ambitions to vigorously defend the power of their institutions. Presidents have persistently expanded their authority with considerable success. Congress has been largely passive or, worse, **complicit** in the draining of legislative authority. Judges have adopted doctrines of avoidance that have removed the courts from important conflicts between the branches. Now is the time for members of Congress and the judiciary to affirm their oaths to "support and defend the Constitution" and to

work to re-establish our delicate constitutional balance."[1] (bold added)

Compelling evidence corroborating this weakening of the Separation of Powers, or checks and balances, between the three Branches of government, can be seen, in part, by the Legislative branch losing its *power of the purse*. In 2013, only thirty-five percent of federal spending was appropriated and voted on by Congress. The other sixty-five percent of federal spending just kind of happened.[2] The need to increase revenue becomes more of the driving force to not only create legislation to secure same, but the need to *enforce* legislation to secure same.

Public policy that is designed to enhance public safety, for example, cannot lawfully undermine fundamental rights, like not having one's person or property unreasonably searched or seized, as a matter of such policy. Again, *unreasonableness* is defined within the 4th Amendment itself, and, the Amendment mandates that for a search or seizure of an individual or their private property to be reasonable, there must be probable cause and a warrant, first, unless the officer directly witnesses a crime. Many times law enforcement officials confuse, on purpose, *reasonable suspicion* with *probable cause*. Reasonable Suspicion does not lawfully secure a warrant to allow the search and seizure of a person, their home, papers, or their effects (car, computer, phone, etc.) But what happens when public policy within the legal system redefines probable cause, or what it means to be reasonable? Or better yet, what happens when *precedent* redefines such terms? The courts have, in some cases, actually redefined probable cause. For example, courts have approved the extension of an officer's olfactory senses, through the implementation of a K9, which supercedes the driver's expectation of privacy, absent the officer's natural ability. It's like saying its ok for a cop to x-ray your home to see inside, and then use what they see to qualify as probable cause. That will come also. This is usurpation at its finest attached to a public safety argument. How about the Patriot Act? Does the Patriot Act meet the Constitutional prerequisites of reasonableness? Of course not! The Patriot Act is actually designed to circumvent the Rule of Law, which is why it is hundreds of pages in length. It takes a lot of argument and a lot of legal, or political language manipulation to redefine and create new terms, all to get around simple Constitutional restrictions. The Patriot Act is representative of the Legal System. The 4th Amendment is representative of the Rule of Law. Ayn Rand said, "We are fast approaching the stage of the ultimate inversion: the stage where the Government is free to do anything it pleases, while the citizens may not act only by permission; which is the stage of the darkest periods of human history, the stage of rule by brute force."[3] It is the legal system that qualifies this brute force. Today, most of society, through social engineering, would find it strange if people did not have to go pay a fee for permission from the people in government to do whatever they want or even to buy whatever they want.

To accept as true that the legal system and the actual Rule of Law is the same thing is comparable to believing that Cheez-Whiz and actual cheese is the same thing. What exactly is the legal system? The legal system in America today is predominantly comprised of all three branches of government working as one, whereby secondary laws, public policy, precedent, Acts, statutes, codes and ordinances, are all enforced equally, at the federal, state and local levels. Secondary laws generally seek to be in command of all the financial, property related, social and behavioral activities of all the people. A sound legal system is second to the Rule of Law, or primary Law. When one goes to court, for example, to answer charges for breaking the law, it is most often not the Rule of Law being challenged by the defendant, it is a statute that is being challenged, or a secondary law, because the statute is actually challenging the Rule of Law. The big problem is, most statutes today trump the Rule of Law, not by Law, but by social engineering and policy enforcement. In addition, ethics are exploited and redefined as a means to sustain forced economic activity. To illustrate, the Rule of Law sets ethics as the base of American economics. The legal system, however, sets economics as the base for American ethics.

The Supremacy Clause vs. Pursuance Thereof

The court's effort, ideally, is to determine if a statute is or is not withstanding to the actual Law. Secondary laws that are *withstanding* to a Constitution are generally always null and void. What does withstanding mean? Webster defines withstanding as "to stand up against: oppose with firm determination; especially: to resist successfully." So, for example, if the actually Law reads, referring to the North Carolina State Constitution, Article One, Section 28, "There shall be no imprisonment for debt in this State, except in cases of fraud," and one is imprisoned for debt, by state statute, which trumps? It should be the State's Constitution. State statutory Laws, Federal statutory Laws, local ordinances, Constitutions, are not all equally law, even though political convention edicts it so. Statutes and ordinances only carry the force of law, which is very different from Law itself. As it relates to federal statute and state statute, the United States Constitution's Supremacy Clause, for example, in Article Six reads,

> "This Constitution, **and the Laws of the United States which shall be made in pursuance thereof**; and all treaties made, or which shall be made, under the authority of the United States, shall be the supreme law of the land; and the

judges in every state shall be bound thereby, **anything in the constitution or laws of any state to the contrary notwithstanding**." (bold added)

What does "in pursuance thereof" mean? What does "notwithstanding" mean? Notwithstanding is the opposite of withstanding. These terms are best defined and understood in their actual context. That is to say, if you recall, that it is by way of letter *and* spirit that the Constitution is soundly interpreted, as should be any law. Thus, to understand what the Supremacy Clause actually means is to not only look to the Constitution itself, but to look to the State Ratification Debates, which actually define such clauses. Alexander Hamilton, at New York's convention, articulates,

> "I maintain that the word supreme imports no more than this — that the Constitution, and laws made in pursuance thereof, cannot be controlled or defeated by any other law. The acts of the United States, therefore, will be absolutely obligatory as to all the proper objects and powers of the general government...**but the laws of Congress are restricted to a certain sphere, and when they depart from this sphere, they are no longer supreme or binding**" (bold added)

Hamilton also stated in Federalist Paper 33, "It will not, I presume, have escaped observation that it expressly confines this supremacy to laws made pursuant to the Constitution...." Is the enforcement of a corporation's financial interest in an individual's debt a lawful charge of the federal government? It can be, under law of contract. Is such a federal statute Supreme to a State's Constitution if such authority for the statute is the result of complying with special interests? Is a statute deriving from special interest also pursuant thereof? What happens when a federal statute is enforced when the State Constitution is contrary? Moreover, what happens when a federal statute is enforced when the Federal Constitution is contrary? James Iredell, at the first North Carolina convention said, "When Congress passes a law consistent with the Constitution, it is to be binding on the people. If Congress, under pretense of executing one power, should, in fact, usurp another, they will violate the Constitution." Would not "pretence," generally, encompass special interests? Also, in Federalist paper 78, Alexander Hamilton tells us, "There is no position which depends on clearer principles than that every act of a delegated authority, contrary to the tenor of the commission under which it is exercised, is void. No legislative act, therefore, contrary to the Constitution, can be valid." In addition, Thomas McKean, at the Pennsylvania convention said, "The meaning [of the Supremacy Clause] which appears to be plain and well expressed is simply this, that Congress have the power of making laws upon any subject over which the proposed plan gives them a jurisdiction, and that those laws, thus made in pursuance of the Constitution, shall be binding upon the states." So even when Congress establishes jurisdiction over people or property, such federal statutes are still void if they are not made *in pursuance thereof* to the Constitution itself. This is not the same thing as the jurisdiction secured in Article 1, Section 8, Clause 17, as it relates to absolute authority over the District of Columbia and its enclaves, which are absent any State consent. Many people in government like to think it so, however.

Pursuance thereof consists of federal and state secondary laws that do not hinder or prevent the people from freely exercising their fundamental rights, which are the whole intent of the primary Laws, or Constitutions. Federal and state secondary laws that are not pursuant thereof specifically undermine or interfere with the people freely exercising their natural, or inalienable rights. Not *pursuant thereof* is when state or federal legislation prevents the exercise of inalienable rights absent a crime, *a priori*. Only crime committed and convicted by the individual is what justly suspends their inalienable rights. When the Legal System is withstanding or not pursuant thereof to the US Constitution, or a State Constitution, it is working against the Rule of Law. Legislative tyranny invades free people, through the uniform, when the enforcement of the legal system takes priority over the enforcement of the Rule of Law. The Legal System today solidifies the corporate takeover of life, whereby any and all activity, any and all property, any and all everything, which sadly includes the basic necessities to exist, are subservient to monetary policy and regulations, by way of government enforcement.

Webster defines *notwithstanding* as "without being prevented by." Black's Law Dictionary, Eighth Edition, defines notwithstanding as "Despite; in spite of." What is an example of a secondary law that is withstanding to primary law? Primary Law, for example, secures the right of the individual to be free of unreasonable search and seizure of both their person and property. The federal, secondary law called *The Patriot Act*, or a federal law banning an individual from smoking pot in their home, or state laws that permit *civil asset forfeiture*, or state laws that allow cops to search property without a warrant, or secondary laws that arbitrarily infringe on the right to carry a gun, or an ordinance that prevents local protests without permission, are all examples of laws that are *withstanding* to primary Law, rather than an enhancement. Federal and State laws, city and county ordinances, can easily be withstanding to the US Constitution, and in fact most probably are. The fact is, politicians sit around and get bored, so they dream up stuff to satisfy those who want to make society the way they want it to be, or they create some regulation to make society the way they themselves want it to be. This is near equal to cops getting bored and setting up a license checkpoint.

What is an example of a state law, or city ordinance that is notwithstanding to Federal Statute, or even to the US Constitution? Be advised that the US Constitution is not the same thing as Federal Law. Federal Law consists of secondary statutory laws or Acts made by Congress, which are restricted to a certain sphere, as Hamilton says. This "sphere" is Article One, Section Eight, of the US Constitution, known as the *Delegated Powers*, as mentioned before. An example of a state law that is notwithstanding to a sound federal statute is a statute that regulates the privilege of driving. This is separate, however, from the regulation of the vehicle. The reason I refer to the act of driving often is because most of what local cops do is enforce traffic laws, which can potentially enhance the right to travel. However, the secondary law designed to regulate the privilege of driving can easily deviate into *withstanding* when the officer spends equal effort enforcing a statute that infringes upon the right of an individual simply exercising a fundamental right, absent any PC or reasonable suspicion. This dichotomy, or conflict between the Legal System and the Rule of Law is largely unseen by the public, and unseen by law enforcement itself.

Lawrence Davidson, a professor of history at West Chester University in Pennsylvania, recently stated that, "Americans are culturally conditioned to believe that their country is the foundation of freedom and truth and they have neither knowledge nor interest to fact-check what their leaders and media tell them."[4] The media is there to sell you something, to determine the issues that make it into the public forum, and to shape the perception of whatever it is the media decides to report. Moreover, the media divides people against each other, all while leading them psychologically into consent of whatever the underlying agenda might be. Recently in Time Magazine, Thom Swanker, a Pentagon correspondent with the New York Times, stated that, "The government really needs to get its message out to the American people, and it knows that the best way to do that is by using the American news media. The relationship between the government and the media is like a marriage; it is a dysfunctional marriage to be sure, but we stay together for the kids."[5] So are our "leaders" like our parents? The corporate media and political leaders with "good intentions" will tell you that such statutory laws are actual Law and are necessary for public safety. "Good intentions," said Daniel Webster, "will always be pleaded for every assumption of authority. It is hardly too strong to say that the Constitution was made to guard the people against the dangers of good intentions. There are men in all ages who mean to govern well, but they mean to govern. They promise to be good masters, but they mean to be masters."[6] What really matters to those who desire to govern authoritatively is mass ignorance and state dependency. Like Thomas Sowell noted, "we are in a post-thinking era." Non-thinking is evidenced in forced fairness and forced political correctness, which again, socially engineers people into what to think, rather than how to think.

The Oath

Throughout history governments have always done what they wanted to the people through enforcement. America was to be different, then and today. Individual soldiers and law enforcement officers take a constitutional oath, to instantiate virtue and the intent of the Rule of Law, to be a check and balance against the Judicial and Legislative branches. To weaken possible despotism and/or tyranny. This is not the case today. For

Law Enforcement to blindly do the bidding of legislators defeats this whole purpose of an oath and thus nullifies it. What does the Law Enforcement Oath read? I will use the State of North Carolina as an example. Law Enforcement Officers generally swear two Oaths: one federal and one state. The North Carolina Oath of Office for Law Enforcement (G.S. 11-11) Article VI, Section 7, of the NC Constitution reads;

> "I, _____ do solemnly and sincerely swear that I will support the Constitution of the United States; that I will be faithful and bear true allegiance to the State of North Carolina, and to the constitutional powers and authorities which are or may be established for the government thereof; and that I will endeavor to support, maintain and defend the Constitution of said State, **not inconsistent with the Constitution of the United States**, to the best of my knowledge and ability; so help me God."

> "I, _____ do solemnly swear (or affirm) that I will be alert and vigilant to enforce the criminal laws of this State; that I will not be influenced in any matter on account of personal bias or prejudice; that I will faithfully and impartially execute the duties of my office as a law enforcement officer according to the best of my skill, abilities, and judgment; so help me, God."

The intent of this Oath confirms all the aforementioned, as it relates to the dichotomy of secondary laws working against primary laws. Moreover, the intent of this oath suggests that the officer shall not enforce law that works against, or is withstanding to the US Constitution or to the

State Constitution. The Oath is intended to be concurrent review in action: bad laws die when enforcement is denied.

What about Federal Law Enforcement? What is their Oath? Recall, that all law enforcement, at all levels, exist within the Executive branch of government. All Federal Employees, which includes all federal law enforcement, must take the following Oath, in accordance with U.S.C., Title 5, 3331: An individual, except the President, elected or appointed to an office of honor or profit in the civil service or uniformed services shall take the following oath:

> "I, ___, do solemnly swear (or affirm) that I will support and defend the Constitution of the United States against all enemies, foreign and domestic; that I will bear true faith and allegiance to the same; that I take this obligation freely, without any mental reservation or purpose of evasion; and that I will well and faithfully discharge the duties of the office on which I am about to enter. So help me God.'"

Again, even the Oath that federal law enforcement officials must swear to, entails this dichotomy of secondary laws working against primary laws. In other words, there exists a Legal System that works against the Rule of Law and it is paramount that Law Enforcement at all levels posses the Constitutional discretion and discernment between the two. Otherwise, the oath is a mere formality. What does "defend the Constitution of the United States against all enemies, foreign and domestic" actually mean? This is not the same thing as defending the United States itself from enemies foreign and domestic. Again, going back to chapter one, what did Madison say? "The branches of the National Government are coordinate, each must, in the exercise of it's functions, be guided by the text of the Constitution according to its own interpretation of it." Federalist 49. Madison reaffirmed this in 1834. The opposite of this nullifies the Separation of Powers, a fundamental aspect of the Rule of Law. Thus, law enforcement no longer defends the Constitution of the United States from enemies domestically when constitutional discretion plays no role in their enforcement actions. Law Enforcement takes this Oath, because their individual discretion, or lawful and Constitutional discernment, shall be exercised as a means to *check and balance* the power of the other two branches. A domestic enemy of the US Constitution will most likely be within the government itself, as Madison says in Federalist 44, "…the success of the usurpation will depend on the executive and judiciary departments, which are to expound and give effect to the legislative acts…." Therefore cops need to wise up so they are no longer exploited by the legal system.

The Declaration of Independence argues against the blending together of the Law of the Land with secondary laws as one power, absent a secondary law's consistency with the Law of the Land's intent. The Constitution also argues against this, the Founders' argued against this, Locke's philosophy of liberty argues against this, the Ratification Debates argue against this, the Federalist Papers argue against this, the State Constitutions argue against this. Then why is this sound dichotomy so weak now in America? Throughout the history of the world, enforcement efforts have always worked against its own founding ideology. Why? Because unchanged aspects of negative human nature have always dominated government efforts. And, the founding ideology in America, the Declaration and the US Constitution, have succumb to the same fate, which is that shady people get into government and think that they know what is best for everybody else, and, then they use the monopoly of force to make it happen. History always repeats itself.

Recall that a recent study done at Princeton and Northwestern University has declared that America is no longer a democracy or a republic, that America has become an oligarchy. An oligarchy is a system of government where the financial elite establishes financially leaning public policy over its foundational system of laws, and that the average citizens have no real political effect on public policy whatsoever. Thus the study, in part, reads, "When the preferences of economic elites and the stands of organized interest groups are controlled for, the preferences of the average American appear to have only a minuscule, near-zero, statistically non-significant impact upon public policy." The study continues,

> "In the United States, our findings indicate, the majority does not rule — at least not in the causal sense of actually determining policy outcomes. When a majority of citizens disagrees with economic elites and/or with organized interests, they generally lose.... Moreover, because of the strong status quo bias built into the U.S. political system, even when fairly large majorities of Americans favor policy change, they generally do not get it."[7]

This is the system of government that cops enforce today, by way of exploitation, without even knowing it. Cops today enforce an oligarchic system of government, which is evidenced in the equal enforcement of secondary laws that seek to regulate legal privileges and civil rights above and beyond inalienable rights, thus ultimately plundering property and undermining the Rule of Law. The legal system today is this oligarchy and it comes from judges ruling in favor of policy contrary to Law, thus creating a type of judicial despotism. Recall also what Jefferson said, "To consider the judges as the ultimate arbiters of all constitutional questions is a very dangerous doctrine indeed, and one which would place us under the despotism of an oligarchy."[8] Those people who are corruptible generally transmit this legal system. David Brin said, "It's said that 'power corrupts,' but actually it's more true that power attracts the corruptible. The sane are usually attracted by other things than power. When they do act, they think of it as service, which has limits. The tyrant, though, seeks mastery, for which he is insatiable, implacable."[9] In short, an enemy of the United States Constitution is either a foreign or domestic group of people or individual that supports and enforces this oligarchic system of government over the Law of the Land. What type of government official can specifically be defined as a domestic enemy of the US Constitution? A domestic enemy, for example, operating on the greed for power, but not limited to same, can be when a judge seeks to attach their name to arbitrary precedent. Greed for power can be when the legislator seeks to attach their name to a piece of arbitrary legislation. Greed for power can be when the cop seeks to enforce arbitrary statutes blindly or to execute their will simply because they can and want to exercise control. All such actions are capricious in nature. *Arbitrary* is simply defined as "acts based solely on personal wishes, feelings, or perceptions, rather than on objective facts, reasons, or principles." J.R.R. Tolkien says, "The proper study of Man is anything but man; and the most improper job of any man, even saints (who at any rate were at least unwilling to take it on), is bossing other men. Not one in a million is fit for it, and least of all those who seek the opportunity."[10]

Liberty has become more of an abstract idea, again, of the past, as opposed to a reality for now and the future. How can this American oligarchic legal system of government be stopped? Voting does not constitute consent by the governed anymore because elections are generally rigged by special interests and too costly for the average citizen. How can we as a free and open society reconcile the constitutional intention of individual freedom with the present-day "Might makes Right" legislation designed to protect special interests? The blatant greed for power and financial domination by the elite has weakened the standards and liberties our Constitution is designed to secure. This has happened through the exploitation of our law enforcement men and women, who I personally believe become cops with genuine intentions, to do good, and to go after bad people who commit genuine crimes. But in effort to secure this legal system socially and financially, virtually everything people do, or do not do, has to become a crime. Another interesting question to ask is this, how is it possible that the government can amend the Constitution to give itself more power when the intent of the Constitution is to limit the government's power? Or better yet, how is it that the government can take the Constitution literally, like, "...from any source derived," in the 16th Amendment? But, when it comes to the people taking the Constitution literally, like, "...shall not be infringed," in the 2nd Amendment, the people are deemed extremist or right wing nuts? This is because incompetence in government has become a staggering reality.

Surveillance

The right to be left alone is fundamental. Spying, or surveillance, has been around since the rise of Mesopotamia, where local societies sent out spies to monitor and gather information on other communities. Look how much we have changed. America has been in a declared "state of emergency" since 9/11, a never-ending state of perpetual war against an enemy abroad, justifying the mass surveillance of Americans, or does it? We can all remember very specifically where we were and what we were doing on September 11, 2001. I was actually sitting in the Communications black of instruction in Basic Law Enforcement Training (police academy). I recall quite a few reserves being reactivated and having to drop out. President Bush shortly afterwards declared a state of emergency,

> "A national emergency exists by reason of the terrorist attacks at the World Trade Center, New York, New York, and the Pentagon, and the continuing and immediate threat of further attacks on the United States. NOW, THEREFORE, I, GEORGE W. BUSH, President of the United States of America, by virtue of the authority vested in me as President by the Constitution and the laws of the United States, I hereby declare that the national emergency has existed since September 11, 2001 . . . ."

President Obama continued this state of emergency in 2009, "The terrorist threat that led to the declaration on September 14, 2001, of a national emergency continues. For this reason, I have determined that it is necessary to continue in effect after September 14, 2009, the national emergency with respect to the terrorist threat." Following the re-declaration of a state of emergency, Dan Hamburg, a former US Congressman argued in 2009 that,

> "Congress and the judiciary, as well as public opinion, "can restrain the executive regarding emergency powers," nothing of the sort has occurred. Under the 1976 National Emergencies

Act (50 U.S.C. 1601-1651), Congress is required to review presidentially declared emergencies. Specifically, "not later than six months after a national emergency is declared, and not later than the end of each six-month period thereafter that such emergency continues, each House of Congress shall meet to consider a vote on a joint resolution to determine whether that emergency shall be terminated." Over the past eight years, Congress has failed to obey its own law, a fact that casts doubt on the legality of the state of emergency. The Obama administration is essentially arguing that the United States is currently in a state of resisting foreign invasion a full eight years after the attacks of 9/11! This is ludicrous. [Dr. Harold C. Relyea, a specialist in national government with the Congressional Research Service (CRS) of the Library of Congress] argues that Congress and the judiciary, as "co-equal branches of constitutional government," serve as a check on the executive power. As we have seen, Congress has either been shut out of this process, or, as in so many cases, it has capitulated. Dr. Relyea then offers that public opinion can restrain the executive. But the public doesn't even know they're living under a state of emergency. The media doesn't report it, and the government is certainly not in the business of providing information that might raise the hackles of real Americans."[11]

Here simple checks and balances, or the *Separation of Powers*, a fundamental aspect of tripartite government, established by James Madison, is continually being undermined by the Executive Branch's sustained mass surveillance of Americans. Black's Law Dictionary, 8th Edition, defines surveillance as, "Close observation or listening of a person or place in the hope of gathering evidence." This *evidence*, or information that is collected is also called *intelligence*. The question to ask now is, is this *intelligence* actually intelligent? Intelligence, as it relates to foreign surveillance, decreed that Iraq had weapons of mass destruction. Was this *intelligence* intelligent? What does the actual basic term intelligence mean, not referring to information collected by way of spying? Webster's defines intelligence as, "the ability to learn or understand or to deal with new or trying situations: reason; also: the skilled use of reason. The ability to apply knowledge to manipulate one's environment or to think abstractly as measured by objective criteria." Has surveillance been an exercise of skilled reasoning? Reasoning from what? There must be a foundation. Unfortunately, within the scope of psychology, there are only theories of what intelligence actually is. Thus, intelligence is defined by whichever theory one likes best. I favor psychologist Robert Sternberg's theory of what intelligence is. Sternberg defines intelligence as, "mental activity directed toward purposive adaptation to, selection and shaping of, real-world environments relevant to one's life."[12] He also says,

> "Successfully intelligent people discern their strengths and weaknesses, and then figure out how to capitalize on their strengths, and to compensate for or remediate their weaknesses. Successfully intelligent individuals succeed in part because they achieve a functional balance among a "triarchy" of abilities...Moreover, all of these abilities can be further developed."[13]

Sternberg divides this theory into three aspects of what intelligence is, or what he calls "triarchy:" *Analytical intelligence* refers to problem-solving abilities. *Creative intelligence* involves the ability to deal with new situations using past experiences and current skills. *Practical intelligence* refers to the ability to adapt to a changing environment. "...all of these abilities can be further developed," he says.[14] Now, take this understanding of what intelligence is and apply it to surveillance. Context is necessary correct? Keith Laidler, a PhD anthropologist, says in his book, *Surveillance Unlimited: How We've Become the Most Watched People on Earth*, that "The rise of city states and empires…meant that each needed to know not only the disposition and morale of their enemy, but also the loyalty and general sentiment of their own population." From here, one can reasonably infer that the context of American surveillance, as a whole, is to secretly gather information on people in other countries as well as to secretly gather information on people within the country, which actually is the case. Thus, as it specifically relates to the mass domestic surveillance of Americans, who have committed no crimes, either those who spy see Americans as the enemy or the intent is to learn of who is loyal to the legal system and its consorts, and to learn of those who exercises political dissent. Both of these, then, support a *divide and conquer* agenda, propagated in the media (FOX vs. MSNBC). This is evidenced in the left/right paradigm within the American political landscape. Actualizing intelligence in the cognitive sense evolves and advances human beings ethically. This intelligence, as it relates to information gathered, appears to devolve and digress human beings away from natural ethical behavior into a left/right paradigm that in turn, socially engineers a new and divided "ethical" behavior. This is a conspiracy, however, says the neo-progressive. Yet, the evidence shows that this surveillance is then rationalized through collected *intelligence* designed to also socially engineer mass fear of an enemy, which has always been the case for all governments for nearly 6,000 years of human history. Negative human nature reigns, still. James Madison said,

> "A standing military force, with an overgrown Executive will not long be safe companions to liberty. The means of defence against foreign

danger have been always the instruments of tyranny at home. Among the Romans it was a standing maxim to excite a war, whenever a revolt was apprehended. Throughout all Europe, the armies kept up under the pretext of defending, have enslaved the people."[15]

Again, as Madison stated, the monopoly on legal violence and force are secured within the Executive branch's attempt to combat an enemy, which in turn crushes dissent and restricts liberty of those at home, all in the name of *National Security*. American surveillance advocates either Americans as an enemy or it seeks to crush dissent. The safety argument is generally rhetoric, especially in light of the latest crime statistics. Also in a letter to Thomas Jefferson, Madison said that, "Perhaps it is a universal truth that the loss of liberty at home is to be charged against provisions against danger, real or *pretended* from abroad."[16] (italics added) Acquiring intelligence intelligently and lawfully is a sound and necessary practice within the scope of the responsibility of the government to the people it is charged to protect from foreign and/or domestic invasion/danger. This compromise between the people in government with the people not in government is another aspect of the social compact, where neither side, in practice, holds absolute authority. Moreover, sound domestic intelligence must be acquired ethically. Ethically is when individual liberties are not infringed upon in the absence of verifiable probable cause. To unethically acquire intelligence through surveillance is also generally unconstitutional. This is because the US Constitution is a moral force codified to restrict the exercise of the negative aspects of human nature within the people in government, which includes, but is not limited to, the greed for power and money, the arbitrary use of violence, the desire to control other people's lives, the lust for war, the arbitrary invasion of privacy, etc.

Ann Cavoukian, a PhD and *The Information and Privacy Commissioner* of Ontario, Canada, argued in a paper, via Ryerson University in 2014, entitled: *Get Smart: Embed Privacy, by Design to Avoid Unintended Consequences*, that creativity, a primary driving force of prosperity requires personal privacy. In other words, personal privacy is essential to prosperity and well-being, that "individual human rights, property rights and civil liberties, the conceptual engines of innovation and creativity, could not exist in a meaningful manner." Moreover, she argues that, "privacy is the essence of freedom," and that "surveillance is the antithesis of privacy".... "a negative consequence of surveillance is the usurpation of a person's limited cognitive bandwidth, away from innovation and creativity."[17] A similar report done by the *Financial Post* noted that, "Big Brother culture will have adverse effect on creativity, productivity."[18] Personal privacy is not only a fundamental right, it is an essential key to America's economic success. Even Edward Snowden remarked that, "The success of economies in developed nations relies increasingly on their creative output, and if that success is to continue we must remember that creativity is the product of curiosity, which in turn is the product of privacy."[19] Mass surveillance not only destroys trust and undermines the Rule of Law, it violates one of the most fundamental of human rights, the right to be left alone. Mass spying slowly shuts down an open society, and it shuts down because the enforcement necessary to do it is exploited. In addition, blackmail becomes a bureaucratic tactic against many well-intended politicians who seek to stop mass surveillance by law, but because their private lives are already monitored and "collected," their attempts are thwarted.

As it relates to Edward Snowden, the former NSA employee, revealing the massive spying apparatus on innocent Americans by the federal government, I believe he was simply exercising his *right of conscience*, which is an inalienable right. The right of conscious in action is to put into effect what one believes is fundamentally and specifically right and wrong. The Rule of Law secures the exercise of the right of conscience, while the legal system tries to squash it, or at least control and minimize its effects. This is where policy comes in as a virus and directly infects the Rule of Law, making a right of conscious nearly impossible to exercise absent the oversight of those who work against it. William Livingston, one of the signers of the US Constitution, declared that, "Consciences of men are not the objects of human legislation." John Jay, the first Chief Justice and founding father also said, "Security under our constitution is given to the rights of conscience and private judgment. They are by nature subject to no control but that of Deity, and in that free situation they are now left." Likewise, Thomas Jefferson stated that the 1st Amendment was an, "expression of the supreme will of the nation in behalf of the rights of conscience."[20] James Madison inferred that right of conscience was property,

> "Conscience is the most sacred of all property; other property depending in part on positive law, the exercise of that, being a natural and unalienable right. To guard a man's house as his castle, to pay public and enforce private debts with the most exact faith, can give no title to invade a man's conscience which is more sacred than his castle, or to withhold from it that debt of protection, for which the public faith is pledged, by the very nature and original conditions of the social pact."[21]

But someone like Karl Marx, on the other hand, the communist philosopher, radical socialist and economist says,

> "In the social production of their existence, men inevitably enter into definite relations, which are independent of their will, namely relations of production appropriate to a given stage in the development of their material forces of production. The totality of these relations of production constitutes the economic structure of society, the real foundation, on which arises a legal and political superstructure and to which correspond definite forms of social consciousness. The mode of production of material life conditions the general process of social, political and intellectual life. It is not the consciousness of men that determines their existence, but their social existence that determines their consciousness. At a certain stage of development, the material productive forces of society come into conflict with the existing relations of production or – this merely expresses the same thing in legal terms – with the property relations within the framework of which they have operated hitherto. From forms of development of the productive forces these relations turn into their fetters. Then begins an era of social revolution. The changes in the economic foundation lead sooner or later to the transformation of the whole immense superstructure."[22]

"It is not consciousness of men that determines their being, but, on the contrary, their social being that determines their consciousness." Here is when consciousness and conscience are intertwined, I believe. Rather than the right of conscience being a natural right determined by one's moral and political convictions, Marx infers that such a right is not a right at all, but false, that an individual's moral and political convictions should be determined and shaped by social and political interactions that are controlled and manipulated by the people in government. This is the philosophical foundation of the modern security state. Such a worldview tends to reinforce the efforts related to such a security state in spite of the foundational principles that created the authority of the state from the start, resulting in a complete *transformation* of society, which is what's happening now in America through the legal system. This is also what in the end, destroys nations from within. Imagine if Marx' statement, as mentioned above, for example, was applied to the Constitution as the source of one's moral and political convictions. Would it still be Marxism? Technically this can be inferred as a whole, to a contrary view. Can't constitutionalists simply apply this Marxist ideology, that the Declaration of Independence and the US Constitution, are the sources for the constitutionalists' "social being," and is thus determining their "conscious." Oh now it changes. The fact is, it is the power and control that matters for statism, not the principles.

Recently Snowden did an extended interview on NBC with Brian Williams, of which some significant points regarding the federal government's surveillance of the American people were edited out. Answering Williams question about 9/11 and what a non-traditional enemy qualifies as, Snowden remarked,

> "You know, and this is a key question that the 9/11 Commission considered. And what they found, in the post-mortem, when they looked at all of the classified intelligence from all of the different intelligence agencies, they found that we had all of the information we needed as an intelligence community, as a classified sector, as the national defense of the United States to detect this plot."

As it relates to the intelligence of the *US Intelligence* apparatus, Snowden continued,

> "The problem was not that we weren't collecting information, it wasn't that we didn't have enough dots, it wasn't that we didn't have a haystack, it was that we did not **understand** the haystack that we have. The problem with mass surveillance is that we're piling more hay on a haystack we already don't understand, and this is the haystack of the human lives of every American citizen in our country, If these programs aren't keeping us safe, and they're making us miss connections - vital connections - on information we already have, if we're taking resources away from traditional methods of investigation, from law enforcement operations that we know work, if we're missing things like the Boston Marathon bombings where all of these mass surveillance systems, every domestic dragnet in the world didn't reveal guys that the Russian intelligence service told us about by name, is that really the best way to protect our country?" (bold added)

If the "haystack" is not understood, than the *intelligence* is not intelligent. However, even understanding the "haystack" in the context of contemporary surveillance would be morally inapprehensible. One point Snowden made that did air during the prime time interview, in which he questioned the effectiveness of modern intelligence gathering under the guise of being a counterterrorism tool,

> "It's really disingenuous for the government to invoke and sort of scandalize our memories to sort of exploit the national trauma that we all suffered together and worked so hard to come through to justify programs that have never been shown to keep us safe, but cost us liberties and freedoms that

we don't need to give up and our Constitution says
we don't need to give up."

Additional documents revealed later by Snowden show that the NSA has swept up far more information on American citizen and foreigner's private communications content than on actual targets, nine to one. Yeah, nine to one. This information includes people's photos, medical records, resumes, emails, etc., all by way of unlawful, but "legal" surveillance.[23] Then again, this whole Snowden revelation could very well be another PSYOP, a psychological operation, where people in government, under the thumb of a ruling class, seek to influence audiences' sentiments, reasoning, behaviors and the like, to encourage and strengthen behaviors that are favorable to certain objectives, which may also be an intended distraction from something bigger. I believe such intent encourages a classic *divide and conquer* philosophy that has become solidified within the left/right paradigm of the American political landscape, and unbeknownst to the cops, they are pulled into this whole scheme and patted on the back as the "gun in the room."

A 2014 International Gallup poll of 65 countries conducted in Zurich, Switzerland, concluded that the United States is considered to be the greatest threat to world peace, next to Pakistan and China.[24] Why? Sadly, even Americans that were polled concluded that America was the 4th greatest threat to world peace.[25] Why? The annual Global Peace Index, which quantifies the relative peacefulness of 162 countries, puts the United States at 101.[26] Why? If America is the land of the free, why would we be such a threat to world peace, or a world power that is lacking in stabilizing world peace? The answer is, money, or the lack thereof, because everything has a price. Steve Killelea, founder and executive chairman of the *Institute for Economics and Peace*, and who participated in the study above, stated that,

> "Many macro factors have driven the deterioration in peace over the last seven years, including the continued economic repercussions of the global financial crisis, the reverberations of the Arab Spring, and the continued spread of terrorism. As these effects are likely to continue into the near future, a strong rebound in peace is unlikely. This is resulting in very real costs to the world economy. Increases in the global economic impact of violence and its containment are equivalent to 19 percent of global economic growth from 2012 to 2013. To put this in perspective, this is around $1,350 per person. The danger is that we fall into a negative cycle: Low economic growth leads to higher levels of violence, the containment of which produces lower economic growth."[27]

The study also concluded, as to why the US has become 101 on the Global Peace Index, that,

> "The economic impact of containing the levels of violence cost the U.S. economy $1.7 trillion, or more than 10 percent of the GDP in 2013, translating to more than $5,455 per U.S. citizen. Despite a scaled-back military presence overseas, the country's high degree of militarization, unmatched incarceration rate and an increase in the impact felt from terrorism caused the U.S. to descend into triple digits."[28]

So the War on Terror and the lack of peace around the world may be a result of a lack of funds? Really? I can't help but think it goes deeper than that, philosophically. Tyler Cowen, the Chairman and General Director of the Mercatus Center, holds a rather cynical and irrational perspective on how we can increase world peace and strengthen the US and global economy. In the New York Times, Cowen argues,

> "The world just hasn't had that much warfare lately, at least not by historical standards. Some of the recent headlines about Iraq or South Sudan make our world sound like a very bloody place, but today's casualties pale in light of the tens of millions of people killed in the two world wars in the first half of the 20th century. Even the Vietnam War had many more deaths than any recent war involving an affluent country.
> Counterintuitive though it may sound, the greater peacefulness of the world may make the attainment of higher rates of economic growth less urgent and thus less likely. This view does not claim that fighting wars improves economies, as of course the actual conflict brings death and destruction. The claim is also distinct from the Keynesian argument that preparing for war lifts government spending and puts people to work. Rather, the very possibility of war focuses the attention of governments on getting some basic decisions right — whether investing in science or simply liberalizing the economy. Such focus ends up improving a nation's longer-run prospects."[29]

So more war is the answer to creating world peace and moving the economy forward? So inciting more warfare internationally can decrease the *War on Terror*? Really? When the economy directly benefits from the death and destruction of war, there is something terribly wrong with the financial system as a whole. There is also something terribly wrong with the people that prop up and support such a financial system. This financial system, in part, comes down to the use of government force, cops, to secure private power and investments, which is a corporate protection racket, even abroad. Noam Chomsky notes,

"One current illustration is the huge trade agreements now being negotiated, the Trans-Pacific and Trans-Atlantic pacts. These are being negotiated in secret — but not completely in secret. They are not secret from the hundreds of corporate lawyers who are drawing up the detailed provisions. It is not hard to guess what the results will be, and the few leaks about them suggest that the expectations are accurate. Like NAFTA and other such pacts, these are not free trade agreements. In fact, they are not even trade agreements, but primarily investor rights agreements. Again, secrecy is critically important to protect the primary domestic constituency of the governments involved, the corporate sector."[30]

More war, it appears, secures the private investments and benefits of the wealthy investors here and abroad. This financial system is the backbone of the legal system, and the government's monopoly on force is exploited to secure both as one. Violence begets violence is the standard of all human history and the direct result of the negatives aspects of human nature. Force is extremely overrated and fallacious in a government that argues ethical standards as its premise. Here is a basic moral question to ask. Is it morally right to punish someone for doing nothing wrong? Then why reward people for doing nothing right? The legal system is predicated upon the punishment of people who do nothing wrong, as well as rewarding people for doing nothing right. This is because such criminalization secures revenue and enhances a political philosophy that separates people in government from people not in government. Arbitrary force becomes the means of control, which is in and of itself, immoral.

What we have here is modern, technologically advanced humans resorting to an ancient and destructive means for peace and security:

violence. Oh how we humans have evolved out of our negative human nature. It is not money, or the lack thereof that is the real problem. It is the lust for money that is the problem. Why? The lust for money didn't come about by nature. It came by way of conditioning the masses that currency is god. This conditioning says that everything has monetary value attached to it. We all are the problem. In addition to the lust for money, or rather the need of it for the basic necessities of individual existence within a manufactured control grid, the easily corruptible people get into American government, who are morally deficient and hold no affinity to the Rule of Law or to individual liberty, or to the principles associated with same, and who are sentimentally predispositioned to violate the Constitution, for example, by inciting wars of aggression, generally for the purpose of gratifying domestic and global special interests and for securing financial incentives for themselves and their colleagues. Thus, a philosophical perspective like Marxism, as cited earlier, is attractive, as are views like Blackstone, Hobbes, and the like, because they can be "pragmatically" implemented to control rights of conscience, property and movement abroad. America has become the Leviathan.

As it relates to stopping people who get into government and who seek to manipulate and transform the Rule of Law into some other political ideology, what does Madison say? "A mere demarcation on parchment of the constitutional limits (of government) is not a sufficient guard against those encroachments which lead to a tyrannical concentration of all the powers of government in the same hands."[31] This "tyrannical concentration of all the powers" is the legal system. The Constitution itself does not guard against those who seek to destroy it. Rather, the people in mass must understand it and enforce it, as well as hold accountable those who actively undermine it after swearing to uphold it. But this is not the political system today. Rather, government creates for itself the power to interpret and enforce the constitution for it's own sake, centrally, in effort to circumvent its restrictions. The fundamental question to ask now is, is it legitimate to sacrifice liberty for security? The whole of the security state now emphatically commands yes. But, Benjamin Franklin said no, "Those who would give up essential Liberty, to purchase a little temporary Safety, deserve neither Liberty nor Safety."[32]

It takes a lot of social engineering and silent encroachments to thwart the collective conviction of liberty from the masses. Fear is the greatest tool to implement encroachments. And so we have the *War on Terror*, a tool within the tool of law enforcement, at all levels, for implementing absolute control over a populace conditioned into being "kept safe" from an enemy, by force. Many extremists interpret this as tyranny. But what is happening in America today is not tyranny in the historical sense, whereby a dictator monopolizes violence through trained minions to crush society under his thumb, as founded upon some political ideology, in the people's "best interest," so goes his rhetoric. Similarly, what we are seeing is *legislative tyranny*. This is when special interests and/or corporate lobbyists, and the like, have by and large authored Bills, which become "law," with the help of their attorneys, and then exploit cops for their enforcement. Moreover, representatives do not, for the most part, even read the Bills. These Bills then become secondary laws, statutes, Acts, ordinances, rules, regulations, public policies and the like. These "laws" then develop into the government's "legal" frame of reference and justification to execute its arbitrary will of control rather than to secure the pursuit of happiness. John Quincy Adams said that, "The laws of man may bind him in chains or may put him to death, but they never can make him wise, virtuous, or happy."[33] Thus, this legal system becomes the axis of unlawful power. These "laws" also allow for the "legal" sidestepping of blame or direct responsibility of government officials, whereby such enforcement actions against personal liberty and property rights are referred to the legislation itself as the "authority" for such enforcement. The legal system itself has become the tyrant.

The increasing inequality between the people in government and the people not in government can be seen, for example, when cops exercise surveillance and tracking of Americans through technology like *Stingray,* without a warrant or probable cause, or when they arrest people for filming them on duty, while in public. Stingray technology, for example, collects in mass, cell phone data within a specific area. Surveillance works both ways, however, and for good reason: accountability. State, local and federal courts have ruled time and time again that law enforcement does not have a reasonable expectation of privacy while on duty and that filming cops on duty is protected by the 1st Amendment. For example, in *Gericke vs. Begin* (2014), the court argued,

> "As we explained above, claims of retaliation for the exercise of clearly established First Amendment rights are cognizable under section 1983. See Powell, 391 F.3d at 16. Thus, under Gericke's version of the facts, any reasonable officer would have understood that charging Gericke with illegal wiretapping for attempted filming that had not been limited by any order or law violated her First Amendment right to film.12 "'[T]he contours of [the] right [were] sufficiently clear' that every 'reasonable official would have understood that what he [was] doing violate[d] that right.'" Ashcroft v. al-Kidd, 131 S. Ct. 2074, 2083, 179 L. Ed. 2d 1149 (2011) (quoting Anderson v. Creighton, 483 U.S. 635, 640, 107 S. Ct. 3034, 97 L. Ed. 2d 523 (1987)). Hence, at this

stage of the litigation, the officers are not entitled
to qualified immunity.13"

Recently a photojournalist won a settlement of $200K against police for his arrest while filming them on duty. In *Datz vs. Suffolk County*, Datz said,

> "This settlement is a victory for the First Amendment and for the public good. When police arrest journalists just for doing their job, it jeopardizes everyone's ability to stay informed about important news in their community. Journalists have a duty to cover what the police are doing and the settlement strengthens the ability of journalists and the community to hold the police accountable for their actions as well as protecting First Amendment rights of the public."

Another such case at the federal level is *Boston vs. Glik*, which ruled that State Laws banning the recording of public officials, including police officers while on duty, is unconstitutional and in violation of the First Amendment. There are many such cases where the courts have ruled at the state, federal and local levels against people being arrested for filming cops on duty. To get around this, many cops use the "wiretapping" laws to justify the arrests. Yet falsely arresting people for violating wiretapping laws are only an unethical means to justify such enforcement. Filming cops on duty does not qualify as "wiretapping." Under the Law, citizens can freely film and record cops on duty at any time, provided a reasonable distance is between the cops and citizens, and such filming does not blatantly interfere with an officer exercising his or her duty. Under the Law, cops cannot film or employ surveillance on citizens without probable cause and a warrant because cops are the government.

Over the last decade or so, cops have taken mobile devices from people under *incident to arrest* and searched them for incriminating evidence. Cops generally argue that searching through a cell phone is like searching a person's pockets, a "pat down." This is false. As mentioned before in chapter two, this is unlawful, not only because the mobile device is property subject to 4th Amendment protection, but because a search incident to arrest is only to check for weapons and the like, and not an actual search.

The United States Supreme Court, *Riley vs. California* (2014) banned all law enforcement from looking through mobile devices, or cell phones without a warrant, even during incident to arrest. Chief Justice Roberts argued, "The fact that technology now allows an individual to carry such information in his hand does not make the information any less worthy of the protection for which the Founders fought. Our answer to the question of what police must do before searching a cell phone seized incident to an arrest is accordingly simple — get a warrant."[34] Justice Roberts also stated that, "The term "cell phone" is itself misleading shorthand; many of these devices are in fact minicomputers that also happen to have the capacity to be used as a telephone. They could just as easily be called cameras, video players, rolodexes, calendars, tape recorders, libraries, diaries, albums, televisions, maps, or newspapers."[35] This also includes the Stingray from collecting cell phone data without a warrant. The Court also ruled that only in cases of life threatening, exigent circumstances could a phone be searched absent a warrant, for example to look for a family member's number, or medical information.

The *Riley* ruling is a huge victory for 4th Amendment privacy, and the protection of personal information, which is property, in a technological age where so many people are out and about with so much personal information on their mobile devices. The Chief Justice further concluded,

> "We cannot deny that our decision today will have an impact on the ability of law enforcement to combat crime. Cell phones have become important tools in facilitating coordination and communication among members of criminal enterprises, and can provide valuable incriminating information about dangerous criminals. Privacy comes at a cost. Our holding, of course, is not that the information on a cell phone is immune from search; it is instead that a warrant is generally required before such a search, even when a cell phone is seized incident to arrest."[36]

Constitutional Law Professor David Sklansky, at UC Berkeley, said in response to the ruling, "It certainly is true that if the police are just allowed to rummage through the cell phone of any arrestee without a warrant they can find all kinds of things that might be helpful. Sometimes honoring the Constitution means that law enforcement does not have advantages that it otherwise would have."[37]

First of all, law enforcement officials should have known better before the Supreme Court ruled on it. This is simple LEO competence vs. incompetence. Many cops do know better, however, and abided by the 4th Amendment prior to the ruling. Second, such rulings that confine government activity to the *Law of the Land* makes no real difference anyway. This is because no matter what the courts say in favor of actual Law, government officials will do what they want anyway, somehow, someway. Recall Blackstone. They will generally do what they want through manipulating the legal language within secondary legislation, designed to continue any such infringement upon any fundamental rights.

George Orwell wrote in his book, *Politics and the English Language*, that, "Political language…is designed to make lies sound truthful and murder respectable, and to give an appearance of solidity to pure wind." Case in point, and to digress back to the guns issue, when the Supreme Court ruled in *Heller vs. DC*, that DC's ban on firearms, even in the home, was unlawful and that owning a gun is an individual and fundamental right, the DC Mayor is quoted as saying that the ruling was a "disappointment," and emphasized, as did the District's Police Chief, that gun possession in the home must still be "registered."[38] Forced registration of a handgun kept in the home, in and of itself, is still an unlawful infringement. It is an unlawful infringement because the government is still reducing the right to bear arms into a legal privilege, as we have discussed earlier in chapter two. Carrying a gun outside the home, in public, is only where "reasonable" legislation related to possession of a firearm can come into play because it falls under the jurisdiction of genuine public safety. Yet DC even banned Americans from carrying in public. *Palmer vs. DC* ruled, however, that not allowing residents and non-residents of DC to carry "ready-to-use" handguns in public was "unconstitutional." Banning the carrying of a gun in public, as also ruled by the Ninth Circuit Court of Appeals, is unlawful. Recall that registration of property surrenders the rights attached to the property and principal ownership of the property to whoever demands registration of the property. If you really own something, you don't register it by force. In the case of gun registration, registration establishes compulsory jurisdiction of the property itself to the government. Also recall that *jurisdiction* is defined in Black's Law Dictionary, 8th Edition, as "A government's general power to exercise authority over all persons and *things* within its territory." So in the *Heller* case, when you are forced to register a handgun to merely possess within your own home, the right to bear arms becomes a legal privilege instead. This also circumvents the 4th and 5th Amendments. Again, a gun is property first. This is where the neo-progressives and anti-Second Amendment people start kicking and screaming, spouting off "what if" scenarios and citing gun "violence" statistics, which reinforces the inequality they are so comfortable with. Inequality being that government officials can carry guns and the people not in government cannot, in spite of the Oath they swore to uphold, which secures the fundamental right of an individual to keep (own) and bear (carry) arms. Again, a citizen being armed equalizes them to the government official who is armed. Historically, inequality has always comes down to force, not ideology. Registration allows the people in government to know whom they are up against; the people not in government.

A narrow mind easily gravitates to any side of authoritarianism. When this authoritarian logic is applied to the people in government, the "logic" no longer holds as sound reasoning. So to apply authoritarian logic to authoritarians, for example, if there is evidence of a bad cop on the force who made a false arrest, then all the cops should be restricted from making any arrests. Sounds stupid doesn't it? If equality were truly at play, then sound logic would work either way. Recall Blackstonian Theory again; the government does whatever it wants provided a specific government action is not prohibited by its system of laws. So in the *Heller* case, the Supreme Court, or precedent, specifically prohibits DC from banning weapons in the home. So now the DC government comes along with everything its got to continue its infringement on the right to keep arms in the home by forcing registration through threats of violence and being caged, even though the Rule of Law bans government infringement upon the right to bear arms. If permission and registration of property are required to exercise a right, it is not a right, but a legal privilege. It is not the just role of law enforcement to determine who can and cannot participate in their fundamental rights prior to the individual's participation in a fundamental right.

Let me put this into better perspective. The Rule of Law bans the government from infringing upon the right to bear arms. The DC government then bans the right to bear arms, even in the home. The Supreme Court then bans DC from banning the right to bear arms in the home. DC turns around and bans the right to bear arms in the home without registration, which is another infringement, and then continues to ban the right to bear arms in public, which is also an infringement. It's crazy. You have people in government, whether local state, or federal, who *forcefully* prevent or infringe upon the people not in government from exercising their fundamental rights, in the name of getting a few bad ones (authoritarian logic). This is in spite of the people in government having sworn an oath to obey the Law that secures those very rights. Moreover, the people in government actually criminalize the people not in government for exercising their rights without having first requested and paid for permission from those people in government, which ends in the control, monitoring and deciding whether or not people not in government can or cannot exercise their rights. Thus the rights in question have been converted into legal privileges, by threat of force. This is called *might makes right* and it is grossly unethical when applied in mass. Inequality, then, for example, is increased and is corroborated when government officials in a city create and enforce regulations that allow cops to be armed, absent a right, but the citizens cannot be armed without registration of the their property first, in spite of the right. This is what happens when the lawful paradigm of the government to keep people free deviates into the legal paradigm to keep people safe, by force. John Adams, in a letter to his wife Abigail, said that, "a Constitution of Government once changed from Freedom, can never be restored. Liberty, once lost, is lost forever." America is moving forwards in reverse.

Back to surveillance. What is the endgame of the mass surveillance of Americans by the US government? William Binney, a retired NSA employee and a whistleblower, who was also a high-level code breaker during the Cold War, against the Soviet Union, said, "The ultimate goal of the NSA is total population control," that the NSA has a "totalitarian mentality" which has been the "greatest threat" to Americans since the American Civil War. Binney also conveyed, while attending a conference in London on Surveillance,[39] that, "At least 80% of fiber-optic cables globally go via the US. This is no accident and allows the US to view all communication coming in. At least 80% of all audio calls, not just metadata, are recorded and stored in the US. The NSA lies about what it stores." Binney also concluded that, "...I'm a little optimistic with some recent Supreme Court decisions, such as law enforcement mostly now needing a warrant before searching a smart phone."

The Pew Research Centre released a study concluding that by the year 2025, mass surveillance will only worsen, becoming more invasive, deteriorating public trust, and that commercialization will dominate virtually every aspect of the web,[40] all stemming from the War on Terror. As it relates to the commercialization of every aspect of the web and society as a whole, the movie *Idiocracy* comes to mind.

The War on Terror

The powers that be have been systematically reorganizing society and the economy around war, either by active wars abroad like the War on Terror, or by active wars at home, like the War on Drugs, or the War on

Poverty. These are predicted on the ever-present "threat" of an enemy, either assiduously exaggerated or blatantly manufactured, to secure mass control and special interests related to the marriage of corporations to the people in government. The War on Terror has now inevitably replaced the Cold War as the organizing principle of Western society, which includes the increased militarization and repression of open societies, including their fundamental principles, in part, through the *taken for grantedness* of law enforcement. Neo-progressive policies have been built upon the backs of failed progressive policies. Domestic law enforcement itself is being forced to share in this reorganizing of society here at home through the forced enforcement of the legal system, while the US Military is being forced to share in this reorganizing of society abroad through the forced enforcement of foreign policy. For example, in the name of the War on Terror, there has been a dramatic increase of *Delayed-Notice Search Warrants* (DSW) being executed. A Delayed Notice Search Warrant, also called a *sneak and peak* warrant, allows cops to break into a home and search it, collect evidence and leave while nobody is home. Then, the cops have up to 455 days to notify the occupants that their home was searched. Sometimes homes are even made to look like actual break-ins. These DSWs have increased from about 25 in 2002 to about 5,601 in 2012. As it relates to the Constitutionality of such a warrant, law professor Jonathan Witmer-Rich has said that, "There is no evidence of judicially-authorized covert searching, through a delayed notice warrant or any similar mechanism, in the history of search and seizure through 1791, the drafting of the Fourth Amendment."[41] This, coupled with surveillance, *no knock* warrants, and GPS tracking, encompasses, in part, this reorganizing of society into what Supreme Court Justice Sonya Sotomayor noted, that the, "awareness that the Government may be watching chills associational and expressive freedoms."[42]

Let's face the facts; there are some very dangerous people in the world. There always has been and there always will be. There are those who exist within an array of very demented worldviews, whereby the means to achieve their endgame, which is usually some kind of utopia, is to harm or end life that is contrary to what they specifically define as *rightful*. These worldviews are generally sourced in religious or political texts, absent the exercise of reason and absent the exercise of benevolence towards other human beings who think differently. Free speech no longer counts when such speech couples itself with violence, period. The charge of protecting the country from such people who make such threats to end life, harm life, destroy property, and the like, all as a means to enforce their worldview, is a legitimate and lawful responsibility of government. Such security efforts are a quintessential aspect of the social compact, whereby people come together out of chaos to protect themselves and their property from such people who are hell-bent to commit harm and that threaten peaceful existence. On the other hand, when such efforts are exploited as a means to fundamentally shift the fabric of society into another one, or to use this reasoning irrationally to infer same on the freedom of speech generally, then such efforts become capricious and unlawful. Security is fundamental, but not at the expense of an open and free society. Especially when the probability of such threats being actualized are extremely low, compared to the totality of all potential harm. Within the context of causation, a singular event is not evidence enough to make causal inferences from an effect, which is then used to argue backwards or in a circle. This twist in logic restructures one's sound perspective of causation. Something else is at play, especially when no pattern has emerged. If individual liberties become restricted in an effort to prevent another similar, singular event, then such efforts are fallacious because liberty is superior to security. The oppression of liberties, in the name of aristocracy and totalitarianism, has been the pattern of history, as it relates to governments. Therefore, just and sound causal reasoning argues against the contemporary security apparatus within the modern state. On the contrary, this new style of argument, where one argues backwards and circular, from the effect alone, and within the unsound context of causation, is not only a bad argument, it is the foundation of neo-progressive policy, which actually spawns more violence, more extremism and more injustice. Causation itself has become a bad argument exploited for ulterior motives, generally one that attaches to control of the masses and monetary policy. Robert David Steele, former Marine, CIA case officer, and US co-founder of the US Marine Corps intelligence movement, says of the *War on Terror*,

"In identifying and discussing the mechanisms of contemporary terrorism (organizational system, communication, etc.) and establishing a scorecard for how each of the disciplines does against them, you will be severely handicapped because those who spend great sums on secret sources and methods will lie to themselves, to their policy masters, and to the public, in order to protect those budgets. In my experience, most terrorist events are false flag events organized by the Mossad, the CIA, the FBI, or the local national intelligence or security force, generally under the guise of a drill that has unwitting "patsies" — and of course labeling legitimate opposition and insurgent groups as "terrorists."
The other problem is of course blatant dishonesty, where everyone in opposition to their government — including now US citizens — can be labeled a terrorist and killed without trial. We even have Senators who should know better

talking about "so-called Americans" as if their citizenship were some how invalidated by opinion. At the same time, we have governments that make decisions based on bribes from the recipients of taxpayer money, rather than on the needs of the taxpayer, and secret intelligence really does not matter, except as a crutch to justify spending money in criminally insane ways."[43]

Daniel Ellsberg, while lecturing to Henry Kissinger in the 1970s on how government officials are exploited into these positions of covert operations said, "The danger is, you'll become like a moron. You'll become incapable of learning from most people in the world, no matter how much experience they have in their particular areas that may be much greater than yours, because of your blind faith in the value of your narrow and often incorrect secret information."[44] Thus training is inferior to education. The blind enforcement of law limits one's thinking to their daily experience and to those other minds who make the rules. Training is necessarily the source for not only knowing how to operate within a security based apparatus, instead of a liberty based one, but such training plays off as being sourced from an array of contemporary and varying, educational objectives, chosen by those who design those training standards.

The questions to ask now are, why do other countries dislike or even hate America? Why do other countries see America as the greatest threat to world peace? Why do Americans view America as the 4th largest threat to world peace? The simplest answer is, the people in American government, at all levels, won't leave other people around the world and here at home, alone. "They hate us for our freedom," president Bush said. If this were true, why aren't other countries that are actually freer than we are also being equally threatened by domestic and international terrorism? Sweden doesn't have military bases all over the world. Do you get up in the morning and see New Zealand forces, or Chinese forces at Wal-Mart, asking to see your papers? The history of unconstitutionally declared wars of aggression, the violation of treaties, dictatorial power and the financial exploitation of sovereign nations through the *Bretton Woods System*, military bases all over the world, to name a few, are all, and in part, why such a consensus of dislike towards America exists. These wars of aggression are propagated by fear, fear of an enemy abroad, even vicariously through other sovereign nations. Recently Northwestern Professor Peter Ludlow wrote in the New York Times, as it relates to fear of an enemy being a tool for authoritarian governments, stated,

> "Philosophers have long noted the utility of fear to the state. Machiavelli notoriously argued that a good leader should induce fear in the populace in order to control the rabble. Hobbes in "The Leviathan" argued that fear effectively motivates the creation of a social contract in which citizens cede their freedoms to the sovereign. The people understandably want to be safe from harm. The ruler imposes security and order in exchange for the surrender of certain public freedoms. As Hobbes saw it, there was no other way: Humans, left without a strong sovereign leader controlling their actions, would degenerate into mob rule. It is the fear of this state of nature — not of the sovereign per se, but of a world without the order the sovereign can impose — that leads us to form the social contract and surrender at least part of our freedom."[45]

As mentioned in chapter one, the dichotomy between Hobbes and Locke during the Constitutional Debates still rages on in America. The Law of the Land, or the Rule of Law, again, is founded upon Lockean political philosophy, not Hobbes. The legal system today is founded upon a Hobbesian and Blackstonian political philosophy, not Locke. The War on Terror's political philosophy is predicated on the collective fear of an enemy. As Zbigniew Brzezinski, a United States National Security Advisor to President Jimmy Carter from 1977 to 1981, notes in his book, *The Grand Chessboard: American Primacy And Its Geostrategic Imperatives*,

> "Moreover, as America becomes an increasingly multicultural society, it may find it more difficult to fashion a consensus on foreign policy issues, except in the circumstances of a truly massive and widely perceived direct external threat. Such a consensus generally existed throughout World War II and even during the Cold War. It was rooted, however, not only in deeply shared democratic values, which the public sensed were being threatened, but also in a cultural and ethnic affinity for the predominantly European victims of hostile totalitarianisms.
>
> In the absence of a comparable external challenge, American society may find it much more difficult to reach agreement regarding foreign policies that cannot be directly related to central beliefs and widely shared cultural-ethnic sympathies and that still require an enduring and sometimes costly imperial engagement. If anything, two extremely varying views on the implications of America's historic victory in the Cold War are likely to be politically more appealing: on the one hand, the view that the end of the Cold War justifies a significant reduction in America's global engagement, irrespective of the consequences for America's global standing; and on the other, the perception that the time has come for genuine international multilateralism, to which American should even yield some of its sovereignty."[46]

Brzezinski infers that society needs to be reorganized because the rise of multiculturalism in America decreases the traditional taste for war.

Thus a new style of threat is, and has become, necessary. It is then the legal system that not only enforces itself around the world through foreign policy, by way of the US Military, this legal system also enforces itself domestically, by way of law enforcement, creating both international and domestic *blowback* in response to the war on terror as a whole. Blowback is generally defined as the unintended consequences of covert operations. As *domestic blowback* increases in response to increased authoritarianism, or the enforcement of arbitrary legislation here at home, the War on Terror must now deviate inwards, through even more arbitrary legislation like the Patriot Act, the National Defense Authorization Acts, increased gun-control efforts, the Homeland Security Apparatus, spying, and the like, all intended to thwart the negative effects of already too much legislation. Thus, an external and internal threat must be a continual premise to such efforts at keeping people "safe," by force. In reality, it's simply about controlling the masses and extracting their wealth. Ron Paul said, as it relates to getting more involved in mid-eastern affairs, specifically Iraq again, "I don't think the solution is being involved even more so once again. I'm afraid it will end up with a lot more violence because they are putting more troops in there right now." He continued, "This is exactly what Osama bin Laden wanted. He wanted to engage us over there because he said, 'I'll bring you down like I brought the Soviets down.' We are doing the same thing because we flat out can't afford it. It's a failed policy. I think after so many years and so many decades we ought to admit the truth." The "terrorists have long intended to take the US down by wasting its resources on campaigns, the likes of which have been called fodder for some by further fanning the flames of anti-American sentiments through military action carried out in far apart countries."[46.5]

In addition to US military action in other countries creating more violence through blowback, a newer study infers that military assistance to foreign governments also does more harm than good by creating more violence. In a New York University research paper entitled, *Bases, Bullets and Ballots: the Effect of U.S. Military Aid on Political Conflict in Colombia*, written by Professor of Politics Oeindrila Dube and professor of Economics at Columbia University Suresh Naidu, both have concluded that,

> "Though we focus on Colombia, our results speak to broad questions in political development and international assistance. Military aid is sometimes proposed as a cure for weak states, as it is presumed to enhance the government's repressive capacity, and facilitate its ability to secure a "monopoly on the legitimate use of violence." Yet our results suggest that, in environments such as Colombia, international military assistance can strengthen armed non-state actors, who rival the government over the use of violence."

This further creates this whole human drama between people in government and people not in government, and this is a reciprocal process that ends in the destruction of a nation from within, as history and sound, causal reasoning shows. University of Chicago professor Leo Strauss, the father of the neo-con movement, said, "A political order can be stable only if it is united by an external threat.... Following Machiavelli, he maintained that if no external threat exists then one has to be manufactured."[47] Is the War on Terror manufactured? Blowback is what creates international terrorists. Domestic blowback is what creates homegrown terrorism. Would such violent groups have ever arisen and would such anti-terrorist policies be in place if the people in government had simply left other people around the world and here alone from the start? Thomas Jefferson said during his 1801 inaugural address,

> "[We're] about to enter, fellow-citizens, on the exercise of duties which comprehend everything dear and valuable to you, it is proper you should understand what I deem the essential principles of our Government, and consequently those which ought to shape its Administration. I will compress them within the narrowest compass they will bear, stating the general principle, but not all its limitations. Equal and exact justice to all men, of whatever state or persuasion, religious or political; **peace, commerce, and honest friendship with all nations, entangling alliances with none**; the support of the State governments in all their rights, as the most competent administrations for our domestic concerns and the surest bulwarks against antirepublican tendencies; the preservation of the General Government in its whole constitutional vigor, as the sheet anchor of our peace at home and safety abroad." (bold added)

The opposite of "entangling alliances with none" is what creates international and domestic blowback. Oh but the world is so different now. No it isn't. It is the same as it has always been. If no domestic blowback existed would law enforcement continually increase its firepower and militarization, even though crime statistics continue to decrease? Neo-progressives argue that it is because of the increase of authoritarian law enforcement that crime has decreased. This is a circular argument and is also fallacious, especially in light of statistical and historical facts argued earlier, for example, by the Supreme Court in *Stanford v. Texas* (1965), that such oppressive efforts have always been to crush written political dissent, or what the court calls *libel,*

"While the Fourth Amendment [of the U.S. Constitution] was most immediately the product of contemporary revulsion against a regime of writs of assistance, its roots go far deeper. Its adoption in the Constitution of this new Nation reflected the culmination in England a few years earlier of a struggle against oppression which had endured for centuries. The story of that struggle has been fully chronicled in the pages of this Court's reports, and it would be a needless exercise in pedantry to review again the detailed history of the use of general warrants as instruments of oppression from the time of the Tudors, through the Star Chamber, the Long Parliament, the Restoration, and beyond.

What is significant to note is that this history is largely a history of conflict between the Crown and the press. It was in enforcing the laws licensing the publication of literature and, later, in prosecutions for seditious libel, that general warrants were systematically used in the sixteenth, seventeenth, and eighteenth centuries. In Tudor England, officers of the Crown were given roving commissions to search where they pleased in order to suppress and destroy the literature of dissent, both Catholic and Puritan. In later years, warrants were sometimes more specific in content, but they typically authorized of all persons connected of the premises of all persons connected with the publication of a particular libel, or the arrest and seizure of all the papers of a named person thought to be connected with a libel."

The totality of history must come into play when making inferences like the neo-progressives do in justifying the enforcement of arbitrary policies. The people in government do not like competition. The Constitution is the greatest competition for people in government who want to initiate new policies based upon advances in society when those policies specifically go against the freedoms the Constitution secures. The War on Terror helps them do this.

There are always going to be violent people who want to harm others in existence. The challenge is to deal with them individually, or within their specific group, without closing down an open society, as a whole, in that attempt. Legislation that thwarts freedoms in mass in the effort to restrict a few "bad apples" is, in part, the cause of all this political and social madness. Thus, the *lawful* effort of government officials to protect and secure fundamental rights deviates into the *legal* effort of government officials to protect and secure themselves and their legal system at the expense of fundamental rights.

This *new style* (neo) of policy, in part, is evidenced by the increase in the vast fire power and war machinery within local law enforcement agencies and federal regulatory departments, all in spite of statistics that show violent crime across the country has consistently decreased. Moreover, federal bureaucratic agencies within the Executive branch are increasingly becoming armed and more paramilitary as well, like the Department of Labor, the Food and Drug Administration, the Department of Education, the Social Security Administration, and even the National Oceanic and Atmospheric Administration. Why? This is in response to 9/11 and the arming of the Inspector General's Office in 2002 by Congress under the Homeland Security Act. Combine this with the War on Drug's minimum sentencing created by politicians who want to appear tough on crime. There have been quite a few attempts in Congress to demilitarize federal bureaucratic agencies, none of which have passed. Most recently, congressman Chris Stewart of Utah put forth another such Bill, which would scale back the SWAT and military style tactics of federal regulatory agencies. Stewart has said,

"When there are genuinely dangerous situations
involving federal law, that's the job of the
Department of Justice, not regulatory agencies like
the FDA or the Department of Education. Not only
is it overkill, but having these highly-armed units
within dozens of agencies is duplicative, costly,
heavy handed, dangerous and destroys any sense of
trust between citizens and the federal
government.... The militarization of agencies is
only a symptom of a much deeper and more
troubling problem within Washington – that the
federal government no longer trusts the American
people.... When all of us feel that we are no longer
seen as citizens but as potential dangerous suspects
– a relationship of trust is impossible.... I'm
working to restore and rebuild trust – beginning
with this effort to defund paramilitary capabilities
within federal regulatory agencies."[48]

This is a good thing, unless you are an authoritarian and like to feel
tough. Why has there been an increase in SWAT (special weapons and
tactics) and military tactics, like *no knock*, for non-violent, white-collar
crimes? As it relates to *no knock* warrants, in *Richards vs. Wisconsin*
(1997) the United States Supreme Court upheld that law enforcement,
under common law tradition, must knock and announce themselves before
entering a home to serve a search warrant. The Court also rejected
categorical waivers for "knock and announcement" cases involving drug
investigations. These *waivers* allowed cops to not announce themselves.
Thus the Court stated,

"The Fourth Amendment does not permit a blanket
exception to the knock and announce requirement
for felony drug investigations. While the
requirement can give way under circumstances
presenting a threat of physical violence or where

officers believe that evidence would be destroyed if advance notice were given, 514 U. S., at 936, the fact that felony drug investigations may frequently present such circumstances cannot remove from the neutral scrutiny of a reviewing court the reasonableness of the police decision not to knock and announce in a particular case." No. 96-5955. Argued March 24, 1997

However, for police to continue to execute a "no knock" warrant, they must lawfully show on a case-by-case basis that they have reasonable suspicion of *exigent circumstances*. So what many cops do to secure a *no knock* warrant, for example, is to claim the possibility of "illegal guns," which a magistrate uses to secure the warrant. Complicit?

One example of the law enforcement use of military style force to serve white-collar crime warrants, and there are many, took place in June of 2014, in Sandy UT, where twelve military style SWAT officers with assault rifles drawn, broke through the front door and raided the home of a lawyer and his children to execute a warrant for the allegation of campaign finance fraud. The District Attorney explained, "There are certain things that you have to do when you go into an area that is unfamiliar to you. This is what every citizen out there is subjected to when it comes down."[49] So to serve a warrant in an unfamiliar area on a non-violent individual for an *alleged* white-collar crime, who is, by Law, innocent until proven guilty, it takes twelve officers in a military style raid, which nearly always includes property damage? This is where the exploitation of law enforcement comes in; in response to the social outcry for such abusive tactics, in this case, the Utah Department of Public Safety stated that the officers/agents "followed proper procedure" and "acted in accordance to **policy** and utilized the minimum force necessary to execute the warrants."[50] (bold added) These types of tactics are being taught to officers as "training standards" and then executed all over the country for very minor criminal and civil allegations. Even such tactics have been executed to serve warrants for unpaid student loans and /or government fines. All by way of theoretical threats, or what *might* happen. Such "what if" scenarios, AKA "legal" arguments, are not argument enough to violate the Rule of Law. Legal does not equal lawful.

Many times non-violent 1st Amendment protected protests and demonstrations turn ugly and violent simply because the movement is covertly infiltrated by cops who then turn it ugly by yelling obscene remarks, provoking violence by shoving people and other uniformed cops around, peeing in the street, damaging property, etc. They do this to end the protest prematurely, because such a demonstration may be a nuisance to local businesses, they also do this to make the movement appear ridiculous to the masses and to prevent interest in the message. Many times cops infiltrate protests simply as a means to exercise the show of force. Authoritarians love an excuse to wear their cool military style gear and to exercise their "hands on" training. This is very common. The presence of provocateurs during civil unrest, and the like, is not limited to law enforcement, however. Provocateurs also include outsiders who want to turn a simple act of civil disobedience, a protest or movement ugly for personal or political gain. Another neo-progressive way to thwart a 1st Amendment protected demonstration or protest is to *unlawfully* contain it within "free speech zones" by the same force covertly thwarting it. Retired Police Captain Ray Lewis said in an interview with Vice Magazine in August 2014, as it relates to law enforcement's military style tactics in response to peaceful protests,

> "Here you have a protest that's very peaceful. You don't need cops driving up and down the street. It's an insult to the community. It's not

just a slap in the face to the community; it's a punch in the face. And the body suits they have, they look like robots. When you look like robots, you're going to act like a robot. Your sensitivity is reduced. If you start dressing a police force like an occupying army they're going to start acting like an occupying army. And we all know how occupying armies act. Look at the atrocities that this country has committed in occupied countries that we're in now. You lose perspective."

As it relates to protests or demonstrations in general, Sociologist and fellow Nick Adams at the University at California at Berkley and who heads the University's *Institute for Data Science* study has inferred that police are more often the cause of escalating violence during rather peaceful demonstrations. "Everything starts to turn bad when you see a police officer come out of an SUV and he's carrying an AR-15, it just upsets the crowd. We're finding police have a lot of capacity to set a tone. When police show up in riot gear you get a different kind of interaction than when they show up in their regular uniforms."[50.5] Moreover, when such a demonstration or protest ends badly, people sitting at home watching on the TV will less likely show any interest in that movement. Thus, the provocateurs were successful.

Law enforcement raids in private homes involving military style tactics are increasing to more than one hundred families per day, and for several reasons.[51] One, I believe, is to justify the use of donated military surplus from the federal government. Second, law enforcement agencies must justify their budgets, where over-spending for such non-surplus military style equipment and training standards have taken place. Some of this spending comes from asset forfeiture. These are based upon the theoretical threats conveyed within and derived from the War on Terror. Moreover, such use of force is utilized to negatively reinforce or condition the populace to be accustomed to such raids for non-violent crimes as a means to gain a mass fear advantage, which is utterly authoritarian. Cops don't receive genuine military training. Cops don't train for real war. Americans are not enemies of the state, or are they? The gearing up in military-style wear is a show of force, its psychological. Even the former police chief of Seattle said that when cops dress up in military gear it is an "act of provocation."[51.5] Of course the argument is going to be, "for your safety." This helps solidify further inequality between the cops and the citizens. Militarization of local law enforcement is also a boon to contractor profits, which help play into Homeland Security (DHS) grants. Evan Bernick of The Heritage Foundation recently pointed this out in an article titled *Overmilitarization: Why Law Enforcement Needs to Scale Down Its Use of Military Hardware and Tactics*,

> "The federal government has also encouraged state and local law enforcement officials to concentrate on other categories of crimes that are perceived as particularly threatening. In recent years, for example, the Department of Homeland Security has handed out anti-terrorism grants to cities and towns across the country, enabling them to buy armored vehicles, guns, armor, aircraft, and other equipment."

The exaggerated enforcement of "other categories of crimes" plays into the justifications needed for such military-style tactics and hardware. How else are local law enforcement agencies acquiring tons of military surplus, like tanks, assault weapons, gas masks, and the like, all designed for war? Time Magazine recently articulated in an article that,

> "As the Iraq and Afghanistan wars have wound down, police departments have been obtaining

military equipment, vehicles and uniforms that have flowed directly from the Department of Defense. According to a new report by the ACLU, the federal government has funneled $4.3 billion of military property to law enforcement agencies since the late 1990s, including $450 million worth in 2013. Five hundred law enforcement agencies have received Mine Resistant Ambush Protected (MRAP) vehicles, built to withstand bomb blasts. More than 15,000 items of military protective equipment and "battle dress uniforms," or fatigues worn by the U.S. Army, have been transferred. The report includes details of police agencies in towns like North Little Rock, Ark., (pop: 62,000), which has 34 automatic and semi-automatic rifles, a Mamba tactical vehicle and two MARCbots, which are armed robots designed for use in Afghanistan."[52]

Neo-progressives argue that such an escalation of potential force against the public is necessary because so many Americans have accessibility to many types of sophisticated weaponry, that the root of these raids being a problem comes down to how Americans traditionally interpret the 2nd Amendment. Think about that. It's the Constitution's fault. Again, the escalation in the probability of force is reciprocal of both people in government and people not in government. US Senator Rand Paul wrote a separate article in Time Magazine regarding the militarization of law enforcement and said that, "When you couple this militarization of law enforcement with an erosion of civil liberties and due process that allows the police to become judge and jury—national security letters, no-knock searches, broad general warrants, pre-conviction forfeiture—we begin to have a very serious problem on our hands." Paul also inferred the primary cause of this problem,

"Not surprisingly, big government has been at the heart of the problem. Washington has incentivized the militarization of local police precincts by using federal dollars to help municipal governments build what are essentially small armies—where police departments compete to acquire military gear that goes far beyond what most of Americans think of as law enforcement."[52.5]

One method law enforcement agencies utilize to avoid public accountability on the escalation of force, is to *incorporate*. To incorporate protects the entity that is incorporating from liability. Some agencies with record levels of property damage and brutality actually file 501(c)(3) status, a classification of incorporation they say makes them exempt from public records requests, for example. These law enforcement agencies are then operated by Law Enforcement Councils (LECs) at taxpayer expense, absent taxpayer accountability, with the specific intent to combat the War on drugs, the War on Terror and to crush political dissent.[53] Many law enforcement superiors and politicians also argue for an increase in a paramilitary style of force because of homegrown terrorism, which is a style of political dissent that utilizes violence, but is not itself limited to political dissent. For example, Sheriff Michael Gayer of Pulaski County, IN, argues,

"The United States of America has become a war zone. There's violence in the workplace, there's violence in schools and there's violence in the streets. You are seeing police departments going to a semi-military format because of the threats we have to counteract. If driving a military vehicle is going to protect officers, then that's what I'm going to do."[54]

The government itself is escalating this perception of violence through such military style tactics on non-violent, alleged "crimes." Such perception is also created by mass media reporting every little violence incident that happens around the country. Likewise, the purchasing of war type firepower and the purchasing of paramilitary equipment by bureaucratic agencies feeds into such a perception. In addition, this view of the citizenry as enemies, by definition, is a conspiracy theory in action, except advocated by government officials, contrary to what the evidence may suggest otherwise. The evidence contrary to police militarization is, again, that violent crime is decreasing, according to the FBI, CDC, and other political think tank statistics. So to increase the threats of probable violence founded upon "what if" scenarios and by way of military surplus and firepower against a threat that "might" be there, makes no sense. For law enforcement agencies, and for the government in general, to operate based upon the statistics of violent crime actually on the decline, would mean that government and their budgets would have to shrink. So more crimes are created and the threats related are exaggerated as a means to prevent this.

Nor does it make sense when such increase in military style tactics are founded upon the few incidents that occur from crazed gunmen, for example. Authoritarian logic infers that government "prepping" for civil unrest is necessary. But, then the same logic, however, infers the citizen who stockpiles ammo, or who themselves "prep," is a possible *domestic terrorist* threat. This is the reinforcement of the source of inequality, and such logic is designed to sustain the legal system. Again, more people have died in the 20th Century from *democide,* also known as murder by way of a government's enforcement apparatus, than from any other source of death.[55]

So does it makes more sense to work against government logic with government logic?

This escalation of force through the militarization of local law enforcement increases the dichotomy between the people in government and the people not in government. Paul Szoldra, a Marine, wrote an article on the subject and asked the question,

> "While serving as a U.S. Marine on patrol in Afghanistan, we wore desert camouflage to blend in with our surroundings, carried rifles to shoot back when under enemy attack, and drove around in armored vehicles to ward off roadside bombs. We looked intimidating, but all of our vehicles and equipment had a clear purpose for combat against enemy forces. So why is this same gear being used on our city streets?"[55.5]

One method the feds use to circumvent State Law via local law enforcement authority is to swear officers into the Drug Enforcement Administration (DEA) as a dual agent, for example, transitioning pseudo-authority to the DEA, as it relates to fighting the war on drugs. This war on drugs, and the war on terror especially, are creating a standing, domestic military police force through agencies like DHS, the DEA, the IRS and the like. As it relates to the DHS, the Rutherford Institute's commentary, quoting from analyst Charles Kenny, who suggested that there are six reasons to abolish DHS,

> One, the agency lacks leadership; two, terrorism is far less of a threat than it is made out to be; three, the FBI has actually stopped more alleged terrorist attacks than DHS; four, the agency wastes exorbitant amounts of money with little to show for it; five, "An overweight DHS gets a free pass to

infringe civil liberties without a shred of economic justification"; and six, the agency is just plain bloated.[56]

Even James Madison stated that, "A standing military force, with an overgrown Executive will not long be safe companions to liberty."[57] Unless there is another hidden agenda, which would also, because of the lack of coherent evidence, be called a conspiracy theory. Why such threats of violence against free people? A retired Albuquerque Police Sergeant recently said, as it relates to terrorism being exploited to create a domestic police force, "Here [in New Mexico], we are moving more toward a national police force. Homeland Security is involved with a lot of little things around town. Somebody in Washington needs to call a timeout."[58] Like I've stated earlier, its reciprocal, and it will grow. Even Hillary Clinton, during a CNN Town Hall discussion in June of 2014, exploited the use of the word *terror*, saying in response to a question about firearms, "I'm well aware that this is a hot political subject. And again, I will speak out no matter what role I find myself in. But, I believe that we need a more thoughtful conversation. We cannot let a minority of people – and it's, that's what it is, it is a minority of people – hold a viewpoint that terrorizes the majority of people." Really? The minority she refers to are gun owners. First of all, the Rule of Law is designed to protect the minority from the majority. This is an example of where social engineering utilizes terms like "terrorize" to invoke fear into the public's perception of gun owners. It's ridiculous. I could see if gun owners were running around America shooting and killing people randomly as an insurrection. "As a general rule, tyrants, far more than democratic rulers, need guns, ammunition, spies, and police officers. Their decrees will rarely be self-implementing. Terror is required," writes Cass Sunstein.[59]

The War on Terror has and is slippery sloping into legislative tyranny, whereby all legislation at all levels is virtually designed to prevent theoretical, domestic acts of violence, to radically suppress protests of political dissent, and to sustain a social grid, all at the expense of fundamental rights and property ownership. Law enforcement is then exploited as the "gun in the room," to make sure the job gets done. Recall from Locke, the founding fathers, and the debates; do secondary laws designed to undermine the Rule of Law, for the sake of controlling a few bad apples, equate to exercising Justice? Political dissent, absent any threat or suggestions of violence, will soon become a mental illness, established as justification for the people in government to not only disarm individuals exercising free speech, which is protected by the 1st Amendment, but to exploit law enforcement even further by enforcing such policy through military style tactics, in a free and open society that is secured by a Constitution designed to thwart such arbitrary force. When the people in government self-referentially apply the definitions of terrorism, conspiracy theory, or domestic violence, or self-referentially apply laws against theft or violence, for example, all of the sudden, such definitions and laws either change or don't apply. This is inequality.

The point is this, there is a fundamental difference in insurrection caused by legitimate government action than by arbitrary actions designed to secure special interests at the expense of sound and moral government. Exploitation comes in by way of the latter. What does the Constitution say, as it relates to same? Article 4, Section 4 reads, "The United States shall guarantee to every state in this union a republican form of government, and shall protect each of them against invasion; and on application of the legislature, or of the executive (when the legislature cannot be convened) against domestic violence." What does the Constitution mean by domestic violence? Homegrown terrorism? In James Madison's *Notes of Debates*,[60] there is no suggestion that the framers proposed that Article 4, Section 4 shall be limited to brief insurrections and massive criminal assaults. Alexander Hamilton believed that *domestic* violence was "more alarming than the arms and arts of foreign nations," and that the entire resources of the nation are to be made available to deal with a condition of domestic violence. Therefore, spending should be appropriated for whatever domestic danger arises, "As the duties of superintending the national defense and of securing the public peace against foreign or domestic violence involve a provision for casualties and dangers to which no possible limits can be assigned, the power of making that provision ought to know no other bounds than the exigencies of the nation and the resources of the community."[61] Therefore acts of domestic violence clearly were not intended only towards physical challenges to government, but visa versa when such government violence towards the people threaten liberty, thus the security of militias and the individual right to bear arms. Domestic violence, or danger, is neither only limited to groups the government sees as potential threats. Again, it works both ways, which is why the Rule of Law must remain the paradigm.

Lincoln made the point that, "All the armies of Europe, Asia and Africa combined could not by force take a drink from the Ohio or make a track on the Blue Ridge, in a trial of a thousand years. At what point then is the approach of danger to be expected? I answer, if it ever reaches us, it must spring up amongst us. If destruction be our lot, we must ourselves be its author and finisher."[62] To somewhat illustrate this point, the Japanese attacks at Pearl Harbor did not invade America by land because they knew American homes were heavily armed. In addition, and likewise, a *domestic invasion* from within can be potentially thwarted because Americans are armed individually and by way of organized militias. Thus, the probability of such domestic threats, if government remains Constitutionally limited, is very low indeed. In addition, today, and then, domestic violence encompasses the modern understanding of domestic terrorism, or homegrown terrorism. What is domestic terrorism? According to the FBI's *Terrorist Research and Analytical Center in 1994*, domestic terrorism was defined as "the unlawful use of force or violence, committed by a group(s) of two or more individuals, against persons or property to intimidate or coerce a government, the civilian population, or any segment thereof, in furtherance of political or social objectives."[63] Now, what happens when this definition is applied to government itself? Unfortunately, this definition generally changes according to the necessary terminology needed to justify enforcement actions apart from the definition applying to government itself. Causal reasoning shows that as government authority increases arbitrarily, government will use this type of reasoning and the people's lawful response to such arbitrary authority as an excuse to shut the people's response down, and to enact stricter policy to restrain same. This is the Hegelian Dialectic in action. Government creates a problem through law, then creates a solution through law, thus further encroaching upon fundamental rights, through law, which then further shuts down a free and open society.

Recall that Locke said people come together to create government to establish peace and to secure natural rights and property ownership. The goal for American government, as declared in the Declaration, is to secure life, liberty and the pursuit of happiness. This can only happen in a free and open society. The Framers knew that America would become radically different than other countries around the world, then and in the future. Therefore, the Constitution establishes legitimate power to the people and their representatives to secure their rights and to secure their safety and happiness. This was reaffirmed in the U. S. Supreme Court case *Texas v. White* (1868) that the people's rights and happiness are guaranteed by this protection. But what happens when government deviates from this for the sake of what *might* happen, compared to what has happened outside of backwards causation? The people have a fundamental right to rise up when their government threatens their freedom. Then the neo-progressives in government use this to shut society down even more, by way of violence and the threats of violence.

When domestic blowback, also called domestic or homegrown terrorism, becomes the justification for policy that infringes upon the liberties of the people in mass, then government loses its validity and has deviated into authoritarianism. Sound policy works against such domestic threats absent the undermining of individual liberties, like the right to travel abroad freely. Valid policy abides by the Rule of Law, rather than by the legal system alone. For example, the War on Terror has led to vary invasive policies that no longer respect privacy. Of course, the neo-progressives will also argue that one can avoid such policy enforcement by not putting themselves into those situations where such policy enforcement exists. So, if you want to avoid having all your personal belongings searched by TSA agents, don't fly. Stay home. If you want to avoid being pulled over and searched by cops who seek sweet reward for fighting the War on Drugs, don't drive through certain states or through certain areas. If you want to avoid unreasonable search and seizure of your home for voicing your political opinion on a social network, shut up. If you do not want your guns taken from you for simply carrying in public, or if you do not want your home raided by SWAT for having guns that are cosmetically "illegal," avoid exercising your 2nd Amendment. If you don't want your emails read by government officials, or if you don't want your phone calls listened to by government officials, don't communicate with other people by email or phone. If you don't want government officials telling you want you can and can't do with your property, don't own any. If you want to avoid government's micromanagement of your finances, avoid earning income. If you don't want to be arrested and put in jail for a day or two to then have the charges dropped, than don't exercise your 1st Amendment right to protest. Yes, civil disobedience in now a crime, unless permission is paid for and the government can maintain *absolute* control. Ridiculous isn't it. This redefines civil disobedience. Especially in a society that entraps people within a monetary system by force. This social engineering of people away from their rights, through force, is the endgame of what the War on Terror and the legal system accomplishes. It's like concrete in the roadway directing cars into a certain formation. The War on Terror helps convert rights into privileges and it's all for your safety. Real life is risky. Fake life is less risky. As government authoritarianism increases, so does resentment within the masses.

In June of 2014, Louisiana Governor Bobby Jindal said in a speech, "I can sense right now a rebellion brewing amongst these United States, where people are ready for a hostile takeover of Washington, D.C., to preserve the American Dream for our children and grandchildren."[64] This "sense of rebellion" is not limited to one man who is the head of one state. In fact, this "sense of rebellion" has been the primary motivating factor for the intensified and militaristic training of law enforcement. Even the Pentagon has been preparing for mass civil disobedience (domestic blowback) and a breakdown of law and order by way of the *DoD 'Minerva Research Initiative*.[65] Imagine a parent that systematically abuses a child over his or her adolescence. Who is to blame when the child becomes an adult and then retaliates for the years of abuse? Recall the Declaration of Independence's stand against King Charles the III of England,

> "Governments are instituted among Men, deriving their just powers from the consent of the governed, That whenever any Form of Government becomes destructive of these ends, it is the Right of the People to alter or to abolish it, and to institute new Government, laying its foundation on such principles and organizing its powers in such form, as to them shall seem most likely to effect their Safety and Happiness. Prudence, indeed, will dictate that Governments long established should not be changed for light and transient causes; and accordingly all experience hath shewn, that mankind are more disposed to suffer, while evils are sufferable, than to right themselves by abolishing the forms to which they are accustomed. But when a long train of abuses and usurpations, pursuing invariably the same Object evinces a design to reduce them under absolute Despotism, it is their right, it is their duty, to throw off such Government, and to provide new Guards for their future security."

What is truly disturbing about this quote from the Declaration is, that men and women in uniform are being socially engineered and "trained" that those individuals who honor this *preamble* that quintessentially defines America, are the roots of domestic terrorism. This can be no further from the truth. Mere patriotism today is interpreted as a crime. Patriotism today must adhere to the status quo, which is what government defines as patriotism. Genuine patriotism seeks to protect country from invasive government. This pseudo-patriotism, as advocated by the neo-progressives, is to support the status quo, without question. This is un-American.

As it relates to homegrown or domestic terrorism, law enforcement agencies are routinely informed through "in-house" documentation, for law enforcement's eyes only, of possible domestic threats, and rightfully so. Because there are those who want to execute violence on innocent people, including those innocent people in government, as a way to pacify their frustrations. Therefore, it becomes a noble effort for cops to go after those Americans who hold extreme views that incite and commit to threats of violence against innocent people. For example, "CTB 14-07: Recent Spike in Violence Targeting Law Enforcement," published by New York State Intelligence Center, stated in June of 2014,

> "Over the last week there have been three attacks – one in Canada and two in the United States – in which law enforcement officers were targeted, leading to the death of five officers and one civilian…. Based upon reporting it appears all the suspects in these incidents were motivated by elements of a far right anti-government ideology with a particular fixation on law enforcement."

Communication between law enforcement agencies is vital to helping stop and/or thwart such acts of violence. However, exploitation comes in when such enforcement efforts restrain the free movement of individuals, *a priori*, who hold beliefs that resemble those who are targeted as extreme right-wing or left-wing. Suspicion does not equal probable cause, and neither do statutes justify the enforcement of such a surveillance and enforcement apparatus. The Southern Poverty Law Center (SPLC) now infers that people who politically dissent in their speech, holding that the Constitution is continually violated by government, for example, or who believe and voice the opinion that government should be limited, are right-wing extremists and are potentially violent threats to society, especially when such speech has not made any actual threats of violence. The SPLC also demonizes and socially engineers into the public that the very view of the militia system established by the founders, as a means to check power, is "domestic extremism." This is ludicrous thinking and completely designed to reinforce, negatively, the War on Terror, and to condition and reinterpret the public's perspective of such fundamental principles like limited government. This conditioning makes its way into the minds of cops by way of *Law Enforcement Sensitive* material such as one recent document released by HLS entitled, *Domestic Violent Extremists Pose A Threat To Government Officials And Law Enforcement*. Law enforcement then, generally and unlawfully, but "legally," enforces regulations related to such "theoretical" threats, based upon suspicion, limiting the free movement of people simply voicing their opinions. Heavy abuse of property rights also comes into play. Corporate media is additionally to blame, in part. Both theoretical assertions of what might happen, coupled with and compared to the statistics of what has happened, are then propagated by media, into the public's perception, thus creating fear and encouraging the gradual shut down of free speech that creates friction upon the status quo. The legal system is representative of the status quo, and law enforcement is *trained* and then exploited to uphold same.

What are some of the statistics of homegrown or domestic terrorism? During the years between 1990 and 2013, the University of Maryland infers that far-right extremists have committed about 155 homicides within the United States, and that thirteen percent of these were related to anti-government sentiment, including the Oklahoma City bombing, which averages out to about 368 individuals killed. Thus, on average, 16 people a year, since 1990, have become victims of domestic terrorism.[66] Now compare this number to the over 300 million people who live in the United States. So, to put this into perspective, which is absolutely necessary, as it relates to mass restrictions upon liberty, the following statistical facts will end an individual's life prior to the possibility of domestic terrorism: heart disease, accidents and injuries, intentional self-harm, assault by firearms, walking, choking, fire, post-surgical complications, alcohol, falling down stairs, exposure to forces of nature, cycling, exposure to excessive natural cold, accidental firearms discharge, storms, lightning, and dog bites.[67] Is domestic terrorism, then, enough to enforce statutes aimed at preventing same, when such enforcement limits and restricts the individual liberty that the Constitution secures?

A recent May 2014 study entitled *Inventing Terrorists, The Lawfare of Preemptive Prosecution*, researched and written by the *National Coalition to Protect Civil Freedoms* and *Project SALAM*, have concluded that nearly 95 percent of the arrests of "terrorists" have been the result of the FBI foiling its own entrapment plots, in the name of fighting the War on Terror and to justify budgets. Many of these have also taken place with homegrown terrorist activities, whereby near indigent individuals who voice political dissent, are exploited under these *entrapment* plots. Most of these arrests have implicated the unjust prosecution of targeted Muslim Americans. The study analyzes 399 individuals from the year 2001 to 2010, which are also included on the Department of Justice's list. The study concluded,

> "According to this study's classification, the number of preemptive prosecution cases is 289 out of 399, or 72.4 percent. The number of elements of preemptive prosecution cases is 87 out of 399, or 21.8 percent. Combining preemptive prosecution cases and elements of preemptive prosecution cases, the total

number of such cases on the DOJ list is 376, or 94.2 percent."

The authors define 'preemptive prosecution' as "a law enforcement strategy adopted after 9/11, to target and prosecute individuals or organizations whose beliefs, ideology, or religious affiliations raise security concerns for the government." Such "security concern" efforts of law enforcement as cited by the study do not equate to probable cause, but mere suspicion. So to illustrate, as it relates to homegrown terrorism, flying the Gadsden Flag that reads "Don't Tread on Me," combined with voicing one's opinion that government should be limited and that government is thwarting the Constitution for the sake of special interests, may be a security concern for law enforcement officials, thus their surveillance is "necessary." This is a bad argument. Moreover, the Human Rights Watch released a report in July of 2014 that concluded, "In some cases the FBI may have created terrorists out of law-abiding individuals by suggesting the idea of taking terrorist action or encouraging the target to act."[68] Entrapment is not only unethical, it is unlawful. It is unlawful because such entrapment efforts work against the Constitution.

Fortunately, the Constitution has been slowly working against such unlawful government tactics in the name of the War on Terror. For example, the "no fly list" was recently declared unconstitutional in Federal Court. U.S. District Court Judge Anna Brown declared the "no fly list" violated the Constitution's promise of "life, liberty and pursuit of happiness,"

> "One need not look beyond the hardships suffered by Plaintiffs to understand the significance of the deprivation of the right to travel internationally. Due to the major burden imposed by inclusion on

the No-Fly List, Plaintiffs have suffered significantly including long-term separation from spouses and children; the inability to access desired medical and prenatal care; the inability to pursue an education of their choosing; the inability to participate in important religious rites; loss of employment opportunities; loss of government entitlements; the inability to visit family; and the inability to attend important personal and family events such as graduations, weddings, and funerals. The Court concludes international travel is not a mere convenience or luxury in this modern world. Indeed, for many, international travel is a necessary aspect of liberties sacred to members of a free society."[69]

Studio Prey columnist Rebecca Mickley, wrote an interesting article called *We the Problem*. In it she concludes,

"We, the people, must reject the false paradigms offered as easy panaceas by our leaders. Gun Control, Ubiquitous Surveillance, and free speech zones are snake oil, meant to poison and distract the people all the while we are tied down by oppressive laws and fatal memes that security only comes through slavery. Terrorists will not stop because we are being watched, extremists will not be silenced because the law abiding are crowded into free speech zones, and shooters will not stop the murder of our children because the law abiding are denied essential rights and protections. These problems will only grow as our liberties enter their twilight, and ultimately sunset because if we are not a free people than we are ready victims being led to the slaughter by those not only outside of our culture but by those we will beg to defend us."[70]

The Moral Compass vs. Qualified Immunity

Legislative tyranny can only take hold through the badge, uniform and gun. Over time, the blind submission to secondary legislation as real authority, coupled with the equally blind enforcement of such legislation, calluses and then reshapes the officer's moral compass, whereby any and all necessary actions taken, including violence, become the "ethical" standards of "enforcing the law." This also applies to overzealous prosecutors. James Madison once said that,

> "The aim of every political Constitution, is or ought to be first to obtain for rulers men who possess most wisdom to discern, and most virtue to pursue, the common good of society; and in the next place, to take the most effectual precautions for keeping them virtuous whilst they continue to hold their public trust."[71]

The US Constitution itself is the ethical source for the common good, the collective moral compass, which secures life, liberty and the pursuit of happiness. Making reference to any and all legislation itself as the justification for every law enforcement action, including the use of violence, apart from self-defense and the defense of another, and in contrast to the very oath sworn, is itself the avenue by which legislative tyranny engulfs a free and open society. Legislative tyranny is a corruption of the Rule of Law, by the Legal System, and it bullies Americans into thinking that right and wrong are determined by what is legal and illegal. "Might makes right" nullifies any standard of ethics, especially as it relates to the people in government being a *moral force* for goodness and justice. In an article entitled, *Escalating Domestic Warfare*, Brian J. Trautman concludes that,

"Modern policing, which frequently treats citizens like enemies of the state, should deeply concern every American, regardless of political affiliation. Over the past two decades, the violent crime rate in the United States has decreased sharply. Innovations in computer technology have provided law enforcement with new crime prevention tools, especially in surveillance. The excessive militarization of American policing, then, is counterintuitive.

The drug war and counter-terrorism efforts may represent two of the official justifications for current trends in policing. Historically, however, nations have militarized their police to rapidly quell potential mass civil uprisings against tyranny and injustice.

Whatever the reasoning, abusive, hyper-aggressive policing against communities, particularly economically disadvantaged communities of color, as well as the stripping of civil liberties, are real threats to freedom and democracy and thus urgently require serious national attention and meaningful action."[72]

The monopoly on violence is a *might makes right* worldview. And, it is a very old worldview, one that the founders fought against. To illustrate the actualization of how legislative tyranny infects the populace through the uniform, I want to cite an actual case; during the summer of 2014, a campus police officer stopped and asked a female professor for her ID because she crossed the road without using the "designated" crosswalk. The cop explained to her that crosswalks are there for her "safety" and because he had almost hit her in his patrol car, he needed to see her ID. Then, when the woman refused to show her ID, an argument issued. The cop then grabs her to arrest her for not showing her ID, and because she resists, he picks her up into the air and body slams her on the ground. Mind you, she did not lunge at him, nor did she try to assault him anytime prior to him grabbing onto her to arrest her. She simply pulled away. After the cop body slammed the woman, he charged her with *assault on a government official*, resisting arrest, and jaywalking. His justification for the violence? He cited a statute that reads one must show an ID to a law enforcement officer when asked. Was his use of arbitrary violence rational? Of course not, it was arbitrary. When a mere statute can justify a law enforcement officer to commit a violent *assault on a female*, or any assault period, absent the context of self-defense or her being a verifiable threat to the officer or to society, then legislative tyranny commences. It commences because secondary laws are used to rationalize whatever violent means is necessary to enforce them, for "public safety" of course. Moreover, his superiors concluded that he was acting within his "lawful" duty because she "resisted" and refused to show an ID, again citing the statute as justification for body slamming a woman half his size. Recall that Locke mocked the idea that any and all governments, whether tyrannical or not, operate by a system of laws. What determines a law to be sound, or moral, as it relates to its consistency to the American Rule of Law? The problem is, cops don't know. Moreover, they are not trained to "know."

The question to ask is, if a cop *arbitrarily* executes violence as a means to either inquire information from someone or to enforce a statute by way of arrest, absent violence on the part of the subject, as cited above, would resistance qualify as self-defense, especially if the subject is in fear of their life? The government says emphatically, NO! Or does it? A Texas Grand Jury in 2014 refused to indict a man on capital murder for "knowingly shooting and killing a law enforcement officer." The Grand Jury refused to indict the man on the grounds of self-defense, because the subject reasonably believed that his home was being broken into and that he and his family's lives were in danger. The law enforcement officer that was shot and killed was attempting to execute a "no knock" warrant based upon an informant, who said that the man was growing pot. The "no knock" part of the warrant was secured because the cops then argued the man *might* have "illegal guns." In the end, the man's guns were legal and an officer sadly lost his life over two small pot plants.[73]

Free individuals have a fundamental right to defend themselves against unlawful arrests, according to many State Supreme Courts and according to the United States Supreme Court. The US Supreme court, for example, ruled in *John Bad Elk v. U.S.*, 177 U.S. 529, that,

> "Where the officer is killed in the course of the disorder which naturally accompanies an attempted arrest that is resisted, the law looks with very different eyes upon the transaction, when the officer had the right to make the arrest, from what it does if the officer had no right. What may be murder in the first case might be nothing more than manslaughter in the other, or the facts might show that no offense had been committed."

This ruling stemmed from the Indiana State Supreme Court case *Plummer vs. State*, 136, which ruled, "Citizens may resist *unlawful* arrest to the point of taking an arresting officer's life if necessary." In addition, the North Carolina Supreme Court ruled in *State vs. Mobley*, 83 S.E.2d 100 (1954), "It is axiomatic that every person has the right to resist an unlawful arrest.... Each person has the right to resist an unlawful arrest. In such a case, the person attempting the arrest stands in the position of a wrongdoer and may be resisted by the use of force, as in self- defense." So the question to ask now is, what does unlawful mean? Unlawful is when a secondary law is arbitrary, or not pursuant thereof to the federal or state constitution, or whereby the officer acts within the *color of law*. This type of fiasco, where the cop body slams the woman, in the name of a ordinance, in and of itself socially engineers the masses away from the simplicity of the Constitution being a form of government designed to work against aristocracy and capricious violence. Francis Grund, who wrote in, *The Americans in Their Moral, Social, and Political Relations* (1837),

> "The American Constitution is remarkable for its simplicity; but it can only suffice a people habitually correct in their actions, and would be utterly inadequate to the wants of a different nation. Change the domestic habits of the Americans, their religious devotion, and their high respect for morality, and it will not be necessary to change a single letter in the Constitution in order to vary the whole form of their government."

This "legal" means for law enforcement to commit acts of violence, aka brutality, is not only limited to violence itself; it encompasses other questionable acts necessary to "get the bad guy." To illustrate; another very disturbing case of questionable actions takes place in Virginia. A seventeen-year-old boy and his fifteen-year-old girlfriend sent pictures and videos to each other of their genitals via their cell phones. Charges for *distributing pornography* were initially filed against them because they were minors. The charges were later dropped. The prosecutor and the police filed new charges, charging the boy with felony *manufacturing and distributing of child pornography* and even secured a second warrant to take pictures of the boy's "erect" penis as evidence. Pictures of the boy's non-erect penis were already taken under the first warrant. Jonathan Turley, the Constitutional Law professor, whom I've mentioned before, made this remark on his blog,

"The fact that a Northern Virginia magistrate approved a new search warrant shows the lack of any real review in such cases. This warrant is both abusive and unnecessary. The effort to convict the boy of two felonies shows a complete refusal to exercise an ounce of prosecutorial discretion or for that matter judgment. While this story has been the source of jokes, I do not find it funny in the slightest degree. The people of Manassas need to seriously review the performance of their police and prosecutors in this case. Clearly, crime does not appear to be a serious problem in the city for these officers and prosecutors to take such extraordinary actions in such a case."[74]

The Virginia statute against child pornography is soundly necessary to stop, prosecute and punish an individual engaged in child pornography. However, in this case the statute is being grossly exploited against a teenaged boy, whereby the letter of the statute is not in sync with the spirit of the statute. When *might makes right* couples itself with any and all legislation, absent individual constitutional competence and the light of basic human reasoning, as Locke says, the moral compass, both individually and collectively, becomes demoralized. Thus, *legislative tyranny* becomes the model of "Law and Order." Within the midst of exercising one's duty, these questionable actions, or tactics, not only end in violation of a person's rights and of the Rule of Law, it violates the founding. The founding is the moral underpinning of what the Rule of Law is really for, to secure liberty, property and the pursuit of happiness. This "legal" means for cops to do whatever it takes to get the "bad guy" and get away with it is called *qualified immunity*, and it is hugely subjugated and its is abuse rampant in America today. Qualified immunity combined with an authoritarian spirit creates *predatory* and *passive aggressive* law enforcement. Moreover, a lot of "what ever it takes" actions are actual crimes in and of themselves. The most common abuse of qualified immunity, in the end, that begins the cynical nullification of the moral compass, is lying. I'm specifically referring to manipulatively lying, not the kind of "lying" that may be necessary to protect a witness, someone's identity, sensitive information within an investigation, or the like. In Durham, NC for example, the police Chief had to issue an in-house reprimand to officers for lying to people that the resident had received a 911 hang-up call and were there to make sure everything was ok. They manipulatively lied to people about the 911 calls as a way to get consent for searches and to serve outstanding warrants, or to look for wanted persons. The reprimand read,

> "It has recently been brought to my attention that some officers have informed citizens that there has been a 911 hang-up call from their residence in order to obtain consent to enter for the actual purpose of looking for wanted persons on outstanding warrants. Effective immediately no officer will inform a citizen that there has been any call to the emergency communications center, including a hang-up call, when there in fact has been no such call." – Jose L. Lopez, Sr., Chief of Police[75]

Lying to people as a means to manipulatively acquire consent to search qualifies as "unreasonable search and seizure" and is prohibited by the 4th Amendment. These types of tactics are how kings, dictators, Gestapos and despots historically have always gotten their way, and gotten information. These types of acts are also arbitrary because they are self-serving of government interests, which is unlawful. Getting the "bad guy" is not argument enough to justify same.

Genuine qualified immunity is important and necessary for a law enforcement officer to do their job well. Qualified immunity protects an officer from making honest mistakes while on duty. Lying to people, and picking up a woman and body slamming her, is not an honest mistake that deserves protection under qualified immunity. Qualified immunity should neither protect cops from invasively taking genital pictures of a teenage boy because he sent his teenage girlfriend a naked picture of himself. The cops in this case later decided wisely not to execute the warrant because of public outcry, but did continue with the charges. Nor is such enforcement a justifiable means to violate anyone's right to not be assaulted. These actions oppress the moral compass that attaches society to non-violent or non-invasive common goodness. Such justifications on statute interpretations that go far beyond the 'reasonable,' whereby such interpretations maximize government interests, are born within the bureaucratic halls where the people in government comb through law books and precedent to formulate their arguments as a means to maintain authority in any given incident for an arrest.

The easily corruptible understand that when a statute can become the frame of reference and validation for unethical action, through simple articulation of the letter of the statute, or by way of the specific elements of the statute only, absent the spirit in its sound interpretation, qualified immunity then becomes a key component in the rise of and the justification of a police state.

> "The greatest evil is not now done in those sordid 'dens of crime' that Dickens loved to paint. It is not done even in concentration camps and labour camps. In those we see its final result. But it is conceived and ordered (moved, seconded, carried, and minuted) in clean, carpeted, warmed and well-lighted offices, by quiet men with white collars and

cut fingernails and smooth-shaven cheeks who do not need to raise their voices. Hence, naturally enough, my symbol for Hell is something like the bureaucracy of a police state or the office of a thoroughly nasty business concern." — C.S. Lewis, *The Screwtape Letters*

Police states throughout history have always failed in the end. They have failed because the inequality that increases from such a police state, which dramatically divides the people that are not in government from the people that are in government, and which divides the people from other people in society, in the end, incites mass rebellion and ultimately revolution. History is what it is. Arbitrary violence as a necessary means to enforce a statute outside of there being any comparable threat is "justified" by making reference to the statute itself. Then on top of that, the argument that such enforcement is necessary for the individual's and the public's safety follows. Yet again, this has traditionally been any government's primary logic for nearly all of human history. Nothing has changed. In America the same logic has become the excuse to "get around" the moral compass codified within the Constitution, which the founders hoped would become a universal example. Ben Franklin said, "Only a virtuous people are capable of freedom. As nations become corrupt and vicious, they have more need of masters."[76] I would also add that only virtuous people are capable of "defending" freedom from the need of masters. Nations deviate into viciousness and corruption because its government fills up with the corruptible. When Rosa Parks sat in the front of the bus, did the officer that arrested her enforce her fundamental right to travel and to be left alone, or did the officer enforce the legal system at the time, a statute that said she could not sit in front of the bus? Was Ms. Parks a threat to society? Was not Ms. Parks a free individual? Or, was government itself a threat to Ms.

Park's liberty? Oh let me guess, we have evolved out of such arbitrary legislation through civil rights?

If the legal system were truly in sync with the Rule of Law, criminal records, for example, and depending upon the state, would consist of only convictions, and not also of mere charges that were either dismissed, or where the individual was found innocent in a court of law. Why has no representative changed this? I have yet to hear a *competent* argument for leaving dismissed or acquitted charges on criminal records. Generally, the government's argument for keeping charges on an individual's "criminal" record is that criminal records are a collection of all charges related to any "criminal" activity, whether or not one is convicted. The fact is, other people, companies, schools, banks, employers, and the like, still *judge* an individual based upon the "charges" that stay on their record. This is wrong. This is unethical. One problem with this is, and I have seen it many times, anyone can go to a magistrate and swear out a warrant, or an order for arrest, on virtually anybody for anything, based upon the complainant's mere testimony. This is especially common within domestic disputes. One tries to "get back" at the other by actually fabricating a charge, or not. And, even if the complainant decides to drop the charges, the charges stay on the other individual's criminal record. This is unethical because such a scheme contradicts the liberty premise of "innocent until proven guilty." Moreover, such charges play on negative human nature within practically all the people who are inquiring into someone's record. The mind goes straight into the gutter, so to speak. This in and of itself nullifies the moral compass, because it diminishes the trust in the legal system to be ethically sound and proficient of what it means to uphold the ideology of innocent until proven guilty, to actualize the responsibility of the burden of proof, and it pits people in positions of authority against others unfairly, based upon false information. False in the sense that non-convictions are on a "criminal" record, when such non-convictions are not actually criminal. As it relates to law enforcement, cops, a lot of times, pull up these records and then deal with an individual based upon what was not actually the case, because the charges are not convictions. This is a type of exploitation, because it predisposes an officer to an opinion of someone, even though the person may have been found innocent or the charges being used to judge the individual unfairly, and depending on the circumstances, were dismissed. Expungement procedures are very expensive. Maybe there in lies the answer as to why non-convictions saturate criminal records.

The Color of Law

The officer who arrested Rosa Parks was "executing his official duty" under *color of law*, I believe. Following orders or referring blindly to a statute, as the "lawful" authority for an officer's dealings with an individual, does not necessarily, nor ethically liberate the officer from the responsibility attached to not engaging in color of law. Judges, for example, more and more often, still, restrict due process to their own dictates of what counts as evidence and argument, while at the same time being persuaded by *other* attorneys and corporate lobbyists with deep pockets and political ties. All are intimately, somehow, connected to special interests, or a government official's personal feelings, which is also acting under color of law. For instance, in Connecticut, a Superior Court Judge, within the context of their official duty, asserted that, "No one in this country should have guns, I never return guns," referring to his "temporary" confiscation of weapons. Another Judge, even proclaimed from the bench that, "those who support the Second Amendment should be ashamed."[77] The *special interests* within these two examples were clearly related to gun control efforts, which is unlawful when converted to government interests based upon private beliefs. These judges can easily incite law enforcement action, unlawfully. These are judicial officials who swore an oath to uphold the Bill of Rights. They can't simply pick and choose the ones they like and then uphold those, especially within a Court of Law. When any government official acts contrary to their sworn oath to uphold and defend the Constitution, in the name of a secondary law, and within the context of their own government profession, for the sake of special interests, they are "executing their duty" within the color of law.

Here is a straightforward case in point, at the local level when the law is designed around special interests and law enforcement becomes the "gun in the room." Myrtle Beach, South Carolina, April 2014, the city council passed an ordinance banning any other "shading devices" on the beach except for "approved" umbrellas, thus securing the renting of umbrella spacing on the beach by private business. The ordinance reads in Sec. 5-4, a: "Through the use of 'beach franchise agreements' the City has established the time and placement of lifeguard stands to establish and preserve public safety." Subsection e, then reads in part, "Shading devices, other than circular umbrellas with a diameter of seven and one-half feet or less, shall not be allowed on the beach between Memorial Day through Labor Day." So what the city council has done is secure the revenue of the private business of leasing umbrellas and spacing on the beach by making it illegal for people that have their own "shading devices" or for those who have their own umbrellas, to interfere with the renting of umbrellas, and only during the Summer. A "franchise agreement" is the contract between the local government and a private business, where the private business has probably not only complained about competition with "private shading" on the beach, but has more than likely also lobbied the council to enact such an ordinance as a means to minimize such competition with private people's "shading devices." The council then manipulates the legal language by referring to this ordinance as a "public safety" issue. Subsection *f* of the ordinance 5-4 then reads, "It shall be unlawful for any person to place any shading device or umbrella so as to impede lifeguard line of sight, access or egress from the lifeguard stand." Notice how the word "unlawful" is used? The word should read "illegal." The Myrtle Beach ordinance is clear-cut. It translates that the business of renting umbrellas on any public section of Myrtle Beach shall not be infringed upon by people who do not want to rent umbrellas.

As it relates to the public safety aspect, a lifeguard now spends much of their time as a leasing agent, securing the private business owner's income of renting umbrellas while also trying to pay attention to swimmers. Moreover, those who want to use their own umbrellas must either sit behind the line of rental umbrellas or either sit at the end of the rental umbrella line, which is often in a *no swim zone*. Parents who have their own umbrellas cannot pay close attention to their children in the water because they must sit *behind* the line of rental umbrellas, which is potentially a genuine public safety issue, especially since the lifeguard's attention is also spent on leasing those rental umbrellas. Is not the line of rental umbrellas impeding a parent's line of sight? On top of this, following a "warning" to either leave the *public* beach and/or put away the private shading devise, and on not complying with the warning, law enforcement may then arrest the "criminal" and charge the private shading devise owner with a misdemeanor, coupled with a $500 fine and/or thirty days in jail. This is a quintessential example of when cops are exploited to enforce an ordinance that is designed to secure the revenue of private special interests in the name of public safety. The special interests in this Myrtle Beach ordinance are the private businesses of renting umbrella spaces on the public beach. Color of law here does not necessarily mean that an individual cop is intently using his or her authority for personal gain. Color of law can also encompass a cop's authority being used by other government officials for government's financial gain, which is mostly the case.

The color of law is also executing authority outside of both the spirit and letter of the Law of the Land. Color of law is defined by Black's Law Dictionary, 8th Edition, as, "The appearance or semblance, without the substance, of a legal right. The term implies a misuse of power made possible because the wrongdoer is clothed with the authority of the state." Myrtle Beach City Council is using their monopoly on force as a "legal right lacking substance" to secure revenue for special interests. The substance lacking in the Myrtle Beach City Council is compliance to their oath. Securing revenue for the government does not qualify as substance of a legal right to make law, especially when such government revenue is predicated upon securing private business revenue at the expense of the liberty of the people, and especially on a public beach. Nor doe public safety qualify as substance of a legal right to make law when such intent is also to secure private special interests. If the genuine intent were about public safety at Myrtle's public beach, the lifeguard would not also spend his or her time equally as a leasing agent of umbrella rental spacing. Focus on swimmers is what people pay lifeguards for. Of course, any city councilman would vehemently argue against this, through the misuse of rhetoric.

Excessive force also qualifies as color of law, according to the FBI.[78] Even the enforcement of statutes that equally deprive an individual of their fundamental rights qualifies as acting under color of law, because the officer is generally operating on the mere letter of the statute absent the spirit of it. Recall *John Bad Elk vs. U.S.* Operating on both letter and spirit of law only takes basic intelligence. The following Federal Statute declares the due course of action for those government officials who swore the Constitutional Oath and then by their actions deprive individuals of their rights under color of law. U.S. Code, Title 18, Part I, Chapter 13, 242, *Deprivation of rights under color of law*, reads,

> "Whoever, **under color of any law**, statute, ordinance, regulation, or custom, willfully subjects any person in any State, Territory, Commonwealth, Possession, or District to the deprivation of any rights, privileges, or immunities secured or protected by the Constitution or laws of the United States, or to different punishments, pains, or penalties, on account of such person being an alien, or by reason of his color, or race, than are prescribed for the punishment of citizens, shall be fined under this title or imprisoned not more than one year, or both; and if bodily injury results from the acts committed in violation of this section or if such acts include the use, attempted use, or threatened use of a dangerous weapon, explosives, or fire, shall be fined under this title or imprisoned not more than ten years, or both; and if death results from the acts committed in violation of this section or if such acts include kidnapping or an attempt to kidnap, aggravated sexual abuse, or an attempt to commit aggravated sexual abuse, or an attempt to kill, shall be fined under this title, or imprisoned for any term of years or for life, or both, or may be sentenced to death."[79] (bold added)

For free people to always, by compulsory statute, get permission to exercise inalienable rights, for example, or to even move about freely, or to need a "license" for any and all activities, denotes an individual as a subject, and, denotes the right as a privilege. The lawful licensure apparatus, designed for genuine public safety, has also deviated into a *color of law* resource for government to infiltrate any and every profession, human activity, and the like. Forced licensing, especially within an economic context, is an example of how politicians are lobbied by special interest groups and corporations to concoct legislation designed to minimize sound business competition within other like businesses, professions or groups. Timothy Sandefur, in his book *The Right to Earn a Living*, also asserts this. Sandefur writes, "Unfortunately, despite claims that it would protect the general public, licensing is often used as a tool to prevent competition from disfavored groups."[80] Then, once a pseudo-licensure scheme is set into place, the cops are then *taken for granted* to enforce such *predatory business tactics*, which are now "law." One example of this is when the corporate food world works against farmers and/or the raw food industry. Federal, state and local law enforcement officials enforcing licensure laws have vehemently destroyed tons and tons of food because of this. Is not hunger one hundred percent curable? The "violation" of licensing laws then helps government officials many times get their way prior to any court ruling, or actions of due process. Moreover, such "violation" enforcement actually avoids court and due process of law altogether, because the mere threat of arrest, being caged, violence and seizure of property are made prior, unless the victims of such corporate lobbying tactics decide to fight back in court. The cops in these situations think they are just doing their "job."

Another example of licensure laws designed for special interests are related to trademarked or copyrighted property. This is heavily abused, minimizing the likelihood of any other with similar ideas to be innovative, simply by way of the firm vagueness of such laws, and the astronomical costs associated with getting around such laws, "legally." Buying a license, for example. These are not merely to protect property, but to secure income by minimizing competition. It always comes down to the greed for currency, again. One example of this is that the New York Port authority claims trademark, jurisdiction and ownership of the New York skyline. Yes, the skyline. Small businesses have received *cease and desist* letters to stop selling pictures of the New York skyline, absent a license, or be sued.[81] It's ridiculous. Many simply cannot afford what it takes to fight the legal system, so they comply, which then encourages government officials to avoid any *burden of proof* requirements, and many times encourages lawyer dependency if the one who can afford it decides to challenge the system. There are more lawyers in the United States right now than anywhere else on earth. And, there are more students now in law school than there are actual lawyers.

This does not, however, relate to genuine and lawful licensing as a means to authentically protect the public, such as a license to drive on public roads, or practice medicine, for instance. A licensure scheme created by the greed to minimize competition within a given profession or industry, and then incorporated into the legal system by way of the tactical use of government's monopoly on force, is an example of how the legal system shields itself from the Rule of Law. How is this conversion of rights into privileges not inferred as color of law? It is. But color of law is not *pragmatically* enforced, because, once color of law is self-referentially applied to enforcement, or government in general, it undermines itself, thus reinforcing inequality even more.

Again, what counts as lawful secondary legislation, when it comes to controlling society and/or property? Or, how does one know that a particular statute, ordinance or even an Act of Congress is lawful when it is enforced? A lawful regulation's wording must be consistent with the *original intent* or spirit of the Law of the Land, the US Constitution. Or at a minimum, not be withstanding to the Bill of Rights, which is also the supreme Law of each State. Today, by way of a constitutionally undereducated consensus within most government officials, and by way of a callused moral compass, any and all legislation within the legal system is believed consistent with the Law of the Land. This is hugely unintelligent, especially when the response is, "let the courts work it out." There are several ingredients that a statute must have to be consistent with, or not withstanding to, the Law of the Land. Recall *In Pursuance Thereof.* According to Daniel Webster in the *Dartmouth College v. Woodward* case before the US Supreme Court, he argued how the Law of the Land is defined,

> "By the law of the land is most clearly intended, the general law, a law, which hears before it condemns; which proceeds upon inquiry, and renders judgment only after trial. The meaning is, that every citizen shall hold his life, liberty, property and immunities, under the protection of the general rules, which govern society. Everything, which may pass under the form of an enactment, is not, therefore, to be considered the law of the land. If this were so, acts of attainder, bills of pains and penalties, acts of confiscation, acts reversing judgments, and acts directly transferring one man's estate to another, legislative judgments, decrees and civil forfeitures, in all possible forms, would be the law of the land."

Webster's characterization of the Law of the Land has become the official paradigm of *sound* jurisprudence, as it relates to measuring a statute up to the actual Law. Yet, the opposite of what Webster describes is exactly the case today. All legislation, at any level, whether in a city, a county, a state, or even a public park, is enforced as though all these laws are equally the law of the land. Moreover, all such legislation actually, in practice, takes superiority over the actual law of the land. This has come about because law enforcement has been exploited to do so through a combination of social engineering, the "in house" distortion of the moral compass, abused policies like qualified immunity, and "job security" strategies like pensions and ranking.

Can anyone put into words the difference between law enforcement here in the United States today and law enforcement in England, Italy, China, Russia, Germany, Mexico, or any other country in the world? Can the cops here in America actually articulate how they are different from the cops in other countries? It appears that there is no difference. There is, however, supposed to be a profound difference. This fundamental difference in law enforcement here in the US and law enforcement throughout the rest of the world, at least within political "theory," is the officer's oath, as mentioned earlier, to enforce the state and federal constitutionally mandated Rule of Law, whereby a Bill of Rights (via the incorporation doctrine) greatly limits and restricts the powers that federal, state and local governments have over "free" individuals. And, to enforce secondary laws that are *In Pursuance Thereof.* The Bill of Rights is the Law of the Land and shall not be violated. Most importantly, again, the Constitution is a moral force against the arbitrary actions of people in government. America is the only country that has this, and law enforcement should know this.

Competent law Enforcement is a very necessary and politically important aspect of sound government, and incompetent law enforcement is a very necessary and politically important aspect of unsound government. We must honor and respect those who put their lives on the line to make American society a better and a safer place, by going after those who commit real crimes against other people or against other people's property. We cannot become a place like Somalia. Somalia is evidence enough of the need of some government. Thus, government and its enforcement are very indispensable aspects of a sound social contract, as a means to sustain peace and the pursuit of happiness. There are very bad and violent people in society and we need well-trained cops who not only operate as a moral force themselves, against such people, but are also capable of apprehending such people skillfully and lawfully. It takes a special mind-set to endure the ins and outs of the hidden aspects of society. The everyday perspective of a seasoned cop is fundamentally different, psychologically, than of a common person. Some of the most wonderful people I know, who are my personal friends, are officers and they do the best they can to make life better for other people. And, they do their best to actualize their Oath. However, there are those in power who want to exploit the men and women in uniform as a means to create a society that they think is best, to secure special interests, no matter what our founding virtues and foundational principles hold. They seek to minimize the inconveniences of too much liberty. These "leaders" find the Constitution and its Bill of Rights to be a stumbling block and they always seek new ways around them.

How does this exploitation of law enforcement begin? How is exploitation then prolonged? The exploitation of law enforcement begins psychologically, which then allows, just like in history, the people in government to do as they please through enforcement. Psychologists today infer that the human brain does not fully develop and mature until about the age of twenty-five or twenty-six, that the parts of the brain that restrain "risky behavior, including reckless driving, and thinking skills," are not fully developed yet and are still considered *adolescent*.[82] Prior to the brain maturing, people are subject to irrational thinking; they are likewise foolishly impulsive, generally self-absorbed, and psychologically and emotionally unstable. Why would a government enforcement agency hire an individual to enforce law who, by clinical fact, fits within this general, psychological profile? Because they are "trainable." The psyche test prior to employment does not necessarily help quantify this fact.

Not only are these *rookies*, who are generally about twenty-one or so, driving around on patrol, they are also armed and in all probability, have no formal education, nor do they hold any real life experience. Why hire them? Because they can be "trained" to be the way supervisors and superiors want them to be. This also applies to soldiers, who are hired at a younger age than law enforcement, generally about the age of eighteen. In addition, the minimum education requirement at the local level of law enforcement is usually a GED or a high school diploma. Hiring an officer, at the local level, especially with more life experience, and/or who has a formal education, is not in the best interest of an enforcement agency. The officer will generally be more self-reliant and will also think more critically of orders. In addition, such an officer will think more critically of his or her own actions. For a government agency, an officer who blindly follows orders is essential, especially for those people who are in supervisory positions within such agencies. However, to competently question orders is necessary within a profession where an oath is taken to check power. Yet, to question orders within law enforcement generally incites the kicking and screaming of superiors. Literally, I've seen it. Frequently, *trainable* people, whose job it will become to follow orders, are necessarily and purposely young and undereducated from the start. This is evidenced in the case *Jordan vs. New London*, a 2nd U.S. Circuit Court of Appeals case in New York, which ruled that a law enforcement agency can reject an individual for hire because they score too high on a psyche test. The National Law Enforcement Standards for hire range around 21-22, which equals about 104 on an IQ test. The potential officer that was rejected by New London Police scored 33. The District Court ruled that the City had "shown a rational basis for the policy," and the federal court agreed. Recall the *Rational Basis Test*. The court concluded that the policy may appear unwise, but was a "rational" way to reduce job turnover. Think about that.

A good example of how inequality between cops and the people is reinforced by way of precedent and by way of the *Rational Basis Test* is the recent US Supreme Court ruling in *Heien vs. NC* (2014). The court concluded that cops may violate the 4th Amendment if such a violation results from a "reasonable" mistake, as it relates to an officer's ignorance of the law. Yet, on the other hand, a citizen may not use ignorance of the law as an excuse for innocence. John W. Whitehead, president of The Rutherford Institute, who filed the amicus brief in the case stated, "By refusing to hold police accountable to knowing and abiding by the rule of law, the Supreme Court has given government officials a green light to routinely violate the law."

Combine this *social engineering* with job security, pensions, and other positive reinforcements like camaraderie and ranking, the state then formulates itself a minion. Thus, *trained* officers, in general, will not question the authority or the constitutionality of the orders given to them, nor be cognizant enough to exercise constitutional discernment, particularly in times where such orders may infringe upon the rights of the people. When questioned on the enforcement of a specific statute, cops are trained to refer such inquiry to the courts and to the legislators, which then nullifies the very purpose of taking an oath. Thomas Jefferson specifically argued, "The question whether the judges are invested with exclusive authority to decide on the constitutionality of a law has been heretofore a subject of consideration with me in the exercise of official duties. Certainly there is not a word in the Constitution which has given that power to them more than to the Executive or Legislative branches."[83] Judicial Review does not undermine a government official's oath to uphold their understanding of the Constitution. So where does the idea of "let the courts work it out," come from? Exploitation! Just look at history, again, this has been the case with virtually all enforcement within all governments, principally as it relates to controlling people and plundering their property, all for public safety. In addition, and again, it is an absolute fact, that in history, most human beings have died by way of a government's enforcement apparatus, also known as *democide*.[84] So, the argument that any such capricious means are necessary to get the "bad guy" is unsound and actually an exercise of lawlessness.

The Constitution and its Bill of Rights is, again, the most single greatest threat to today's collectivism and to the enforcement of today's socialized equality and forced fairness. Not only must you now get permission to participate in a fundamental right, you must also pay a fee. This is a result of the Rule of Law being submissive to a neo-progressive, legal system, which generally seeks to mimic policy from other countries, primarily European and even Chinese policies. This legal system has virtually destroyed the Declaration's definition of what liberty means in America, in the name of security and forced equality. Liberty has been redefined, which in turn has destroyed genuine, equal opportunity. True liberty being, as conveyed in the letter and spirit of the Declaration, where the people have the fundamental right to be left alone, to truly own their property and to pursue their own happiness, and to hold the continual power to undo government that threatens such liberty. Officers in the US, as do officers in the rest of the world, simply enforce a legal system created out of the intent to shape society into a collectivist, financially controlled, politically correct community, whereby genuine rights are relinquished and legal privileges are granted and controlled by government itself, all for "public safety." And, this legal system is designed to actually protect itself from the Law of the Land, from which it derives.

Again, the Supreme Court has ruled that it is not the primary role of Law Enforcement to protect citizens from specific harms, but to protect an individual's fundamental rights, as in *Warren vs. DC, Hartzler vs. San Jose, Riss vs. NY City, Susman vs. LA*. These all generally conclude the same thing, that the protection of rights and property are the prime objective of Law Enforcement, not personal safety, that protection from self or harm is a *courtesy*. Such dependence upon being "kept safe" by force conditions the people to feel that it is a cop's duty to protect an individual from *possible* harm, which in turn, undermines an individual's personal responsibility, not only for their own well being, but from their own actions. Since protection by law enforcement is a mere courtesy and not a duty, courtesy has become the justification for invasiveness, which is counterproductive and fallacious. There is, in part, a Second Amendment to help secure an individual's personal safety responsibility. It is the politicians and their lawyers, who manipulate the constitutional language, by way of personal beliefs and special interests, and as a means to circumvent constitutional restrictions, whereby secondary laws, in the end, encourage state dependency. This is opposed to laws encouraging education and responsibility, which should, by such laws, attach to fundamental rights. The former creates and sustains a collective, false ideology, which is a *forced* sense of safety.

There are generally two types of Law Enforcement Officers in America: Officer #1: You operate as an agent of the state and you are animated by the uniform and/or badge. You are an authoritarian. You like having power over other people. Your opinion is that you will enforce any law on the books because you believe the state has given you the power to do so. If the law you enforce is not constitutional or lawful, then let the courts work it out. You maintain that you are not the judge. The Law Enforcement Oath is a mere formality for you, having no serious effect on how you act and think while on duty. Your primary objective is to "do your job" and to keep your benefits. Your good intentions were sincere, to make the world a better place, to go after the "bad guys." But then you became a part of the system, whereby *positive law* criminalizes virtually all human activity and the state becomes the *primary* victim in your efforts of defending "justice." You interpret right and wrong from what is legal and illegal. You always do as your superiors tell you.

Officer #2: You animate the uniform or badge because you are a Peace Officer who operates within the boundaries of your sworn oath to defend, protect and preserve the US Constitution, to the best of your ability. You are non-authoritarian. You exercise constitutional discernment from vigorous study, whereby you practice the power of discretion to faithfully enforce law, provided said laws are sound, and not merely arbitrary, thus actualizing the founder's concurrent review. You operate as a check and balance against the other two branches of government, not in conformity with them. You are not an operative of the legal system, but of the Rule of Law. You protect people's fundamental rights, property and individual freedom, even if from the very government that employs you.

You go full force after those who commit crimes against other persons and/or their property. Natural Law, not positive law, is your *primary* concern. You are willing to lose your job over foundational principles.

Again, Law Enforcement is a part of the Executive Branch, thus the term, to "execute" or enforce. This consists of all Law Enforcement; Federal (NSA, FBI, US Marshals, IRS, HLS, etc.); State (SBI, Troopers, etc.) County (sheriff); City (Police, etc.) and Military (foreign policy enforcement).

Here is a real life scenario comparison of officer #1 and officer #2: In 2011, an Ohio congressman had cops take cell phones and cameras from citizens at a town hall meeting, for "security" purposes.[85] To compare, officer #1 would immediately start taking the people's property at the request of the congressman, not taking into consideration his sworn oath to protect the property rights of the citizens, which supercedes the will of a single federal representative. Officer #2, who is competent in the Rule of Law, understands that recently the US Supreme Court has ruled that State Laws banning the recording of public officials, including police officers while on duty, is unconstitutional and in violation of the First Amendment. In addition, the taking of cell phones does not qualify as a mass "pat down," as some have deliriously argued. Officers in public have no reasonable expectation of privacy while on duty. Also, officer #2 would know that seizing private property without probable cause is in violation of the 4th and 14th Amendments. Officer #2 would simply tell the Congressman that he will not take people's phones, that he is there to keep the peace only.

What we have here is officer #1 being exploited as a pawn, while officer #2 understands his lawful capacity and cannot be taken for granted by the Congressman or the legal system. Officer #1 is conditioned by the legal system and works for the state. The legal system always argues its case from a position of *safety* and *security*. Officer #1 will more than likely be looked upon by his or her superiors as doing a good job. Officer #2, on the other hand, will more than likely be looked upon by his or her superiors as not doing their job.

Liberal and Conservative Enforcement

Liberalism today is not the same thing as liberalism in the past. Being conservative today is not the same thing as being conservative in the past. Both liberal and conservative today are more modern political inventions of the mind. The founding fathers were very socially "liberal" because they emphasized personal "liberty" over and above the history of a ruling class and its aristocracy, which can be actually conservative or liberal. The founders were also "conservative" in that there would be no micromanagement of the private life of the individual by big and evasive government, and there would be great emphasis on an individual's natural rights. They sought to "conserve" the Rule of Law. The founders' mix of both liberalism and conservative views then, is called *classical liberalism* today. "Liberalism" today, for the most part, has deviated into neo-progressivism, which seeks to actually "do away with" anything associated with what the founders understood as genuine liberty, especially as it relates to finances, limited government, the Bill of Rights and the founders' successful attempt to restrict central power. It can be generally inferred that modern liberals want to control your money while modern conservatives want to control your thinking. Many liberals today, for example, tend to bash the 4th of July, for example, because it continues to tie modern Americans to an ideology of personal liberty based in a literal reading of the Constitution. Liberals today also tend to bash the founders and their whole *new world order*, simply because they were not angels and because they made moral mistakes, like we all do. Modern *conservatives* are just as equally a nuisance to the founders' view of liberty because conservatives today refuse to actualize genuine progress by way of arguments that are hell bent on *conserving* views through statutes and similar legislation that are obviously morally "obsolete," especially as it relates to dogma, sexism, culture and skin color, for example. *Classical Liberalism*, on the other hand, and of which I hold favor, attempts to hold to our founding principles, which includes the security and actualization of an individual's fundamental rights, while propelling a free and open society that is technologically advanced into the modern world, combined also with obtaining new knowledge collectively in and of an ever-changing world. The opposite of this is left or right extremism. Liberals and conservatives today are actually extremists compared to founding ideology. For the founders, individual liberty in defense against traditional aristocracy, violence and plutocracy, where free individuals could truly own property, and where the Rule of Law secured their natural rights and personal privacy, was the *New World Order*. The *Old World Order* is one where people are not free, where people do not truly own their property, where people are restricted from exercising their fundamental and natural rights. The Old World Order is where the people not in government are unequal to the people in government. Modern conservatives and modern liberals work against this, and generally want to subconsciously move back into a type of aristocracy, or "forward" into a technology-based oligarchy. In other words, the left/right paradigm works against this progressive New World Order that the framers established in the Declaration of Independence and in the US Constitution.

Neo-progressives can be both liberal and conservative in the modern sense of the words. So to illustrate this difference between a liberal and a conservative view of liberty today, and how they seek to exploit law enforcement as the "gun in the room," here is a mental exercise. Where do you stand? Imagine an American citizen, who is middle-eastern in origin. This person is a non-violent, bisexual atheist. This individual is well educated, financially independent and loves guns. This person even carries a concealed weapon in public, "legally." Also, imagine that this individual is *joyfully* open to and respectful of multiple cultures and races living in America, but despises when cultural dogma forces others who think differently out of social circles. This individual is a political activist who is an *independent* voter. This person believes in limited government, State's rights and holds that prisons should primarily be for rehabilitative purposes, except in repeat cases of violence. Imagine additionally that this person has a benevolent respect of animals and only eats locally raised and naturally grazed animals that he or she believes were treated ethically during their lifetime. Moreover, imagine this individual is very family oriented and is sentimentally attached to the idea of a life long marriage and just has not found the right "partner" yet. This individual believes that loving families are the building blocks of a moral society. Is this person self-contradictory or is the liberal or conservative perspective of who this individual is, conditioned by a very narrow view of liberty? The modern liberal's first problem with this individual is more than likely the person being armed and that they hold to an *original intent* view of the Constitution. The conservative would probably condemn the individual for being mid-eastern, bisexual and an atheist. In addition, the conservative would think this person strange for their view of animals as both living creatures deserving mutual respect and care, while being equally a source of food. Both liberal and conservative would seek to somehow, someway, change this person through legislation, and then enforce it. The classical liberalist, and even the libertarian, would view this person as a free American whose life, worldview, sexuality are secured and protected by the Rule of Law, that government should leave them alone. The classical liberalist and the libertarian would also argue that they do not know what is best for this person and that to force a liberal or conservative view on this person is draconian and unlawful.

But this liberal or conservative intent to change or control a person from being free and from being who they really are, like with the American mentioned above, not only plays its way into secondary legislation, in part, but such legislation also becomes the law in law enforcement. Combine this intent to control an individual's freedom to be whom they really are with the intent to secure special interests and revenue. Revenue and control over other people's freedom, therefore, and in part, is the general driving force behind most the enforcement of petty laws, except in cases of common law, whereby living humans are a victim of crime. Again, in light of violent crimes dropping across the country, and even while populations increase, the federal and state legislatures, and local city and county councils must, for example, "criminalize" more human activities, making the country, state, city or county the primary victim, as a means to raise more revenue and to meet budget restraints, while socially controlling and engineering the populace within the intent of those laws. This exploitation of cops as "revenue collectors" is evidenced by the "slowdown" of the enforcement of petty laws by the NYPD; "Police officers around the city are now threatened with transfers, no vacation time and sick time unless they write summonses.... This is the same practice that caused officers to be labeled racist and abusers of power." One cop in the 105th Precinct is quoted as saying, "And the majority of [new] summonses written aren't protecting the public in any way…. But now they're realizing how much revenue the city is losing and they're enforcing their will upon us."[85.5]

The Congressional Research Service (CRS) reported in June 2014 that 439 new criminal offences were added to the U.S. Code between 2008 and 2013. Yet, between the years 2000 and 2007, the CRS reports an increase in 452 new criminal offences. The government, then, is actually criminalizing more human activities now then before, even though the media conveys that Congress today is a "do nothing" Congress. So as crimes increase, jail becomes a real concern for people who would not generally commit theft, fraud, or do any harm to another person or to another's property. Therefore, it is wise for people, in general, to always have bail money set aside. Because, as governments in America continue to criminalize more and more human activities, we are all more and more potentially criminals, somehow, someway. It is actually a good thing for legislative bodies to do much less nowadays, unless they are repealing laws.

As it relates to enforcement for revenue, in Massachusetts, for example, the state's Supreme Court ruled in favor of charging ticket recipients fines even though they are found innocent in a court of law, all as a way to generate more revenue for administrative processes.[86] This "numbers" effort trickles down to law enforcement efforts, through an array of positive reinforcement tactics, because generally the agency and its "supervisors" seek high numbers of arrests as a means to request greater funding from city councils or county commissioners, even though the true "call volume" of real crime (living, breathing victim) cannot corroborate the "funds" request. Of course this does not count for every agency. Therefore, the enforcement of any and all possible laws can be financially beneficial, not only to the court system, which collects court costs and fines, but to the lawyers who fatten their bank accounts from the "criminals," who need their legal counsel. Many time judges will not charge fines for offences because court costs are too high. From this, city and county officials reprimand those judges because it literally weakens the revenue source for the government itself. These particular judges argue, rightly so, that many fines combined with court costs are just too much to financially bear on average citizens.

The legal system depends mostly on repeat offenders. Thus, *slaps on the wrist* for minor offences are significant for revenue security. Most importantly, the law enforcement agency, in turn, gets greater funding from tax revenues to pay for increased enforcement of new and old crimes, gadgets and other items "necessary" for the safety of the public, even though the real crime statistics are inconsistent with what's on paper. A mere seatbelt ticket, for example, counts as an arrest on paper. So, a cop who generates high numbers and doesn't question his own authority is of great interest to an agency, and to government in general. A cop whose frame of reference is the Rule of Law and who questions his or her own authority is of no interest to an agency, and especially not to government. The key to government always getting its way through the "taking for granted" of law enforcement is, again, a psychological one. Combine the ability to execute power over people with vanity. Once vanity is massaged by the ability to enforce the politician and corporation's will, so too the increase of government as a whole is intensified. Power corrupts, absolute power corrupts absolutely.[87] This is what the legal system consist of today. As it relates to the future, George Orwell said that, "If you want a picture of the future, imagine a boot stamping on a human face—forever."

4

Revolution

"Unhappy it is, though, to reflect that a brother's sword has been sheathed in a brother's breast and that the once-happy plains of America are either to be drenched with blood or inhabited by slaves. Sad alternative! But can a virtuous man hesitate in his choice?"

– George Washington

There are two primary sources of morality in modern society: religion and the state. How is that working out so far? More people have died in the name of either the state or of religion than in all other ways to die. So, if we are to reason causally, as an evolving species, apparently morality is about the ending of life, not the sustaining and well-being of life. As a culture, and as a species, should we rethink morality? For humanity to move forward into the universe, we need to evolve into a single species made up of free individuals. This can only happen in the absence of "rulers," who determine that everything has a price. Being in charge does not equal being a leader. Nor does authority equal being right. Today, mere objects themselves are the avenues of criminalizing behavior absent the corresponding behavior itself. This has become the "ethical" standards behind criminalizing much human activity. If fact, such a view has nothing to do with ethics at all, but has everything to do with control and currency. The American Revolution was an attempt to establish a New World Order. This New World Order says that the individual is free, and this freedom is founded upon the fundamental and natural principles of virtue, which the social compact and the US Constitution seeks to progress.

Virtue

Ralph Waldo Emerson writes in his essay on Self-Reliance,

> "Virtues are, in the popular estimate, rather the exception than the rule. There is the man and his virtues. Men do what is called a good action, as some piece of courage or charity, much as they would pay a fine in expiation of daily non-appearance on parade. Their works are done as an apology or extenuation of their living in the world, — as invalids and the insane pay a high board. Their virtues are penances. I do not wish to expiate, but to live. My life is for itself and

not for a spectacle. I much prefer that it should be of a lower strain, so it be genuine and equal, than that it should be glittering and unsteady. I wish it to be sound and sweet, and not to need diet and bleeding. I ask primary evidence that you are a man, and refuse this appeal from the man to his actions. I know that for myself it makes no difference whether I do or forbear those actions which are reckoned excellent. I cannot consent to pay for a privilege where I have intrinsic right. Few and mean as my gifts may be, I actually am, and do not need for my own assurance or the assurance of my fellows any secondary testimony."[0]

Self-reliance, being who you truly are, and holding to the fundamental principles of liberty, for all, are more than mere idealism, they are acts of virtue, and they are perspective. Like Emerson points out, virtues today are like penances, forced upon the masses by society and by secondary legislation. These are not real virtues. Sam Adams said that once virtue is lost, Americans will easily surrender their liberty, "A general dissolution of principles and manners will more surely overthrow the liberties of America than the whole force of the common enemy. While the people are virtuous they cannot be subdued; but when once they lose their virtue then they will be ready to surrender their liberties to the first external or internal invader."[1] What does it mean for Americans to be virtuous, specifically? Is it virtuous to fit in with everyone else? Is it virtuous to blindly obey government officials? Is it virtuous to always pay your taxes? Fitting in, blindly obeying and not questioning your tax objectives are not virtues, but *penances*, that the status quo socially engineers as virtues. A virtue is simply a quality or trait that reflects a sound moral compass. Blindly obeying government officials has nothing to do with morality. It does have everything to do with self-preservation, however, in light of the government's exploitation of violence.

What is this virtue that the founders established, that Sam Adams is referring to? This *virtue* is *Republicanism*, founded upon the moral philosophy of John Locke. Not republicanism in the political party sense, but the philosophy of the *form* of government, *in action*. American Republicanism is the total rejection of aristocracy.[2] This *virtue* stresses inalienable rights, individual liberty, self-reliance and property ownership as the central and fundamental values of American Republicanism. Coerced Commerce, forced fairness and forced economic activity, are not foundational values, but *penances*. Moreover, this virtue of the founding holds to the natural right of the people to overthrow their "leaders." American virtue vilifies political and commercial corruption. Republicanism also rejects the "tyranny of the majority" that was so prominent in the history of democracies. Jefferson said the first principle of American virtue is the rights of the people, "The first principle of republicanism is the fundamental law of every society of individuals of equal rights.... This law once disregarded, no other remains but that of force, which ends necessarily in military despotism."[3] In other words, a *police state* comes about when securing individual, fundamental rights and educating the people on the responsibility attached to those rights is no longer the primary principles of government action. Rather, today, government action is primarily to secure an individual's exercise of penances, or what the government today defines as "virtuous." Jefferson further emphasized earlier that, "It is to secure our rights that we resort to government at all."[4] This virtue, as founded upon the political philosophy of republicanism, was also agreed upon by John Adams, "Others, again, more rationally, define a republic to signify only a government, in which all men, rich and poor, magistrates and subjects, officers and people, masters and servants, the first citizen and the last, are equally subject to the laws. This, indeed, appears to be the true and only true definition of a republic."[5] Therefore, theft is theft. Assault is assault. Robbery is robbery. Greed is greed. Corruption is corruption. Thomas Jefferson defined republicanism, this original form of American government as,

> "It must be acknowledged that the term "republic" is of very vague application in every language... Were I to assign to this term a precise and definite idea, I would say purely and simply it means a government by its citizens in mass, acting directly and personally according to rules established by the majority; and that every other government is more or less republican in proportion as it has in its composition more or less of this ingredient of direct action of the citizens."[6]

How can we know and how can we verify that this virtue, founded upon republicanism, is no longer the active foundation of law and order in America today? We know this and can verify this because arbitrary force is predicated upon the protection and security of commerce policy, above and beyond inalienable rights and property ownership, whereby commerce itself is predicated upon the enforcement of individual, economic activity. "Where the law of the majority ceases to be acknowledged, there government ends; the law of the strongest takes its place, and life and property are his who can take them."[7] Therefore, America can only operate today by arbitrary force, or the threat of force. Like I said before, once America became a business, a corporation, the virtues of republicanism converted into the virtues of commerce. As John Adams warned in a letter to Mercy Warren,

> "Virtue is the only Foundation of Republics. There must be a positive Passion for the public good, the

public Interest, Honour, Power and Glory, established in the Minds of the People, or there can be no Republican Government, nor any real Liberty…. I have seen all along my Life Such Selfishness and Littleness…that I sometimes tremble to think that, altho. We are engaged in the best Cause that ever employed the Human Heart yet the Prospect of success is doubtful not for Want of Power or of Wisdom but of Virtue. The **Spirit of Commerce**, Madam, which even insinuates itself into Families, and influences holy Matrimony, and thereby **corrupts the morals of families as well as destroys their Happiness, it is much to be feared is incompatible with that purity of Heart and Greatness of soul which is necessary for an happy Republic**…. Even the Farmers and Tradesmen are addicted to Commerce; and it is too true that Property is generally the standard of Respect there as much as anywhere. While this is the Case there is great Danger that a Republican Government would be very factious and turbulent there. Divisions in Elections are much to be dreaded. Every man must seriously set himself to root out his Passions, Prejudices and Attachments, and to get the better of his private Interest."[8] (bold added)

The virtue spoken of by Sam Adams has been lost to commerce and special interests, which are now secured by secondary laws written by politicians and corporate lobbyists, and then these secondary laws are blindly enforced by cops at all levels. Moreover, the opposite of genuine virtue is the execution of arbitrary violence. Arbitrary violence is stupid, just plain stupid. Like choking a guy to death for selling single cigarettes on the street in NYC, because he "resisted."[9] Or, by punching a woman in the face repeatedly on the side of the road, "for her own safety," said the officer. The woman became a millionaire, by the way, following a law suit.[9.5] Such arbitrary violence easily attaches itself to a non-virtuous, simple mind, as though the executioner of such violence must feed upon "justifiable acts" via legislative authority to achieve self-actualization. Violence is never an option except within the context of absolute self-defense of one's own person, of another person or of society in general, like from a violent individual, or from an insurrection. Selling single cigarettes absent an attached tax is not a threat to society that relies upon "necessary" violence. This conversion from our founding virtues secured in republicanism into commerce today secured by the legal system was even feared by President Lincoln. In a letter written to Col. William F. Elkins during the Civil War, Lincoln intimated,

> "We may congratulate ourselves that this cruel war is nearing its end. It has cost a vast amount of treasure and blood.... It has indeed been a trying hour for the Republic; but I see in the near future a crisis approaching that unnerves me and causes me to tremble for the safety of my country. As a result of the war, **corporations have been enthroned and an era of corruption in high places will follow, and the money power of the country will endeavor to prolong its reign by working upon the prejudices of the people until all wealth is aggregated in a few hands and the Republic is destroyed**. I feel at this moment more anxiety for the safety of my country than ever before, even in the midst of war. God grant that my suspicions may prove groundless." (bold added)

And so America today is an oligarchy, and no longer a republic, nor a democracy. Democracies have always and only been a temporary transition from one form of government into another. Oligarchic principles are now the law of the land, whereby elites determine and connect any and everything to a medium of exchange, by force. Virtues as determined within classical liberalism are no longer the foundational principles of liberty because liberty must be free from any compulsory connections to currency, bureaucracy and the enforcement of economic activity.

In nearly six thousand years of human history and evolution, humans are now capable of surfing the Internet, going into space, developing invisibility through mere fabric, and other mind-boggling achievements. A child today has fingertip access to virtually all of human history and information related to same. Yet, humans have not evolved out of stupid violence. The irony is, the government, as an entity made up of other humans, who justify the use of violence by way of the mere title of government, is just as guilty of using violence for personal gain as the mugger on the street. And, it uses a "moral" argument to justify such violence.

To illustrate, as it relates to *arbitrary violence* specifically, in response to protesting, which is a fundamental right, one "veteran" cop remarked, "I'm a cop. If you don't want to get hurt, don't challenge me… if you don't want to get shot, tased, pepper-sprayed, struck with a baton or thrown to the ground, just do what I tell you…even if we are violating your rights"[10] This of course does not encompass all officers' attitudes. I can actually understand where this cop might be coming from, but he is unashamedly wrong. This kind of *superiority complex* is then rationalized by either "experience" or "public safety," which feeds into and reinforces the *inequality* between law enforcement and the people. This is also an attitude whereby the understanding of morality comes by way of social engineering and "training," and not by way of genuine education in ethics. Again, more people have died by *democide* in the 20th century than all other sources of death. Democide is death by government.

Authoritarians in government, and authoritarian governments in general, create the illusion of being a "moral" force founded upon acts of virtue, while still using violence to get what it wants, just as all governments have done throughout history. This illusion is easier for governments to manage than the truth. Violence is feeble minded and attracts those people with very limited cognitive function and plays on psychotic and authoritarian human nature. This is why, again, and in part, our Constitution is a moral force designed and codified to thwart negative human nature and the desire for power of those who are in government, who then create policy to rule arbitrarily. Of course not one government official believes that they act or "rule" arbitrarily. Thus Jefferson, in response to the *Alien and Sedition Act*, confirms that the Constitution is a moral force to restrain or chain down such efforts,

> "Resolved.... That these and **successive** acts of the same character, unless arrested on the threshold, may tend to drive these states into revolution and blood, and will furnish new calumnies against republican governments, and new pretexts for those who wish it to be believed that man cannot be governed but by a rod of iron; that it would be a dangerous delusion were a confidence in the men of our choice to silence our fears for the safety of our rights; that confidence is every where the parent of despotism; free government is founded in jealousy, and not in confidence; it is jealousy, and not confidence, which prescribes limited constitutions to bind down those whom we are obliged to trust with power; that our Constitution has accordingly fixed the limits to which, and no farther, our confidence may go.... In questions of **power, let no more be heard of confidence in man, but bind him down from mischief by the chains of the constitution.**"[11] (bold added)

Apparently Jefferson's resolution against arbitrary power has not been working. Governments throughout America today feed upon the undereducated, young officer and soldier, who are not only easily trainable, but is either a potential sociopath or is someone who sees government as a way to live out an authoritarian spirit. The people who are working in government and who enjoy controlling other people's lives should not be there. And, the one's who should be in government "leading" free people, don't want to be there. This has become a problem in our modern culture. How do we change this? Voting no longer works because only the wealthy can afford to run for office. Does being wealthy reflect better leadership skills? Does running a business reflect a better chance at running a government office? Only if that public office is business oriented. There in lies the problem.

We surely should not resort to violence like past cultures have, because then nothing changes. Violence always ends in destruction, death and pain, and any positive outcome is only temporary, as with the American Revolution against a Monarch. America, under the organic Constitution, only lasted about a hundred years or so. America has now become more authoritarian than the system of government it fought to be liberated from. Go figure. The repetition of history is the result of stupid violence and stupid people, because the feeble minded resort to violence arbitrarily, absent self-defense, as a means to curtail or end the situation they are in from the previous execution of violence. It is a vicious circle. However, to illustrate genuine self-defense, were it not "virtuous" for the Jews to not fight back? If they had they been "allowed" to be armed, nearly six millions Jews may not have been slaughtered. This it contextually sound violence, because self-defense against the Nazis by the Jews would have been absolutely justifiable.

Revolution Prerequisites

How do we deal with such a culture today, that is predicated on the feeble minded in power, the authoritarian executing and enforcing its laws, and the laws being designed to perpetuate the legal system as a means to empower a plutocracy that is hell bent on global dominance and the forced economic activity of the individual? Revolution? America needs a new revolution, not by way of violence, but by way of knowledge through self-education. A revolution can come about by intelligent independence through self-reliance. These are moral and honorable powers. Arbitrary violence is not an honorable power. Violence to achieve power alone ends in dishonorable power, a means to an ugly end, an ending with the monopoly of fear over people, power in the hands of the shameful. Again, violence is only necessary in absolute self-defense of one's own person, or of another, and of one's property. Recall John Parker's words as the British soldiers entered Lexington, "Stand your ground. Don't fire unless fired upon, but if they mean to have a war, let it begin here."

The US Military is generally years ahead of society in weapons technology. Always has been. If the neo-progressives in the federal government decide to finally enforce the fact that the Bill of Rights is no more and has been overridden by a newer world order, and in response, in part, to the illusion of a failed healing economy, the cry of "from my cold dead hands" will take fruition. The only chance Americans have against the US Military's use of violence, especially within a scenario of massive gun confiscation, for example, is if most military and law enforcement personnel defect. Reasonably and ethically, more than half of all enforcement would probably defect if such a violent calamity were to take place against the American people, because the military and law enforcement are made up of other humans who have family and friends living in society. Plus, most of these men and women still strongly believe in our Constitutional principles. Therefore, for the powers that be, social engineering, or "brainwashing," is imperative to training. So, revolution in today's America needs to be smart, ethical and not violent. The founders were near brilliant, and the use of violence against Britain then was in the context of self-defense and of securing liberty from a King's will, which was also the very arbitrary Law of his Land. However, such a revolution like then could not happen today because war is not about soldier against soldier, musket against musket, but of hi-tech strategy and weaponry against hi-tech strategy and weaponry. This type of warfare can't possibly or reasonably apply to Americans who possess only small arms. This fact, coupled with political sanctions and the like, all come by way of credit, which is a fundamental weakness on the part of warmongers in government. So why does America, for example, keep selling weapons of war to virtually all of the middle eastern countries who then keep fighting one another, making terror threats to America, when at the same time politicians argue for peace in the Middle East? Predatory crony-capitalism? Absent the forced extraction of wealth from the people, the probability and success of such pre-emptive war weakens significantly. It is necessary therefore, that such warmongers covertly play on sentiments, like "defending freedom."

Former Marine and Central Intelligence Agency (CIA) case officer, Robert David Steele, whom I've mentioned earlier, is the co-founder and former deputy director of the US Marine Corps Intelligence Command. Steele helped form the *Open Source Intelligence* (OSINT) model, where he wrote the handbooks for the US Defense Intelligence Agency, NATO and the U.S. Special Operations Forces. Steele has also published several books on US Intelligence: *A More Secure World: Our*

329

Shared Responsibility, Report of the UN High-Level Panel on Threats, Challenges, and Change, The War on Truth: 9/11, Disinformation and the Anatomy of Terrorism, and his latest book, *The Open-Source Everything Manifesto: Transparency, Truth and Trust*. Steel's general ambition is to reveal the truth of US Intelligence to the public by way of his Open Source Manifesto. Nafeez Ahmed wrote an intricate article on this subject in *The Guardian*, where he states that, "The open source revolution is coming and it will conquer the 1 percent."[12] In *The Open Source Everything Manifesto,* Steele writes,

>"We are at the end of a five-thousand-year-plus historical process during which human society grew in scale while it abandoned the early indigenous wisdom councils and communal decision-making.... Power was centralized in the hands of increasingly specialized 'elites' and 'experts' who not only failed to achieve all they promised but used secrecy and the control of information to deceive the public into allowing them to retain power over community resources that they ultimately looted.... Over the course of the last centuries, the commons was fenced, and everything from agriculture to water was commoditized without regard to the true cost in non-renewable resources. Human beings, who had spent centuries evolving away from slavery, were re-commoditized by the Industrial Era.... Sharing, not secrecy, is the means by which we realize such a lofty destiny as well as create infinite wealth. The wealth of networks, the wealth of knowledge, revolutionary wealth - all can create a nonzero win-win Earth that works for one hundred percent of humanity. This is the 'utopia' that Buckminster Fuller foresaw, now within our reach. ...concentrated illicitly aggregated and largely phantom wealth in favor of community wealth defined by community

knowledge, community sharing of information, and community definition of truth derived in transparency and authenticity, the latter being the ultimate arbiter of shared wealth."

Ahmed writes, "Open source everything...offers us the chance to build on what we've learned through industrialization, to learn from our mistakes, and catalyze the re-opening of the commons, in the process breaking the grip of defunct power structures and enabling the possibility of prosperity for all."[13]

Steele conveyed this at a Libtech conference in NY, relating to a thesis he wrote in college, that, "I want to start with a brief overview of where we are in human history, touch briefly on the preconditions of revolution, most of which exist in the USA today, and then conclude with 'What Is To Be Done.'" Steele asserted that the following *negative trends*, or preconditions for revolution, exist in America and Europe today. He says, "These trends can be attributed to corruption and the loss of public integrity and public agency. The 1 percent are sucking the life out of the planet and blocking all attempts to escape from their matrix of control, greed, genocide, and other atrocities." Steele's *Key Negative Trends*, as power-pointed at the conference, are:

1. **The collapse of complex societies**: catastrophe from disaster for lack of resilience & adaptation as well as corruption.
2. **Acts of man creating acts of God**: natural disasters will be more frequent & more severe as we cement more land.
3. **Acceleration of earth's demise**: changes that used to take 10,000 years now take three years; absent real time science and real time public policy (online, deliberative, transparent) we die.
4. **Shock capitalism**: continues to loot the earth and has turned USA into a third world country – UAE (Dubai) is the new Switzerland.

5. **Political corruption ascendant**: 44 dictators, both Republican and Democratic parties are "running on empty" and very corrupt, elites in towns across America have sold us out.[14]

Steele went on to say that,

> "There is good news. The best news is that there are not enough guns on the planet to repress the public, something Howard Zinn, Vaclav Havel, and others have understood. We are not listening. It is within our power to shut down the stock market, end all foreign currency transactions, end all income and sales taxes, end government borrowing, end government war-mongering, end government abuses against the public interest. We have the power – we are simply not using that power nor conceptualizing good and achievable ends."[15]

Steele then went on to communicate some *Key Positive Trends*:

1. **Wealth of Networks**: fortune at the bottom of the pyramid, peace through connectivity, wealth from sharing information.
2. **GreenMind**: Biomimicry, beneficial bacteria, green chemistry.
3. **Moral Capitalism**: natural capitalism, green to gold, cradle to cradle, home rule, eat local, end of corporate personality.
4. **Democratic Information**: "true costs" at point of sale.
5. **Left hand of God**: faith based dialogue and diplomacy, obvious need to end our support to 42 of 44 dictators, shunning of cults.
6. **Peer to Peer People Power**: from the Tao of democracy to localized wisdom councils to blessed unrest to the clock of the long now.[16]

Steele continues on by pointing out two key ingredients for a new revolution in America today. Number one, Steele says, "Most critical is leaders that betray the public trust and legalize crime while undertaking elective wars that are about enriching the 1 percent rather than protecting the public interest." Legalizing crime happens, in part, through *qualified immunity* within the Executive Branch, the *rational basis test* within the Judicial Branch, and the appealing to *special interests* within the Legislative Branch, all of which are non-compliance to the Rule of Law, and all complicit to each other in forming an American police state. Justification of these are also made, in part, by adopting new ways of interpreting the Rule of Law, like through the *Living Constitution* view, or through Blackstonian Theory, where government can virtually do anything it wants if the act is not specifically prohibited by law. The public interest that is not protected is inalienable rights, absolute property ownership, equal opportunity and the pursuit of happiness. The lust for war, which ends in death, but great financial gain and power for warmongers, happens through government's use of credit, at the expense of labor debt, and public complacency by way of social engineering.

Second, Steele argues that, "Across all mission areas today, from agriculture and the economy to education, energy, family, health, and water, among others, the US Government is in constant betrayal of the public trust." You no longer truly own property, and everything from the very basic necessities for human existence has a price. Steele concludes that, "At the highest level of thinking, it boils down to a loss of government legitimacy, and a majority of the public being unemployed, abused, and increasingly desperate. We are out of balance."[17]

Neo-progressive ideology combines both republican and democratic political parties. The conservatives' love of war and of social controls combined with the democrats' love of money and the love of non-individual ownership of property, is itself, securing government interests over public interests. The legal system today is neo-progressive, from where all the prerequisites of revolution derive. And this dichotomy between the Law and the Legal system will only get worse, eventually crashing down. Moreover, all the specifics of the aforementioned could have never happened if the one's who execute the force with guns and weapons of mass destruction were not exploited to do so. Essentially, law enforcement is "trained" to protect the arbitrary will of the wealthy in power, the ruling classes and their "special" interests.

To be clear, when I refer to the wealthy, I do not mean the wealthy in general. There are some very wonderful, respectable, loving and benevolent wealthy people in the world and in America. They give and give and give. Because of their wealth, their hard work and pioneering skills, many people have jobs and careers. Wealthy people are much of the driving force behind the innovation and progression of society as a whole. Steve Jobs comes to mind. On the other hand, when I refer to the arbitrary will of the wealthy, I'm referring to those who feed off of the poor, the indigent, the ignorant, the desperate, and who seek to make money from any tragedy, purely for selfish gain. Those who see themselves as better than the rest of us, and who seek to use government to secure their wealth at the expense of everyone else. And of those who are in government who seek to actually change government from within into something else, for the sake of the former. One example of this is when the right to remain silent is arbitrarily interpreted as an admission of guilt. The US Supreme Court in *Salinas vs. Texas*, has allowed pre-Miranda silence to be used against a defendant accused of a crime, completely absent the *beyond a reasonable doubt* and *burden of proof* required by the state. You no longer have a right to remain silent prior to being told you have a right to remain silent, which is absurd. Be silent anyway.

A conscientious millionaire and a member of the one percenters club authored an article in Politico.com, aimed at his fellow one percenters, about the very realism of inequality in America today, and, its possible repercussions. Nick Hanauer is a wealthy man, an early investor in major internet companies like Amazon. As it relates to his wealth, he states that, "I'm not the smartest guy you've ever met, or the hardest-working. I was a mediocre student. I'm not technical at all—I can't write a word of code. What sets me apart, I think, is a tolerance for risk and an intuition about what will happen in the future. Seeing where things are headed is the essence of entrepreneurship." He continues, "And what do I see in our future now? I see pitchforks." Mr. Hanauer sees what many others see happening in America, a potentially violent response to the resurrection of aristocracy that the American Revolution fought against. He continues,

> "But the problem isn't that we have inequality. Some inequality is intrinsic to any high-functioning capitalist economy. The problem is that inequality is at historically high levels and getting worse every day. Our country is rapidly becoming less a capitalist society and more a feudal society. Unless our policies change dramatically, the middle class will disappear, and we will be back to late 18th-century France. Before the revolution."[18]

One response was from the Dailey Ticker, where Rick Newman stated,

> "The rich ought to chill out. While the masses may envy their wealth, there's no evidence of a revolution brewing, or even a well-behaved civil disturbance. Americans are clearly dismayed at the direction the country seems to be heading, but they are also docile in the face of decline and confused about possible solutions. Hanauer fears mobs heading for the castles of Greenwich and Palo Alto, but America's disaffected these days are more likely to vent their rage behind closed doors as they shake their fists at Fox News or MSNBC and leave

cranky comments on websites such as this one. If there's a populist threat to the plutocrats, it's years or even decades away."[19]

Most people who get involved in government for purely employment purposes today are generally not very smart. They are more often attracted to the financial job security that comes with forced taxation, especially within bureaucracy, absent the genuine motive to secure individual liberty and fundamental rights. Such concepts are foreign to their daily, intellectual experience. A recent study done by Johns Hopkins University Political Scientists as research for a new upcoming book called, *What the Government Thinks of the People*, shows that federal employees, for example, earn 48 percent more in compensation than does the private sector. These statistics are also sourced by the U.S. Bureau of Economic Analysis. Benjamin Ginsberg, one of the authors of the study, intimated,

"Official Washington views the public through jaundiced eyes, believing that ordinary Americans are uninformed and misguided and that policy makers should ignore them. The government's lack of trust in the people reflects the civic distance between the American people and their government as much as any political reality. Nevertheless, what the government thinks of the people affects how it governs, especially the chance that policy will be influenced by citizen preferences. Some say American democracy would be strengthened if the people received better civic education," Ginsberg continues. "We argue that it is America's governing elite that needs civic education, focusing on the responsibilities of officials in a democracy."[19.5]

In addition, many people also get into American government to change the essence of it from within. Independent thinking has become a minimum. Biological scientists and anthropologists with Cambridge University say that humans in general are actually getting dumber and weaker, that the human body and brain is actually shrinking.[20] Evidence is not only in biological evolution, but is also reflective within mere SAT scoring[21] and human IQs in general. Dr Nijenhuis with the University of Amsterdam infers that people, primarily in the west, have lost an average of 14 IQ points since the Victorian Age, that we have quite possibly reached our intellectual peak, that human intelligence is on the decline.[22] Why? On a personal note, I'm pretty damn sure teenagers today are a hell of a lot smarter than teenagers forty years ago. But, is easy access to information what counts as intelligence? Today, when you take a teen's access to Google away, they are clueless. Moreover, is this decline in IQs because education is no longer fueled by the desire for truth, as in studying philosophy, for example? The pursuit of truth, abstractly, and not just scientifically, was very common in the Victorian Age. Sure more people read and write today, but there are also seven billion people on the planet. Rather than the abstract pursuit of the truth, education today is driven more by the individual's need of specific skills, as a way to acquire steady income, which has superceded the desire for the pursuit of truth. There needs to be balance. Acquiring skills by themselves takes less brainpower, because then "knowledge" becomes very limited to daily experience, and relies more on input from instructors rather than exercising critical thinking skills abstractly. As it relates to objective truth, George Orwell said, "The very concept of objective truth is fading out of the world. Lies will pass into history." We are relying upon technology too much. Technology does our thinking for us nowadays. Moreover, the constant need of income is destroying mankind. This, in part, derives also from learning what to think rather than how to think. As I have mentioned before, technological advances in society does not necessarily equal humans evolving into a more mature, moral and biologically advanced species, as it relates to overcoming negative human nature. Otherwise, we would not be the same in our natures as we were nearly 6,000 years ago, while carrying around smart phones now. In addition, like I've also mentioned earlier, we are actually digressing back into the type of society that our founders fought Independence from. There is a growing divide between the people in government and people not in government, all based in power, wealth and the monopoly of information and of force, or violence. This is not positive evolution. In consequence, as Orwell also said, "In a time of deceit, telling the truth is a revolutionary act." I add to that, that trying to find the truth is becoming a revolutionary act.

This devolution and lack of intelligence in the masses slithers its way into government. Ignorance of the Rule of Law, American history and its related philosophical principles have become rampant within government at all levels. Government officials operate by training only rather than by education and knowledge. Government officials are also taught what to think rather than how to think, just like they are still in grade school. Even the one's who supposedly "write" the laws don't even really "know" the Law. This is because corporate lawyers and lobbyists usually write the laws, manipulating the legal language, which plays into securing corporate incomes and power. The politicians then just sign off on them, depending on their own financial incentives and kickbacks. This is fact. Go up to any cop and ask them what the 17th Amendment is, how it works and should it exist. Or, ask the cop what the difference is in an American cop and a British cop, or a cop in Mexico. They will probably regurgitate what they are "trained." Or, while at a local town hall meeting, ask the politician or the potential politician what the difference is in a

British representative and an American Representative. If they respond within the context of monarchy vs. democracy, they don't really know. Go up to any judge and ask his or her opinion of the founders' *concurrent review* compared to *judicial review*. They'll look at you funny. I have actually done this quite often while working in court. They simply don't know. Law school teaches precedent, or interpretations of the Law, not actual Law. Knowledge is a communal enterprise. One person cannot possibly know everything about everything. But when it comes to one's profession, knowledge related to that profession, not necessarily by way of training, should be paramount. This has not been the overall case within government jobs. Knowledge appears to be only limited to "training" and one's daily experience, which is helping America repeat history.

Any individuals who take an oath to uphold and defend the constitution against enemies foreign and domestic are directly participating in, and continuing in, the American Revolution against aristocracy, inequality and the oppression of the fundamental rights of personal and religious liberty, which directly encompasses the ownership of self and of property. As the levels of government trickle down, many people assume that because one can cite statutes that they "know" the law. This is ridiculous. It is like someone who cites various scriptures claiming to "know" all about God, or about a particular religion, or what it means to be spiritual or not spiritual. Atheists and agnostics can easily cite scriptures. Likewise, government officials can easily cite statutes. Of course this works the other way also. Neo-progressives will argue that anyone can cite the Constitution or the founders.

The liberty redefined by the neo-progressive legal system comes by way of fiat money, and/or currency. Freedom today is not secured by Law, but by wealth. Many claim any type of critique against the illegitimacies of government or against the *status quo* are conspiracy theories, or right wing extremism. This is stupid. Conspiracies are very real. The "theory" part may be questionable. In fact, if conspiracies are not real, why are there laws against them? The idea of conspiracy *theory* was actually created by the CIA as a way to demonize and ridicule the questioning of JFK's assassination, and to give authority and credibility to the government's explanation.[23] Manipulation of the public's perspective away from the truth is essential to minimize mass inquiry. In fact, Barbara Honegger, a policy analyst in the Reagan Administration, stated in her notes of a staff meeting between Reagan and then CIA Director William Casey in 1981, whereby Reagan asked Casey what his goal was for the CIA, Casey responded, in part, "We'll know our disinformation program is complete when everything the American public believes is false."[23.5]

Control of the masses also comes when the people's collective energy and their thinking are spent in the efforts of complying with debt and the continuous need of income to simply exist, coupled with the social engineering of right and wrong being determined by what is legal and illegal. So what can be done? Revolution? The feeble minded generally laugh at non-violent revolutions because they get to use violence against non-violent people, which is raw authoritarianism and animalistic, absent any inclination of a superior mindset, or even mere intelligence that is beyond negative human nature. A superior mindset is thus reflected in non-violence. Unfortunately, force has been the tipping point within most revolutions. This dichotomy of *right action vs. legal action* is what propagates, in part, the negative aspects of human nature that we as a species must eventually evolve out of. Virtually all of your thinking and experiences are the indirect result of what someone else wants you to be, which is also the essence of conflict, as you try to be different from what someone else wants you to be. That "someone else" is why the United States is now an Oligarchy. Be who you are anyway.

Stephan Molyneux, whom I've mentioned before in Chapter two, is a contemporary ethicist and political philosopher, who writes extensively on ethical and political issues. One such work is his paper called *The Handbook of Human Ownership*. In it he argues that because humans are mere animals, power over other people began in ancient cannibalism, which can be historically corroborated by anthropologists, generally under exo-cannibalism. This power over, and the ownership of, other humans disappeared, however, temporarily, when there were no more meals.

> "In the dawn of history, this predation occurred in the most base manner, through brute cannibalism. While this may have proven effective in the short run, it fell prey to the problem of consuming your seed crop, in that it provided only a few meals, whilst re-growing more human livestock took over a decade. And, it was pretty gross. Sometimes, even after you washed your food, it was too smelly to eat. (Interesting fact: deodorant was first invented as marinade.)" [24]

There were and are many other reasons behind ancient cannibalism, like religious reasons, which falls under endo-cannibalism. Anyway, Molyneux continues, "The husbandry of human ownership took a giant leap forward with the invention of slavery, which was a step up from cannibalism because instead of using people as food, it used people to grow food, which was a much more sustainable model, to say the least." Thus, "the basic reality of human ownership is this: First, you must first subdue the masses through force. Then, you maintain that subjugation through the psychological power of ethics."[25]

As it relates to ethics, I see reflections of Friedrich Nietzsche in what Molyneux says. I am very much an admirer of Nietzsche. In fact, I have a large framed photo of Nietzsche and one of David Hume on my wall in my office. Unfortunately, some people have grossly misread Nietzsche as a means to rationalize their arbitrary power. The Nazis' "superman" or, *Übermensch* comes to mind. Anyway, Friedrich Nietzsche was a late 19ᵗʰ century German philosopher who argued, in part, that morality, as we know it today, derives out of the *resentment* within the weakness of the slave classes in ancient times. Slaves could do nothing about their enslavement, because the ruling classes held the monopoly on force, which was also, ironically, "ethical" behavior for the masters. So morality for slaves was formed as a means to cope, so to speak, in opposition to the master classes' view of morality, which was that it is "good" to conquer, to oppress the weak and to rule over others, simply because they are pathetic. Nietzsche writes in the *Genealogy of Morals,*

"If the suppressed, the down-trodden and the wronged, prompted by the craft of impotence, say to themselves: "Let us be different from the bad, let us be good! and good are all those, who wrong no one, who never violate, who never attack, who never retaliate, who entrust revenge to God, who, like us, live aloof from the world, who avoid all contact with evil, and who, altogether, demand little of life, as we do, the patient, the humble, the just" — this means, viewed coolly and unprejudicially, no more than : "We, the weak, are - it is a fact- weak; it is well for us not to do anything, *for which we are not strong - enough."*
But this stern matter of fact, this meanest kind of prudence, shared even by insects (which occasionally simulate death, in order not to do " too much " in case of great danger), has, thanks to the trickery and self-imposition of impotence, clothed itself in the apparel of renouncing, silent, abiding virtue, as if the weakness of the weak one

itself, *i.e.,* presumably his *being,* his action, his entire, unavoidable, inseparable reality – were a voluntary performance, a thing self-willed, self-chosen, a *deed,* a *desert.* To this kind of man, the *necessity* of the belief in an indifferent, free-willed "subject" is prompted by the instinct of self-preservation, self-assertion, - an instinct by which every falsehood uses to sanctify itself. The subject (or, speaking more popularly, the *soul)* has perhaps been, so far, the best religious tenet on earth, even for the reason that it made possible for the majority of mortals, the weak and oppressed of every description, that sublime self-defraudation of interpreting weakness itself as freedom, the fact of their being thus and thus as a *desert.*"[26]

Similarly, Molyneux writes,

"People think that ethics were invented to make people good, but that's like saying that chastity belts were invented to spread STDs. No, no – ethics were invented to bind the minds of the slaves, and to create the only true shackles we rulers need: guilt, self-attack and a fear of the tyranny of ethics. Whoever teaches ethics rules the herd, because everyone is afraid of bad opinions, mostly from themselves. If you do it right, no judgment will be as evil or endless as the one coming from the mirror."[27]

Over time, and in the end, what we have today, are "human tax farms," where people are controlled by government's version of morality, and that the legal system has become the source of right and wrong, as a means to sustain these "tax farms" psychologically. Nietzsche argues that this harsh control of the masses, which essentially created "morality," also derived from the priestly class. Thus, the concept of *good vs. evil* made its way into the realism or mentality of the slave classes, or of the weak, whereby the masters or the ruling classes, were viewed as *evil*, not just bad. Yet the masters thought of themselves as good. Molyneux likewise writes,

> "After the Dark Ages, when the ruling classes had to suffer the indignity of retreating into the dank attics of the Church, the feudal model emerged. The feudal approach improved on the direct slave-owning model by granting the human livestock ("serfs") nominal ownership over land, while taking a portion of their productivity through taxes, military conscription, user fees for grinding grain and so on. So instead of owning folks directly, we just let them sweat themselves into puddles on their little ancestral plots, then took whatever we wanted from the proceeds – all the while telling them, of course, that God Himself appointed us as masters over them, and that their highest virtue was meek subservience to their anointed masters."[28]

So we have this similar model today, secured in the American legal system, the near equivalent model of soft serfdom/feudalism that was created during the medieval era and thus adopted by the British Monarchy, which our Framers revolted against by establishing the Rule of Law, secured in the Declaration and the US Constitution. Molyneux infers that,

> "…the evolution of medieval serfdom split society into four basic groups: The ruling class (aristocracy); The church (propaganda); The army (enforcement) – and; The serfs (livestock). The aristocracy – of which you are now a proud member – reaped the rewards; the Church controlled the slaves through ethics; the Army attacked those not subjugated through ethics, and the Serfs paid for the whole show. (The modern equivalents are: the political masters, the media, the police and the taxpayers.)"[29]

Propaganda today, secured in the media, tends to either be good or bad itself. It can either heighten the spirits of the masses or it can create conflict. The media today, then, tends to dumb information down into *good vs. bad*, which then helps the masses conceptualize what otherwise need not be understood. And so what happens is, the masses get a controlled and thwarted view of the truth. How do we "know" today that right and wrong, in the "legal" sense, are actual reflections of morality? How do we know that what Emerson called *penances*, are right and wrong in the actual moral sense? Are *penances* genuine reflections of morality? The evidence against genuine reflections of morality in the legal system is overwhelming. What is genuine morality? Rather than dive into moral theory, I believe Jesus himself conceptualized what genuine morality was best when he said to "love your neighbor as yourself." This is the moral compass *in action*, which is the point Jesus makes, *in action*. To "treat others as you would like to be treated" takes benevolent initiative, and not the lack thereof. As it relates to the question, "what is truth," Frances Bacon said it best, "The human understanding is not composed of dry light, but is subject to influence from the will and the emotions, a fact that creates fanciful knowledge; man prefers to believe what he wants to be true."[30] This is what is exploited as penances or virtues within the legal system today.

Silent Encroachments

Practical steps can be taken by people today that institute subtle changes (silent encroachments) in reverse and in like manner to the silent encroachments that have been taken against American liberty over the last century or so through this neo-progression or *new style* of progress. Self-reliance is a revolutionary act in a society where its legal system is predicated upon state dependency. Non-state dependency has much more revolutionary effect on those authoritarians in power then does mere acts of violence. So much so that the probability increases that such acts of self-reliance become more in line with "criminal" activity as a means to keep the system afloat. Ralph Waldo Emerson writes in his essay on *Self-Reliance*,

> "Trust thyself: every heart vibrates to that iron string. Accept the place the divine providence has found for you, the society of your contemporaries, the connection of events. Great men have always done so, and confided themselves childlike to the genius of their age, betraying their perception that the absolutely trustworthy was seated at their heart, working through their hands, predominating in all their being. And we are now men, and must accept in the highest mind the same transcendent destiny; and not minors and invalids in a protected corner, not cowards fleeing before a revolution, but guides, redeemers, and benefactors, obeying the Almighty effort, and advancing on Chaos and the Dark."[31]

The most revolutionary act for any individual is to be self-reliant, self-sufficient, self-informed, and self-educated. To truly be revolutionary today is to live opposite of state dependency. Yet, how can one be secure from poverty and be self-reliant when everything has a price, and, economic activity is forced upon the individual as the only way to pay that price? In today's American society, absolute self-reliance cannot be. Why not? First, you must own property in absolute to be purely self-sustaining. People can no longer truly own property, thus the force of economic activity is imminent. Second, and mark my words, the more people become self-reliant the more those acts that are necessary to be so will become more "criminalized." Again, the legal system is predicated upon state dependency. Liberty, on the other hand, is predicated upon more personal responsibility, self-reliance, benevolence and like-minded individuals. The state will do anything it can to encourage and even force state dependency, in the name of economic activity, which is generally propagated by self-interested individuals. State dependency is when an individual relies upon government for virtually all of their needs and information from near cradle to grave. More often, someone who is state dependent has most of their thinking done for them, and, they are comfortable being provided "protection" by force. State dependency also includes the unquestioned compliance to nearly all activities being supervised, including the exercise of rights, which require permission and fees. Moreover, state dependents are ok with being subjugated to *forced* economic activity. State dependency, however, does not necessarily limit itself to one's access to public services, public education, entitlements and welfare by way of forced fairness. It also refers to certain types of blind subservience, which is designed to propagate state dependency. To illustrate, how can I, as a self-reliant and personally responsible, benevolent, free individual, exercise my fundamental right to bear arms, if I must first yield my initial responsibility of bearing arms to pay for permission from the state, especially in absence of income and/or money? Having money and having income are two different things. Recall that the Framers established the 2nd Amendment as the Rule of Law to *equalize* force between the people in government with the people not in government. True equality has always come down to force, period. When the people in government tell the people not in government that they cannot be armed equally to themselves, then inequality commences. This is the history of authoritarian governments.

The neo-progressive would argue that paying for permission to exercise a fundamental right *is* being responsible, which is grossly fallacious, of course. It is fallacious because such "responsibility" to seek out and pay for permission first, as required by statute, is absent the instantiation of the right itself, independently, which is pre-existing to law. It is *similar* to a parent demanding that a child be responsible for the care of a new pet bird, while the parent always does the feeding and the cleaning and has not taught the child the specific responsibility associated with caring for the bird. It then becomes revolutionary to be the opposite, which includes, but is not limited to, thinking for one's self and exercising one's inalienable rights without "permission." The inalienable rights of people are not subjugated to the whimsical will of government officials because they think they know what's best for others.

If you exercise your 1st Amendment right to protest without permission, for example, then government minions with guns will come use the threat of violence to end your right to protest. Very asinine isn't it? Part of this comes from the social engineering of the "law abiding" ideology into the public sphere as "ethical." Silent encroachments tend to manipulate such wording over time to actually weaken the right itself by citing and manipulating the words "law abiding" into the context of an authoritarian spirit. To illustrate, is it "law abiding," thus ethical, to exercise one's 1st Amendment right to protest by remaining confined to a "free speech zone" after paying for permission to protest, simply because that is the ordnance? What if the ordinance then says that no protests can take place except on Saturdays? Is it law abiding to comply? Is it "unethical" to not comply? What if you wanted to protest a business and they are closed on Saturdays and this ordinance was written and lobbied by that business? How about a statute that says it is "law abiding" for people to turn in their guns? Such regulations are withstanding to the Amendments themselves. To use the threat of violence, or to use violence itself, to stop an individual from exercising an inalienable right, absent permission and fees, in and of itself, is grossly authoritarian and narrow minded. Lawful authority only comes in when the exercise of such a right proves to be irresponsible, not before. In addition, this irresponsibility, in and of itself, does not logically play into the future suppression of the same exercise of the same rights by others. This is outside of the social contract. Such "authority" arises and derives from silent encroachments coupled with the manipulation of the words "law abiding" and the word "ethical." This manipulation is designed to subtly encourage the blind subservience to such statutes as being a "good citizen," or "law abiding."

What exactly are *silent encroachments*? James Madison used the term often to refer to when government slowly infringes upon individual liberties, and liberty in general. In a speech, for example, at the Virginia Ratifying Convention for the US Constitution in 1788, Madison argued,

> "Since the general civilization of mankind, I believe there are more instances of the abridgement of freedom of the people by gradual and silent encroachments by those in power than by violent and sudden usurpations. On a candid examination of history we shall find that turbulence, violence, and abuse of power by the majority trampling on the rights of the minority, have produced factions and commotions, which in republics, have more frequently than any other cause produced despotism. If we go over the whole history of the ancient and modern republics, we shall find their destruction to have generally resulted from those causes."

Madison also argued that silent encroachments against individual liberty comes through religious organizations, which also lobby government as a way to control certain behaviors in society that they find offensive. Today, these encroachments are also, like in forced economic activity, known as special interests. Thus Madison asserts,

> "Besides the danger of a direct mixture of religion and civil government, there is an evil which ought to be guarded against in the indefinite accumulation of property from the capacity of holding it in perpetuity by ecclesiastical corporations. The establishment of the chaplainship in Congress is a palpable violation of equal rights as well as of Constitutional principles. The danger of silent accumulations and encroachments by ecclesiastical bodies has not sufficiently engaged attention in the U.S."

Thomas Jefferson also had something to say about the gradual erosion of liberty by those in power. Jefferson argued,

> "Whereas it appeareth that however certain forms of government are better calculated than others to protect individuals in the free exercise of their natural rights, and are at the same time themselves better guarded against degeneracy, yet experience hath shewn, that even under the best forms, those entrusted with power have, in time, and by slow operations, perverted it into tyranny; and it is believed that the most effectual means of preventing this would be, to illuminate, as far as practicable, the minds of the people at large, ...whence it becomes expedient for promoting the publick happiness that those persons, whom nature hath endowed with genius and virtue, should be rendered by liberal education worthy to receive, and able to guard the sacred deposit of the rights and liberties of their fellow citizens, and that they should be called to that charge without regard to wealth, birth or accidental condition of circumstance."[32]

Today, such "genius and virtue" is expressed through an individual's self-education and self-reliance, which then can "guard the sacred deposit of the rights and liberties of their fellow citizens," and not by way of state dependency. Silent encroachments, the gradual erosion of individual liberties, the "slow operations" that pervert and deviate government from actualizing fundamental principles, comes primarily, again, by way of reinterpreting the US Constitution and implementing that new interpretation through precedent.

A dissertation entitled, *An Inquiry into the Impact Constitutional Interpretation has on Individual Freedom*, written by Robert G. Beard, Jr., infers this very premise, that "This 'abridgment of freedom' appears to have been accomplished over time through *Constitutional Interpretation*." Mr. Beard cites Mary Ann Glendon, a Law Professor at Harvard,

> "Which is more likely: that unruly majorities will have their way? Or that the democratic elements in our republican experiment will wither away, while new forms of tyranny by the powerful few rise? Whom should we fear more: an aroused populace, or the vanguard who know better than the people what the people should want? Tyranny, as Tocqueville warned, need not announce itself with guns and trumpets. It may come softly—so softly that we will barely notice when we become one of those countries where there are no citizens but only subjects. So softly that if a well-meaning foreigner should suggest, 'Perhaps you could do something about your oppression,' we might look up, puzzled, and ask, 'What oppression.'"

As society advances even more, the need of reinterpreting the Rule of Law from its *original intent* becomes increasingly "necessary" for neo-progressives, especially those neo-progressives in government, which includes both democrats and republicans. Likewise, the more technologically advanced American society becomes, the further political philosophy, in the contemporary sense, will argue the need to undermine such fundamental liberties like property ownership, freedom of speech, trial by jury, the right to travel freely, political activism, the right to own and carry a gun, the right to raise children within their parent's own belief system, the right to earn a living, and the like. Such political and "ethical" arguments will ultimately derive from special interest groups, as they mostly do now. Neo-progressives believe that a technologically advanced society cannot legitimately coexist with our current Constitutional protections, that such liberties must be reinterpreted in such a style that ultimately transitions them into government privileges that are heavily regulated. The latter steps will equally be more effective as the three branches of government become more complicit to one another. Thus, you will hear more about efforts to reinterpret and enforce the new "living" understanding of the Constitution. This social engineering of state dependency for "public safety" and the collectivist well-being philosophy becomes further propagated within public education, more secondary laws, the mass media and even in entertainment.

Revolutionary Acts

Think about the following ways of living as revolutionary acts and self-defense techniques against a legal system designed to drain you of real living, whatever you believe that to be. I believe "real living" to be, in part, the absence of arbitrary force and coercion into economic activity. As a lifelong martial artist, I tend to always think in a *defensive* perspective. I then teach my Aikido and Shotokan students to see past misapprehension, as it relates to one's surroundings, to try and see the truth within a given situation and utilize it. A really great book to read on this subject is entitled, *The Secret Power Within*, written by Chuck Norris. Yes, Chuck Norris, a wonderful person and fellow martial artist, whom I very much respect. I want to apply one thing he says to the following "revolutionary acts" in a self-defense context. Norris writes, "When you are attacked, you give way just enough to unbalance your opponent, and then turn the attack to your advantage by using skill or strategy."[32.5] Consider these revolutionary acts not as going in for the kill, but as a way to unbalance the system from within, in the hopes that such acts help pave the way for further reflection about where America is headed.

So, just as it takes conditioning over time to become state dependant, it will likewise take conditioning over time to become self-reliant. Self-reliance is the best defense against being exploited. This conditioning over time from personal freedom into state dependency is what the founders called, again, silent encroachments. It will take work to reverse the effects of this "new style of progress," It can be done. It needs to be done on a massive scale, one individual at a time. The more people become politically aware and active, knowledgeable, and self-reliant, the more revolutionary the masses become against the status quo. Absent this *conscientious living*, American society continues to deviate fully back into the aristocracy and central power our founders rebelled against. Technological advances in society do not necessarily mean, again, that humans are getting smarter, nor does it mean that we are positively evolving. I want to suggest ten *ways of living* that an individual can still "legally" do, as a means to help gradually reverse the effects of the *silent encroachments* that have steered America, by force, away from its organic Constitution. These *ways of living* can also be understood as "revolutionary acts" that eventually become problematic for the neo-progressives as they attach themselves to the status quo.

Number one: personal responsibility. Personal responsibility for one's own life and actions determine genuine independence and intelligence. To be self-reliant takes work. Being free takes work. Most importantly, the work it takes to be free and self-reliant takes the *rational exercise* of personal responsibility called intelligence. Many people cannot handle personal freedom and personal responsibility, simply because it takes hard work. Therefore, state dependency becomes attractive, unfortunately to the point of no return. Being taken care of from cradle to grave is something that is becoming more and more a normal, cultural phenomenon, and such dependency is encouraged at the beginning of life through public education and even into higher education. This is not intelligence. Recall this discussion on what intelligence is from chapter 3. State dependency is also reinforced within the mass and corporate media, entertainment, secondary law, special interests and by way of social settings like church groups or political organizations. The following actions all encompass being personally responsible, which also encompass knowing how to think rather than simply what to think. Personal responsibility equally emphasizes actions that take into strong consideration the well being of others absent coercion.

Number two: try to avoid the use of credit for miscellaneous purchases of wants and "needs." If you can't afford it, and you don't absolutely need it, don't buy it. Moreover, decrease excessive spending. Save your currency. If your "lifestyle" depends on credit, for example, you are thinking *within the box*. There is nothing wrong with credit itself. Credit can be a necessary financial tool that equally takes personal responsibility, like buying a home, a vehicle, or starting up a business. The responsibility that attaches to such purchases is paying back the currency with interest, within a designated time frame, if one can afford it. When the credit attaches itself to miscellaneous purchases, however, then such purchases become unreasonable and become the further cause of deficits and personal debt that are ultimately destroying this country from within, and the world, I might add. It is credit that created the income tax, for example. The 16th Amendment was originally established along side the Federal Reserve Act to help the federal government pay the interest on the currency it could now borrow from the Federal Reserve. This was established to not only go to war, originally, but to also finance socially engineered political programs. "The modern theory of the perpetuation of debt has drenched the earth with blood, and crushed its inhabitants under burdens ever accumulating," says Thomas Jefferson. It is credit that finances war, all around the globe, because countries that have no real wealth have to borrow the money they need from big banks in order to buy weapons and pay soldiers to fight, then the interest and repayment of that currency becomes the "forced responsibility" of the general public and the unborn, which is immoral. Credit is also used by governments and corporations to pay pensions, while the interest is generated from those not directly associated with the use of that credit. Credit then secures government employment when tax revenue is insufficient, again at the expense of taxpayers. There are only three options to sustain this fiasco; shrink government, increase taxes beyond reason, or go further into debt, at the forced expense of the living and unborn. Which is ethical? Because neither is actually ethical, force becomes the supplementary paradigm for such a society. Like I've stated before, rather than the base of monetary policy and valuation being founded upon ethics, monetary policy and its valuation create the bases of what it means to be "ethical." Once such economic activity is enforced as responsibility into the masses by the threat of violence and being caged, such submission is then defined as "good citizenship." You can thank big government debt founders like Hamilton who criticized small government debt founders like Jefferson as "Jacobin levelers," which was a period term for extremist views. Nothing has changed.

To digress a moment, again, what does it mean, anymore, to be ethical? Is it ethical not to offend another person? Because, then you have no free speech. Is it ethical to not rebel against authority? Because then democide would be justified. Is it ethical to side with the majority? Because then America would not exist. Recall that the majority of the people in the Colonies wanted to remain subjects of the King. Was this because the King was ethical? Is a legal system the answer to the question of ethics? Did not the Nazis have a legal system? Did not every government in history have a legal system? Did not the King of Britain have a legal system? Does not Cuba have a legal system? What does it mean to have a legal system that is ethical? It must go deeper than what has already been done. Recall that Locke criticized that all governments claim "lawfulness" through their legal systems. Again, it must go deeper. It's fundamentally philosophical.

As it relates back to credit, the founders were not perfect and were the beginning of such unnecessary uses of credit in America themselves. Thomas Jefferson, for example, used credit to not only operate his farms, which were necessary, but to buy exotic wines and to live a lavish lifestyle. On the other hand, Jefferson was also fiscally responsible for his debt. An associate professor, Susan Kern, at the College of William & Mary, wrote in her book, *The Jeffersons at Shadwell*, that, "Following the American Revolution, there was still a lot of debt outstanding to creditors in Great Britain. There were a fair number of Americans who did not want to pay them and Jefferson was not one of them. He wanted to pay them. He was very personally responsible for what he owed."[33] Living off of credit for unnecessary and miscellaneous purchases can be very destructive. Like Ben Franklin said, "Beware of little expenses, a small leak will sink a great ship." Fortunately for the people in government, they can override ethics and force taxation on the people's labor to secure their misuse of credit for whatever it wants. The humans not in government cannot do that, it's "unethical," and/or "criminal." Like Madison said, "History records that the money changers have used every form of abuse, intrigue, deceit, and violent means possible to maintain their control over governments by controlling money and its issuance." One should know the difference in currency and money. Money is a medium of exchange that holds its purchasing power over long periods of time, generally absent inflation and debt. Currency is regulated paper money, a medium of exchange that fluctuates through inflation and deflation within short periods of time and attaches each paper note of currency to debt. Paper money loses its purchasing power over time because of that inflation and debt attached to it. Gold and silver, for example, have always been considered real money. Paper money, like the US dollar, is currency. Avoid the use of credit.

This leads to another revolutionary act, number three; save your cash and pay yourself first, out of your income, by purchasing actual commodities like gold and silver. Putting cash away somewhere like a safe or safety deposit box can now become suspect. It is even a crime now to carry certain amounts of cash on your person. This is because currencies, or US dollars, are actually property of the Federal Reserve. Mike Maloney, the author of, *Guide to Investing in Gold and Silver*, gives sound reasons why investing in gold and silver are the most legitimate way of securing wealth within any economic turmoil. Within the next paragraph, and from what Maloney talks about in his book, I want to paraphrase into a very short synopsis some of the reasons why Maloney says investing in gold and silver are sound currency investments: Fiat currencies, or faith-based currencies, have always failed, one hundred percent of the time throughout history. The US dollar will fail. Gold and silver have generally, for centuries, always held its value as a medium of exchange. Gold and silver are considered real money because they have always automatically balanced all economies going back thousands of years. Without gold and silver, banks would have never come into existence. Fiat currencies allow for deficit spending, thus creating national and personal debt. Once the actual US dollar fails, generally all global fiat currencies will follow, creating a global crises and the need of a new world monetary system. Gold and silver are necessarily attached to a bank's guarantee. Once currency is printed into *hyperinflation*, gold and silver will take over as a medium of exchange as it always has done. Outside of gold and silver, all other investments are risky. Gold and silver are not subservient to the market psychology of fear. Gold and silver are generally exceptions to the rules of panics and crashes that are attached to fiat currencies and market investments. Plus, gold and silver are less likely to be manipulated by greed. Gold and silver are liquid and tangible. They can go wherever you go and can be secured in a safe or safety deposit box, or even a rented, secure vault.[34]

Currencies today are becoming more digital, which gives way to even more financial manipulation and micromanagement from an array of third parties. Most importantly, as it relates to purchasing gold and silver, you'll sleep better at night knowing that if the dollar crashes, you still have purchasing power and wealth. The US government ended the gold standard because gold and silver held government and banks accountable to genuine economic standards and monetary valuation. Once American government purged itself of the gold and silver standard, it can manipulate the value of its currency, which is exactly the case, thus giving itself more power to do whatever it wants. Mike Maloney stated at a presentation that first deflation of US currency would result in inflation,

> "I believe there's going to be deflation first, and then all of the world central banks will start printing like crazy to get us out of that deflation. What you see here is that there's a little collapse going on of the currency supply up here, although it's not huge. If everything was fine, the Federal Reserve would not be doing that [buying massive amounts of debt from the Treasury]. They're scared, so it's happening. They're doing anything they can to prevent this deflationary collapse that I predicted in my book. If the public gets scared and they stopped borrowing currency into existence and they save up and pay down debt, the whole thing goes into a deflationary collapse."[35]

Number four is another revolutionary act to subtly reverse the silent encroachments that have slowly withered away at the individual liberty that is secured in the US Constitution. End any and all affiliations with political parties. Register as independent and be active politically as an independent. Political parties do your thinking for you. And, political parties need your participation to continually feed into the classic *divide and conquer* mentality, which is itself a silent encroachment. George Washington warned Americans of political parties within his farewell address in 1796 by asserting,

> "All obstructions to the execution of the Laws, all combinations and associations, under whatever plausible character, with the real design to direct, control, counteract, or awe the regular deliberation

and action of the constituted authorities, are destructive of this fundamental principle, and of fatal tendency. They serve to organize faction, to give it an artificial and extraordinary force; to put, in the place of the delegated will of the nation, the will of a party, often a small but artful and enterprising minority of the community; and, according to the alternate triumphs of different parties, to make the public administration the mirror of the ill-concerted and incongruous projects of faction, rather than the organ of consistent and wholesome plans digested by common counsels, and modified by mutual interests....I have already intimated to you the danger of parties in the state, with particular reference to the founding of them on geographical discriminations. Let me now take a more comprehensive view, and warn you in the most solemn manner against the baneful effects of the spirit of party, generally. This spirit, unfortunately, is inseparable from our nature, having its root in the strongest passions of the human mind. It exists under different shapes in all governments, more or less stifled, controlled, or repressed; but, in those of the popular form, it is seen in its greatest rankness, and is truly their worst enemy. The alternate domination of one faction over another, sharpened by the spirit of revenge, natural to party dissension, which in different ages and countries has perpetrated the most horrid enormities, is itself a frightful despotism. But this leads at length to a more formal and permanent despotism. The disorders and miseries, which result, gradually incline the minds of men to seek security and repose in the absolute power of an individual; and sooner or later the chief of some prevailing faction, more able or more fortunate than his competitors, turns this disposition to the purposes of his own elevation, on the ruins of Public Liberty. Without looking forward to an extremity of this kind, (which nevertheless ought not to be entirely out of sight,) the common and continual mischiefs of the spirit of party are sufficient to make it the interest and duty of a wise people to discourage and restrain it. It serves always to distract

the Public Councils, and enfeeble the Public
Administration. It agitates the Community with ill-
founded jealousies and false alarms; kindles the
animosity of one part against another, foments
occasionally riot and insurrection. It opens the door to
foreign influence and corruption, which find a
facilitated access to the government itself through the
channels of party passions. Thus the policy and the
will of one country are subjected to the policy and
will of another."

Thomas Paine, another founding father, also warned of political parties and their negative effects on foundational principles, and on their gradual erosion of individual liberty by declaring that, "It is the nature and intention of a constitution to prevent governing by party, by establishing a common principle that shall limit and control the power and impulse of party, and that says to all parties, thus far shalt thou go and no further. But in the absence of a constitution, men look entirely to party; and instead of principle governing party, party governs principle."[36] Within a more contemporary view of political parties, Carroll Quigley, who was a professor of American History at Georgetown University, wrote in his book, *Tragedy and Hope*, "The argument that the two parties should represent opposed ideals and policies, one, perhaps, of the right and the other of the left, is a foolish idea acceptable only to the doctrinaire and academic thinkers. Instead, the two parties should be almost identical, so that the American people can 'throw the rascals out' at any election without leading to any profound or extreme shifts in policy." Today, political parties undermine the Bill of Rights, and, political parties deviate from constitutional principles for the sake of the power of the party itself. This can't happen the more that people register as independent and stay away from such social and political factions like party politics. Free people can easily be politically active absent the influence of and participation in a political party, and this should be encouraged within sound public education, and sound political discourse. Political parties only reemphasize the fact that money and power are bigger than principle. Political parties "unlimit" government. So much so that what were originally acts of patriotism are now becoming acts of treason and/or crimes. Party leaders sit around all pampas in their thinking, when in fact their thinking is geared towards empowering the party itself, which then empowers their own selfish desires for power over others. Greed for power and self-admonishment is likewise behind party politics. This is evidenced by the fact, and in part, by one who wants to run for office, and who can only do so with the support and acceptance from a political party. Stay away from them. If you want to run for office, run as Independent, grass roots style. It will catch on.

Number five; nullification of law. On a larger scale, *nullification* is a lawful remedy to avoid being victimized by unconstitutional regulations and secondary laws. This can happen in two ways. One is when a particular state does not adhere to a federal law on the grounds that said law is withstanding to the US or State Constitution, which is, by the way, a state power secured in the 9th and 10th Amendments. The 9th Amendment reads, "The enumeration in the Constitution, of certain rights, shall not be construed to deny or disparage others retained by the people." The 9th Amendment was Madison's way to secure the fact that other rights shall be protected that are not specifically named within the Bill of rights. One of these rights is the right of the people to govern themselves through state governments outside of the delegated powers exercised by the federal government, yet limited to the Bill of Rights. The 10th Amendment reads, "The powers not delegated to the United States by the Constitution, nor prohibited by it to the states, are reserved to the states respectively, or to the people." The 10th Amendment helps purposely define the relationship between the federal government and the states, that the federal government is restricted to those specific delegated powers in the Constitution, Article 1, Section 8, and that the States reserve the right to execute *law and order* outside of those delegated powers, provided state's do not violate the Bill of Rights. Neo-progressives argue fanatically that such power to nullify law does not exist anymore under the 14th Amendment. This is grossly untrue and deceptive. Just because the 14th Amendment makes the Bill of Rights the supreme law of each individual state, as it is also the Supreme Law of the federal government, and that the 14th Amendment also creates federal citizenship as a lawful means to override states that potentially violate an individual's rights, does not in and of itself undermine the right of any state to nullify a federal law that goes directly against state sovereignty, or against the federal or any state constitution. Where does such an argument come from? It's fabricated as a means to centralize power in the aftermath of slavery and the Reconstruction.

A really great book on the subject of nullification is itself entitled *Nullification*, written by Thomas Woods, Jr., who holds his BA and PhD in History from Harvard and Columbia Universities. His master's degree in Philosophy (M.Phil), is also from Columbia University. Woods writes that, "Nullification begins with the axiomatic point that a federal law that violated the Constitution is no law at all. It is void and of no effect.... Nullification provides a shield between the people of a state and an unconstitutional law from the federal government."[37] In a nutshell, Woods also argues that the objection to nullification is a sentimental one that will always exists within those government officials who "favor power over liberty." In addition, such sentimental rebuttals and/or interpretations are contrary to the historical record.

The second aspect of nullification of law that is becoming more and more a revolutionary act is when a jury nullifies a federal, state or local law within a specific case by way of acquittal or a not guilty verdict. This is called *jury nullification*. It is the bedrock of sound law. This also relates to the idea that such a law is wrongfully charged or that said law is withstanding to an individual's fundamental or civil rights. Recall that a fundamental or inalienable right is superior to a civil right. A fundamental right is individualistic in nature while a civil right is collective in nature. In addition, recall that a fundamental right exists prior to and without government, while a civil right exists because of government and in need of government bureaucracy. Both can be equally violated by secondary legislation, however, thus jury nullification is a check upon such arbitrary power. Jury nullification is a fundamental check on power because one: a jury cannot be punished for its verdict if such verdict overrules the government's charges. Second: if such a verdict of not guilty is handed down, the defendant cannot be retried for those same charges, which the 5th Amendment guards against under the *Double Jeopardy* Clause. A good example of this is when juries refused to convict escaped slaves under the Federal, Fugitive Slave Act. This is why, in part, a jury is heavily screened prior to a trial. To illustrate, as it relates to a slave being tried for "escaping" under the Fugitive Slave Act, a potential juror may be asked, "Do you have any 'beliefs' that might prevent you from a decision based strictly upon the law?" If the juror answers, "I believe that slavery is immoral," then that potential juror would be dismissed because the law, at that time, said that slaves couldn't escape from their masters. Likewise, when a particular state would not enforce the Fugitive Slave Act, as Northern states actually did not, this was an act of state nullification of federal law. These powers still exist today and are revolutionary acts when implemented. It is cognitively naïve to even think that law can no longer be nullified on the grounds that such a check on power is no longer sound. The Reconstruction and the Amendments attached to the Reconstruction era in no way revolutionized the system of American government from its original Constitutional intent, they were intended to enhance that intent. It is the neo-progressive who argues for the undermining of that intent through this new style of interpretation.

Number six; people can be more self-sustaining by growing one's own food, if possible. Growing one's own fruits and vegetables, for example, based upon where one lives of course, can be very rewarding on the pocketbook. This cuts out excessive spending at grocery stores and allows for one to put more cash away. Corporate grocery stores are a relatively new phenomena, and for good reason. Because of grocery stores, many people have easy access to healthy and nutritious food, including bad food, that they may have not had access to before. This has allowed for increased life spans and healthier lifestyles in general. On the other hand, as inflation of the dollar increases, many people have less spending power for basic healthy foods. When this happens, what little money some people do acquire, they buy cheap fillers, processed foods in boxes and plastics, which ultimately lead to unhealthier bodies that dominoes into healthcare costs for all of us. This is fact. One can grow simple vegetables and some fruits, even within mega cities, where growing food is a lot of times "illegal." In addition to growing fruits and vegetables, raising small game and chickens, for example, may also be a source of food. Eggs are a very easy way of securing access to protein and a garden is easy access to vegetables, both taking moderate work to sustain. What happens when the grocery stores no longer have food? It is unreasonable to think that will never happen. Those who will overcome the non-existence of easy access food will be those who can grow their own food. This also goes for water. Rain run-off, and the like. Water can be easily collected and stored. Just be innovative. And, here in lies the problem, once enough people begin to grow their own food, collect water and sustain sources of food like eggs, the government will step in with heavy regulations, for their safety of course, ultimately pushing people back into "spending" and state dependency. When people spend less at grocery stores, sales tax, corporate tax, and employees' income tax revenues decrease, and the government must find a way to increase that tax revenue back to where it was. Secondary laws in the name of "public safety" help government do that. Therefore, laws against growing vegetables become important and "necessary" for neo-progressives in government.

This leads me to number seven; be healthy and fit by eating healthy and exercising regularly. Minimize the need of medications and doctor visits. The fact is, most Americans eat terribly and are sedentary. This derives, in part, from the ease of going to the doctor and the ease of purchasing crappy processed foods. There are literally only two ways to be in optimal health: diet and exercise. I don't mean diet in the sense of temporary. I mean diet as in how you eat all the time. Diet and exercise must become a lifestyle, a habit of living, like brushing your teeth, or taking a shower. It is a medical fact today that many common diseases can be reversed through diet and exercise.[38] Simple diabetes type 2, for example, can actually be reversed and has been reversed through hard work. Laziness and ignorance are generally the counter options one takes to rigid diet and exercise.

The fact is, bad health is big business. Big business equals big tax revenues. It doesn't take a rocket scientist to figure this out. Why do you think one of the number one commercials you see on TV is always about prescription drugs? Imagine for a second that a cure for cancer was discovered. Would such a cure be implemented in America? Sadly, I believe such a cure would not be implemented, but hidden and suppressed. Why? Because cancer *treatment* is a big business. If a cure happens, many people will lose their jobs. The big business of cancer treatment will stop, thus the big tax revenues attached to treatment will stop. American government is a corporation, a business now, remember? Therefore, such cures are not good for business. Freedom is not good for business. Take care of yourself, be healthy, and be fit. Your general health and well-being are in your hands and are ultimately your responsibility. As it relates to law enforcement, studies conducted by the FBI show that nearly eighty percent of cops are overweight.[39] This comes from riding around for nearly twelve hours, eating fast food and not exercising. I understand how hard it is to go exercise after working twelve hours, or on a day off from working for days. The number one killer of all law enforcement is heart disease. Being fit and energetic in law enforcement is paramount. Many times a cop gets complacent and gains weight. Once he or she suddenly jumps out of the patrol car to chase someone down, his or her heart gives out. This is fact.

Number eight; educate yourself. Read, read, read books, essays, various studies, documents, historical records, news, alternative news, and the like. Read liberal and conservative articles. Be intellectually well rounded. Self-education is golden and another revolutionary act in today's America. It is revolutionary because educating one's self is outside of the status quo and can become a theoretical threat to what one is taught to think. To illustrate, as a cop, above and beyond my "training," I studied Constitutional Law, American History, I read tons and tons of political philosophy, founding documents like the State Ratification Debates, case law, scholarly legal journals, books and dissertations, all completely on my own. In addition to studying independently, I earned my Master's degree in Philosophy, specializing in Political Theory and Ethics. Why? Because I want to "know" what the truth is. Simple. I did my job based upon the totality of what I "knew" at the time. I did not limit my duty to "training" alone, which I believe ultimately ended my law enforcement career. I have no regrets.

Generally, most educational institutions, especially law schools, tell you what to read and then they interpret what you read, which is in and of itself, a regurgitation of the same process that those who are interpreting what you read, learned how to interpret what you read. Begging the question is imperative to sustaining state dependency and the status quo. Reading is the very basic act of acquiring simple intelligence. Reading is how one uploads information into the brain. Reading coupled with studying, helps one develop reasoning skills, vocabulary, critical thinking skills, and the like. Reason then, theoretically, filters the information you read, given also what you know at the time. Abstract reading, again, can help one learn *how to think* rather than just *what to think*. This works against social engineering, which is the problem for the status quo.

As it relates to "training" again, there is a huge difference in training and education, which is not necessarily equal to what it means to "know" something, as I've mentioned before. Many interpret training and education as one and the same, as they do with knowledge and authority. This is a huge intellectual mistake. Training generally instructs one in what to think, coupled with certain skills that are necessary for certain "jobs," where by *like* thinking, or *group think* is necessary. Education is generally individualistic and allows for personal rebuttal and critical inquiry of sources via interpreting evidence, fact checking and argumentation. Education does not necessarily mean that one must have a degree from a university either. Such thinking is usually conditioned and prerequisite upon the "business model" attached to modern education, which is also "formal" education. Education also comes by way of individual study and determination to know the truth about something. Just look at the great minds of history. In today's world, most of the great thinkers in the past may very likely be considered "uneducated" in the formal sense because their learning did not derive from an established university, or in today's context, an "accredited university," which is utterly stupid to assume. Great minds in history were generally self-taught. So for example, if you want to know what your rights are and how to defend them, you must study them out, on your own. Public and formal education will not teach you this. Training will not teach you this. You have to study the history of governments that have and do oppress people's rights. Study the philosophers that argued for rights, like Locke, and against them, like Hobbes. Study the founders, the federalist papers, the anti-federalist papers, the state ratification debates, and the Declaration of Independence. Read lots of case law. Read the Constitution. Don't just read them, study them. Moreover, study out the varying views on whatever subject matter appeals to you. Read and study out arguments from various legislative assemblies, and the like. Don't take someone's word for it. Too many people take for granted that what they are "taught" is correct, simply by the "status" of whoever is "teaching" them something. This can be a double-edged sword. Read history, philosophy, the sciences, the arts, and the like, on your own, daily. Real education takes hard work. You don't have to spend thousands of dollars to be "educated." That is ludicrous. Learning what to think takes memorization, faith in what instructors tell you and obedience to a particular source of information, generally. Self-education is also an act of faith, but to a higher degree, and absent absolute subservience to a particular source, in its rawest sense. Knowledge gained by self-education develops into more self-reliance and independence than does mere knowledge from training or formal education. Most importantly, avoid constant TV as a method of learning how to be. Too many people think their own life should mimic a sitcom. And, many people do mimic their life after a sitcom, as though such *memes* are reality. This distorts perspective. TV is not reality, it is entertainment. What ever happened to the Socratic method within daily life? The Socratic method can be applied to any profession that is based upon training alone. Once such a method is then actualized, the unemployment line may become the context of your next question. Trust me, I "know."

As it relates to law enforcement, and for anyone else actually, one should try to encompass all of formal education, training and self-education. The question is, will one ultimately make decisions on what one "knows" or by what one is "trained" to do? The fundamental *right of conscious* and one's personal convictions are by and large founded upon what one "knows," and/or "believes" to be the "truth." It is ultimately sentimental in nature. Job security and liability are determined usually by what one is trained to do. Such an understanding between the differences in education and training can help lead to more competent law enforcement, whereby the exercise and discernment of constitutional conscientiousness secures people's fundamental liberties, upholds both the spirit and letter of the Constitution, while avoiding the "taken for grantedness" of the unconscious complicity with the other two branches of government by superiors. This complicity chips away at fundamental liberties, even for the officer. The officer holds a right of conscious, for example. These acts within the enforcement of law, in and of themselves, are also revolutionary acts necessary to undo the effects of silent encroachments.

Number nine; develop multiple sources of income. The reality is, if you are not wealthy, income is necessary to simply exist in today's society. You got to have one, two or three incomes today, or you don't eat. The entire legal system is predicated upon forced economic activity and manipulated monetary valuation. So think of multiple incomes as blending with the system's attack on you, coupled with other revolutionary acts. Multiple incomes can be revolutionary because you stay clear of needing government help when things get tight. Most of my cop buddies have multiple sources of income. My other source of income was and is teaching martial arts. The fact is today, a single income is no longer reasonable or financially feasible because of inflation and the increase of taxation, especially for a middle class family. The truth of the matter is, in America, currency is King. The rule of law now answers to the King. All educational institutions and corporations answer to the King. All government legislation and bureaucracy is designed to serve and enforce the will of the King. We all must answer to the King or become peasants on the street, sadly so. How does one develop multiple sources of income? Depends on one's level of innovation and ambition. Moreover, try to develop sources of income that take less government intrusion. Secondary and further sources of income do not necessarily have to involve certification and/or bureaucracy. That just gets more government involved. The goal is to stay clear of government involvement. So for example, most of my cop friends who have other sources of income encompass work like cutting grass, power washing, detailing cars, cleaning gutters, wood work, private security, DJ-ing, and the like. None of these require any bureaucratic micromanagement, at least not where I am.

Number ten; avoid contracts, or legal agreements, at all possible costs. This is very difficult to do. Contracts kill self-reliance. Contracts restrict innovation and especially ambition. Contracts bleed one of their self-ownership and one's control over property, as it relates to the terms of a contract. Contracts also entrap people into blocks of time that ultimately end in someone *else's* benefit. "Agreements" today saturate modern life, with every single turn one makes. Whether it is with a credit card, getting cable, registering property, leasing a new cell phone, buying a vehicle, getting a job, getting a formal education, going to the gym, downloading software, renting an apartment, and virtually anything else you want to do in life today involves a contract, an "agreement," some way or another. Contracts are consent to surrender something in exchange for something else, but on someone *else's* terms. For example, when you renew your cell phone, ask to negotiate a few of the terms within the contract. Good luck with that. If you do decide to consent to a contract or agreement in exchange for something, be smart about it. These types of mistakes can haunt you for a long time, and drain you of income and personal freedoms. An equity line comes to mind. Avoid contracts at all costs.

Unfortunately, there are some contracts you that cannot avoid, however. A 1040 is an example, because income is no longer absolute private property, but Federal Reserve property. A contract in buying a home or renting an apartment is another example, because you must have somewhere to sleep. Sadly, a place to sleep in today's America is no longer absolute property either, because there is always a cost attached, whether you "own" or rent, which takes income. See the design? The only real way to avoid forced economic activity is to be homeless and don't eat, and even now this is "illegal." Good luck. Like I've mentioned before, refuge from government intrusion and sanctuary from brutish poverty are secured within absolute property ownership, not in welfare, subsidies, entitlements or policy. How do we get this back?

The End Game

If the people in mass don't do something about all the aforementioned, I believe the end game of this new Oligarchy in America will become a complete technologically based, financial and social control grid, over every single individual, whereby all rights have been converted into legal privileges. Society will divide further into good and bad people. The "good" people will be those who accept and encourage this grid, while the "bad" people will be those who work against it. All this in the name of "progress," "public safety," and "law and order." This grid will exist under the boot of this *new style* of law enforcement, which only operates by policy rather than by founding principles and by actual Law. As this new America continues to take place, slowly through silent entrapments and the *reinterpretation* of the US Constitution, America will also become a third world country because extreme poverty is sharply on the rise, as reported in a new study by the National Poverty Center. This study, *Rising Extreme Poverty in the United States and the Response of Federal Means-Tested Transfer Programs*, authored by Kathryn Endin of Harvard University and H. Luke Shaefer of the University of Michigan, infer that,

> "As of mid-2011, about 1.65 million households with about 3.55 million children were surviving on $2 or less in cash income per person per day in a given month. ... Households in extreme poverty constituted 4.3 percent of all non-elderly households with children. The prevalence of extreme poverty rose sharply between 1996 and 2011, with the highest growth rates found among groups most affected by the 1996 welfare reform.... The descriptive analyses presented here cannot clarify the exact causal mechanisms that have led to such a sharp uptick in extreme poverty in the U.S."[40]

Even though this study reveals that this *new style* (neo) of social and financial life in America is on the rise, the authors admit that "causal mechanisms" cannot be clarified. I believe the "causal mechanisms" are, in part, due to the progressive transition of America first from a republic into a democracy, following the Civil War, now neo-progressively transforming into an oligarchy. This latter transition from democracy into oligarchy has taken place in America at the guidance of neo-progressive policies aimed at utopian like ideology; forced fairness, that directly undermines both the letter and spirit of the founders' Constitution. Moreover, and in the spirit of this book, all this has come about because our law enforcement has been heavily taken for granted as "the gun in the room." Absent the exploitation of those who utilize the government's monopoly on violence within the legal system, such transitions in American government may not have ever taken place. The only recourse now is smart revolution. Starve the beast. The beast's diet is state dependency, social and political control, the manipulation of currency, and the theft and destruction of property, including self-ownership.

It's only going to get worse. One reason is, expatriatism is on the rise. Sadly so. More and more people, including big corporations, are renouncing their US Citizenship and leaving the country. Why? The Casey Research Institute infers in an essay entitled, *Corporations Join Droves Renouncing US Citizenship* that this renouncing of citizenship is because, "The US has the highest effective corporate tax rate in the developed world."[41] Nick Giambruno, the author, also writes that, "While the US should be enacting policies that make it attractive for productive people and companies to come to the US—rather than driving them away—don't hold your breath for positive change. It's more likely that nothing but more taxes and regulations are coming." With more taxes and more regulations comes more exploited, arbitrary violence necessary to enforce same.

I would like to end this book with one final example of the exploitation of law enforcement by the legal system. While attending a public, City Commission meeting in Florida, one man remained seated while everyone else stood for the pledge of allegiance. The Mayor then told the man to either stand or leave. The man remained seated. The Mayor then asked the Chief of Police to physically remove the man from the public meeting, which the cop did.[42] Where is the problem and who broke the law? The mayor and the cop both exist and work within the Executive Branch. Does not *concurrent review* work also within one branch itself? Absolutely.

The Mayor and the Chief both broke the law and violated their Oaths to uphold the Constitution by using arbitrary force to remove the man from the meeting, thus violating his 1st Amendment right to free speech and free assembly. Period. This arbitrary force, in response to no real crime, defense of self, or of another, followed failed attempts to also forcefully coerce the man from exercising his 1st Amendment right. It is any individual's free choice not to participate in the pledge of allegiance.

My personal pet peeve here is that the cop should have "known" better, but then blindly removes the man at the Mayor's request. Why? Did the Mayor "take for granted" that the cop would follow his orders? The cop should have "knowingly" refused to remove the man as a way to "protect" the man's right, as he swore to do. Job security and the Mayor being his "boss" is not a legitimate reason to violate the man's rights. We can easily go back in history and look at the excuses of "following orders."

I want to close with a quote from David Hume, whom has had the most profound impact on my own life, philosophically. As it relates to morality and its connection to actual "crime," of which any rule of law should be quintessentially founded upon, Hume answers the question, "From what source, reason or sentiment, is the action or character trait of another considered either good or bad?"

> "Reason judges either of matter of fact or of relations. Inquire then first, where is that matter of fact which we hear called crime? Point it out. Determine the time of its existence, describe its essence or nature. Explain the sense or faculty to which it discovers itself. It resides in the mind of the person who is ungrateful. He must therefore feel it and be conscious of it. But nothing is there except the passion of ill will or absolute indifference. You cannot say that these of themselves always and in all circumstances are crimes. No. There only crimes when directed towards persons who have before expressed and displayed good will towards us. Consequently we may infer that the crime of ingratitude is not any particular individual fact. But arises from a complication of circumstances, which being presented to the spectator excites the sentiment of blame by the particular structure and fabric of his mind."[43]

Did the man who refused to stand for the pledge actually commit a crime, or did the act of not standing for the pledge incite a sentimental or a reasonable response in the mayor, who then used his power to exploit the officer's "legal" use of force? Or, was this merely being offended? And there in lies the problem of incompetence. In the case of *Cops vs. the Constitution*, should the government have the right to an appeal?

The Declaration of Independence

The Unanimous Declaration of the Thirteen United States of America
In Congress, July 4, 1776

When in the Course of human events, it becomes necessary for one people to dissolve the political bands which have connected them with another, and to assume among the powers of the earth, the separate and equal station to which the Laws of Nature and of Nature's God entitle them, a decent respect to the opinions of mankind requires that they should declare the causes which impel them to the separation.

We hold these truths to be self-evident, that all men are created equal; that they are endowed by their Creator with certain unalienable rights; that among these are Life, Liberty, and the pursuit of Happiness; that, to secure these rights, governments are instituted among Men, deriving their just powers from the consent of the governed; that whenever any form of government becomes destructive of these ends, it is the right of the people to alter or to abolish it, and to institute new government, laying its foundation on such principles, and organizing its powers in such form, as to them shall seem most likely to effect their safety and happiness. Prudence, indeed, will dictate that governments long established should not be changed for light and transient causes; and accordingly all experience hath shown that mankind are more disposed to suffer, while evils are sufferable than to right themselves by abolishing the forms to which they are accustomed. But when a long train of abuses and usurpations, pursuing invariably the same object, evinces a design to reduce them under absolute despotism, it is their right, it is their duty, to throw off such government, and to provide new guards for their future security. Such has been the patient sufferance of these colonies; and such is now the necessity which constrains them to alter their former systems of government. The history of the present King of Great Britain is a history of repeated injuries and usurpations, all having in direct object the establishment of an absolute tyranny over these states. To prove this, let facts be submitted to a candid world.

He has refused his assent to laws, the most wholesome and necessary for the public good.

He has forbidden his governors to pass laws of immediate and pressing importance, unless suspended in their operation till his assent should be obtained; and, when so suspended, he has utterly neglected to attend to them.

He has refused to pass other laws for the accommodation of large districts of people, unless those people would relinquish the right of representation in the legislature, a right inestimable to them, and formidable to tyrants only.

He has called together legislative bodies at places unusual uncomfortable, and distant from the depository of their public records, for the sole purpose of fatiguing them into compliance with his measures.

He has dissolved representative houses repeatedly, for opposing, with manly firmness, his invasions on the rights of the people.

He has refused for a long time, after such dissolutions, to cause others to be elected; whereby the legislative powers, incapable of annihilation, have returned to the people at large for their exercise; the state remaining, in the mean time, exposed to all the dangers of invasions from without and convulsions within.

He has endeavored to prevent the population of these states; for that purpose obstructing the laws for naturalization of foreigners; refusing to pass others to encourage their migration hither, and raising the conditions of new appropriations of lands.

He has obstructed the administration of justice, by refusing his assent to laws for establishing judiciary powers.

He has made judges dependent on his will alone, for the tenure of their offices, and the amount and payment of their salaries.

He has erected a multitude of new offices, and sent hither swarms of officers to harass our people and eat out their substance.

He has kept among us, in times of peace, standing armies, without the consent of our legislatures.

He has affected to render the military independent of, and superior to, the civil power.

He has combined with others to subject us to a jurisdiction foreign to our Constitution and unacknowledged by our laws, giving his assent to their acts of pretended legislation:

For quartering large bodies of armed troops among us;

For protecting them, by a mock trial, from punishment for any murders which they should commit on the inhabitants of these states;

For cutting off our trade with all parts of the world;

For imposing taxes on us without our consent;

For depriving us, in many cases, of the benefits of trial by jury;

For transporting us beyond seas, to be tried for pretended offenses;

For abolishing the free system of English laws in a neighboring province, establishing therein an arbitrary government, and enlarging its boundaries, so as to render it at once an example and fit instrument for introducing the same absolute rule into these colonies;

For taking away our charters, abolishing our most valuable laws, and altering fundamentally the forms of our governments;

For suspending our own legislatures, and declaring themselves invested with power to legislate for us in all cases whatsoever.

He has abdicated government here, by declaring us out of his protection and waging war against us.

He has plundered our seas, ravaged our coasts, burned our towns, and destroyed the lives of our people.

He is at this time transporting large armies of foreign mercenaries to complete the works of death, desolation, and tyranny already begun with circumstances of cruelty and perfidy scarcely paralleled in the most barbarous ages, and totally unworthy the head of a civilized nation.

He has constrained our fellow-citizens, taken captive on the high seas, to bear arms against their country, to become the executioners of their friends and brethren, or to fall themselves by their hands.

He has excited domestic insurrection among us, and has endeavored to bring on the inhabitants of our frontiers the merciless Indian savages, whose known rule of warfare is an undistinguished destruction of all ages, sexes, and conditions.

In every stage of these oppressions we have petitioned for redress in the most humble terms; our repeated petitions have been answered only by repeated injury. A prince, whose character is thus marked by every act which may define a tyrant, is unfit to be the ruler of a free people.

Nor have we been wanting in our attentions to our British brethren. We have warned them, from time to time, of attempts by their legislature to extend an unwarrantable jurisdiction over us. We have reminded them of the circumstances of our emigration and settlement here. We have appealed to their native justice and magnanimity; and we have conjured them, by the ties of our common kindred, to disavow these usurpations which would inevitably interrupt our connections and correspondence. They too, have been deaf to the voice of justice and of consanguinity. We must, therefore, acquiesce in the necessity which denounces our separation, and hold them as we hold the rest of mankind, enemies in war, in peace friends.

WE, THEREFORE, the REPRESENTATIVES of the UNITED STATES OF AMERICA, in General Congress assembled, appealing to the Supreme Judge of the world for the rectitude of our intentions, do, in the name and by the authority of the good people of these colonies solemnly publish and declare, That these United Colonies are, and of right ought to be, FREE AND INDEPENDENT STATES; that they are absolved from all allegiance to the British crown and that all political connection between them and the state of Great Britain is, and ought to be, totally dissolved; and that, as free and independent states, they have full power to levy war, conclude peace, contract alliances, establish commerce, and do all other acts and things which independent states may of right do. And for the support of this declaration, with a firm reliance on the protection of Divine Providence, we mutually pledge to each other our Lives, our Fortunes, and our sacred Honor.

THE CONSTITUTION OF THE UNITED STATES
AS ORIGINALLY ADOPTED

We, the people of the United States, in order to form a more perfect union, establish justice, ensure domestic tranquility, provide for the common defence, promote the general welfare, and secure the blessings of liberty to ourselves and our posterity, do ordain and establish this constitution for the United States of America.

ARTICLE 1

SECTION 1.

1. All legislative powers herein granted shall be vested in a Congress of the United States, which shall consist of a Senate and House of Representatives.

SECTION 2.

1. The House of Representatives shall be composed of members chosen every second year by the people of the several States; and the electors in each State shall have the qualifications requisite for electors of the most numerous branch of the State Legislature.

2. No person shall be a Representative who shall not have attained to the age of twenty-five years, and been seven years a citizen of the United States, and who shall not, when elected, be an inhabitant of that State in which he shall be chosen.

3. Representatives and direct taxes shall be apportioned among the several States which may be included within this Union, according to their respective numbers, which shall be determined by adding to the whole number of free persons, including those bound to service for a term of years, and excluding Indians not taxed, three-fifths of all other persons. The actual enumeration shall be made within three years after the first meeting of the Congress of the United States, and within every subsequent term of ten years, in such manner as they shall by each State shall have at least one Representative; and until such enumeration shall be made, the State of New Hampshire shall be entitled to choose three; Massachusetts eight, Rhode Island and Providence Plantations one; Connecticut five; New York six; New Jersey four; Pennsylvania eight, Delaware one; Maryland six; Virginia ten; North Carolina five; South Carolina five; and Georgia three.

4. When vacancies happen in the representation from any State, the executive authority thereof shall issue writs of election to fill such vacancies.

5. The House of Representatives shall choose their Speaker, and other officers, and shall have the sole power of impeachment.

SECTION 3.

1. The Senate of the United States shall be composed of two Senators from each State, chosen by the Legislature thereof, for six years; and each Senator shall have one vote.

2. Immediately after they shall be assembled in consequence of the first election, they shall be divided, as equally as may be, into three classes. The

seats of the Senators of the first class shall be vacated at the expiration of the second year, of the second class at the expiration of the fourth year, and of the third class at the expiration of the sixth year, so that one-third may be chosen every second year; and if vacancies happen, by resignation or otherwise, during the recess of the Legislature of any State, the Executive thereof may make temporary appointments until the next meeting of the Legislature, which shall then fill such vacancies.

3. No person shall be a Senator who shall not have attained to the age of thirty years, and been nine years a citizen of the United States, and who shall not, when elected, be an inhabitant of that State for which he shall be chosen.

4. The Vice President of the United States shall be President of the Senate, but shall have no vote, unless they be equally divided.

5. The Senate shall choose their other officers, and also a President *pro tempore,* in the absence of the Vice President, or when he shall exercise the office of President of the United States.

6. The Senate shall have the sole power to try all impeachments. When sitting for that purpose, they shall be on oath or affirmation. When the President of the United States is tried, the Chief Justice shall preside; and no person shall be convicted without the concurrence of two-thirds of the members present.

7. Judgment in cases of impeachment shall not extend further than to removal from office, and disqualification to hold and enjoy any office of honor, trust, or profit, under the United States; but the party convicted shall

nevertheless be liable and subject to indictment, trial, judgment, and punishment, according to law.

SECTION 4.

1. The times, places, and manner of holding elections for Senators and Representatives, shall be prescribed in each State by the Legislature thereof, but the Congress may, at any time, by law, make or alter such regulations, except as to the places of choosing Senators.

2. The Congress shall assemble at least once in every year, and such meeting shall be on the first Monday in December, unless they shall by law appoint a different day.

SECTION 5.

1. Each House shall be the judge of the elections, returns, and qualifications of its own members; and a majority of each shall constitute a quorum to do business; but a smaller number may adjourn from day to day, and may be authorized to compel the attendance of absent members, in such manner, and under such penalties, as each House may provide.

2. Each House may determine the rules of its proceedings, punish its members for disorderly behavior, and, with the concurrence of two-thirds, expel a member.

3. Each House shall keep a journal of its proceedings, and from time to time publish the same, excepting such parts as may in their judgment require secrecy; and the yeas and nays of the members of either House, on any question, shall, at the desire of one-fifth of those present, be entered on the journal.

4. Neither House, during the session of Congress, shall, without the consent of the other, adjourn to more than three days, nor to any other place than that in which the two Houses shall be sitting.

SECTION 6.

1. The Senators and Representatives shall receive a compensation for their services, to be ascertained by law, and paid out of the treasury of the United States. They shall, in all cases, except treason, felony, and breach of the peace, be privileged from arrest during their attendance at the session of their respective Houses, and in going to or returning from the same; and for any speech or debate in either House, they shall not be questioned in any other place.

2. No Senator or Representative shall, during the time for which he was elected, be appointed to any civil office under the authority of the United States, which shall have been created, or the emoluments whereof shall have been increased during such time; and no person holding any office under the United States shall be a member of either House during his continuance in office.

SECTION 7.

1. All bills for raising revenue shall originate in the House of Representatives; but the Senate may propose or concur with amendments, as on other bills.

2. Every bill which shall have passed the House of Representatives and the Senate shall, before it becomes a law, be presented to the President of the United States; if he approve, he shall sign it; but if not, he shall return it, with his objections, to that House in which it shall have originated, who

shall enter the objections at large on their journal, and proceed to reconsider it. If, after such reconsideration, two-thirds of that House shall agree to pass the bill, it shall be sent, together with the objections, to the other House, it shall become a law. But in all such cases the votes of both Houses shall be determined by yeas and nays, and the names of the person voting for and against the bill shall be entered on the journal of each House respectively. If any bill shall not be returned by the President within ten days (Sundays excepted) after it shall have been presented to him, the same shall be a law in like manner as if he had signed it, unless the Congress by their adjournment prevent its return, in which case it shall not be a law.

3. Every order, resolution, or vote, to which the concurrence of the Senate and House of Representatives may be necessary, (except on a question of adjournment,) shall be presented to the President of the United States; and before the same shall take effect, shall be approved by him, or, being disapproved by him, shall be repassed by two-thirds of the Senate and House of Representatives, according to the rules and limitations prescribed in the case of a bill.

SECTION 8.

The Congress shall have power--

1. To lay and collect taxes, duties, imposts, and excises, to pay the debts, and provide for the common defence and general welfare of the United States; but all duties, imposts, and excises, shall be uniform throughout the United States:

2. To borrow money on the credit of the United States:

3. To regulate commerce with foreign nations, and among the several States, and with the Indian tribes:

4. To establish an uniform rule of naturalization, and uniform laws on the subject of bankruptcies throughout the United States:

5. To coin money, regulate the value thereof, and of foreign coin, and fix the standard of weights and measures:

6. To provide for the punishment of counterfeiting the securities and current coin of the United States:

7. To establish post offices and post roads:

8. To promote the progress of science and useful arts, by securing, for limited times, to authors and inventors, the exclusive right to their respective writings and discoveries:

9. To constitute tribunals inferior to the Supreme Court; to define and punish piracies and felonies committed on the high seas, and offences against the law of nations:

10. To declare war, grant letters of marque and reprisal, and make rules concerning captures on land water:

11. To raise and support armies; but no appropriation of money to that use shall be for a longer term than two years:

12. To provide and maintain a navy:

13. To make rules for the government and regulation of the land and naval forces:

14. To provide for calling forth the militia to execute the laws of the Union, suppress insurrections, and repel invasions:

15. To provide for organizing, arming, and disciplining the militia, and for governing such part of them as may be employed in the service of the United States, reserving to the States respectively the appointment of the officers, and the authority of training the militia according to the discipline prescribed by Congress:

16. To exercise exclusive legislation in all cases whatsoever, over such district (not exceeding ten miles square) as may, by cession of particular States, and the acceptance of Congress, become the seat of Government of the United States, and to exercise like authority over all places purchased, by the consent of the Legislature of the State in which the same shall be, for the erection of forts, magazines, arsenals, dockyards, and other needful buildings: and

17. To make all laws which shall be necessary and proper for carrying into execution the foregoing powers, and all other powers vested by this constitution in the Government of the United States, or in any department or office thereof.

SECTION 9.

1. The migration or importation of such persons as any of the States now existing shall think proper to admit, shall not be prohibited by the Congress prior to the year one thousand eight hundred and eight; but a tax or duty may be imposed on such importation, not exceeding ten dollars for each person.

2. The privilege of the writ of habeas corpus shall not be suspended, unless when, in cases of rebellion or invasion, the public safety may require it.

3. No bill of attainder, or *ex post facto* law, shall be passed.

4. No capitation or other direct tax shall be laid, unless in proportion to the census or enumeration hereinbefore directed to be taken.

5. No tax or duty shall be laid on articles exported from any State; no preference shall be given by any regulation of commerce or revenue to the ports of one State over those of another; nor shall vessels bound to or from one State be obliged to enter, clear, or pay duties in another.

6. No money shall be drawn from the treasury, but in consequence of appropriations made by law; and a regular statement and account of the receipts and expenditures of all public money shall be published from time to time.

7. No title of nobility shall be granted by the United States, and no person holding any office of profit or trust under them shall, without the consent of the Congress, accept of any present, emolument, office, or title of any kind whatever, from any King, Prince, or foreign State.

SECTION 10.

1. No State shall enter into any treaty, alliance, or confederation; grant letters of marque and reprisal; coin money; emit bills of credit; make any thing but gold and silver coin a tender in payment of debts; pass any bill of attainder, *ex post facto* law, or law impairing the obligation of contracts; or grant any title of nobility.

2. No State shall, without the consent of the Congress, lay any imposts or duties on imports or exports, except what may be absolutely necessary for executing its inspection laws; and the net produce of all duties and imposts laid by any State on imports or exports, shall be for the use of the treasury of the United States, and such laws shall be subject to the revision and control of the Congress. No State shall, without the consent of Congress, lay any duty of tonnage, keep troops or ships of war in time of peace, enter into any agreement or compact with another State, or with a foreign Power, or engage in war, unless actually invaded, or in such imminent danger as will not admit of delay.

ARTICLE II

SECTION 1.

1. The executive power shall be vested in a President of the United States of America. He shall hold his office during the term of four years, and, together with the Vice President, chosen for the same term, be elected as follows:

2. Each State shall appoint, in such manner as the Legislature thereof may direct, a number of electors, equal to the whole number of Senators and Representatives to which the State may be entitled in the Congress; but no

Senator or Representative, or person holding an office of trust or profit under the United States, shall be appointed an elector.

3. The electors shall meet in their respective States, and vote by ballot for two persons, of whom one at least shall not be an inhabitant of the same State with themselves. And they shall make a list of all the persons voted for, and of the number of votes for each; which list they shall sign and certify, and transmit sealed to the seat of the Government of the United States, directed to the President of the Senate. The President of the Senate shall, in the presence of the Senate and House of Representatives, open all the certificates, and the votes shall then be counted. The person having the greatest number of votes shall be the President, if such number be a majority of the whole number of electors appointed; and if there be more than one who have such majority, and have an equal number of votes, then the House of Representatives shall immediately choose, by ballot, one of them for President; and if no person have a majority, then from the five highest on the list the said House shall, in like manner, choose the President. But, in choosing the President, the votes shall be taken by States, the representation from each two-thirds of the States, and a majority of all the States shall be necessary to a choice. In every case, af ter the choice of the President, the person having the greatest number of votes of the electors shall be the Vice President. But if there should remain two or more who have equal votes, the Senate shall choose from them, by ballot, the Vice President.

4. The Congress may determine the time of choosing the electors, and the day on which they shall give their votes; which day shall be the same throughout the United States.

5. No person, except a natural born citizen, or a citizen of the United States at the time of the adoption of this constitution, shall be eligible to the office of President; neither shall any person be eligible to that office who shall not have attained to the age of thirty-five years, and been fourteen years a resident within the United States.

6. In case of the removal of the President from office, or of his death, resignation, or inability to discharge the powers and duties of the said office, the same shall devolve on the Vice President; and the Congress may, by law, provide for the case of removal, death, resignation, or inability, both of the President and Vice President, declaring what officer shall then act as President; and such officer shall act accordingly until the disability be removed, or a President shall be elected.

7. The President shall, at stated times, receive for his services a compensation, which shall neither be increased nor diminished during the period for which he shall have been elected, and he shall not receive within that period any other emolument from the United States, or any of them.

8. Before he enter on the execution of his office, he shall take the following oath or affirmation:

9. "I do solemnly swear (or affirm) that I will faithfully execute the office of President of the United States, and will, to the best of my ability, preserve, protect, and defend the constitution of the United States."

SECTION 2.

1. The President shall be commander-in-chief of the army and navy of the United States, and of the militia of the several States when called into the actual service of the United States; he may require the opinion, in writing, of the principal officer in each of the executive departments, upon any subject relating to the duties of their respective offices; and he shall have power to grant reprieves and pardons for offences against the United States, except in cases of impeachment.

2. He shall have power, by and with the advice and consent of the Senate, to make treaties, provided two-thirds of the Senators present concur; and he shall nominate, and, by and with the advice and consent of the Senate, shall appoint ambassadors, other public ministers, and consuls, judges of the Supreme Court, and all other officers of the United States whose appointments are not herein otherwise provided for, and which shall be established by law. But the Congress may, by law, vest the appointment of such inferior officers as they think proper in the President alone, in the courts of law, or in the heads of departments.

3. The President shall have power to fill up all vacancies that may happen during the recess of the Senate, by granting commissions which shall expire at the end of their next session.

SECTION 3.

1. He shall, from time to time, give to the Congress information of the state of the Union, and recommend to their consideration such measures as he shall judge necessary and expedient; he may, on extraordinary occasions, convene both Houses, or either of them, and, in case of disagreement between them, with respect to the time of adjournment, he may adjourn

them to such time as he shall think proper; he shall receive ambassadors and other public ministers; he shall take care that the laws be faithfully executed; and shall commission all the officers of the United States.

SECTION 4.

1. The President, Vice President, and all civil officers of the United States, shall be removed from office on impeachment for, and conviction of, treason, bribery, or other high crimes and misdemeanors.

ARTICLE III

SECTION 1.

1. The judicial power of the United States shall be vested in one Supreme Court, and in such inferior courts as the Congress may from time to time ordain and establish. The judges both of the Supreme and inferior courts, shall hold their offices during good behavior; and shall, at stated times, receive for their services a compensation which shall not be diminished during their continuance in office.

SECTION 2.

1. The judicial power shall extend to all cases in law and equity arising under the constitution, the laws of the United States, and treaties made, or which shall be made, under their authority; to all cases affecting ambassadors, other public ministers, and consuls; to all cases of admiralty and maritime jurisdiction; to controversies to which the United States shall be a party; to controversies between two or more States; between a State and citizens of another State, between citizens of different States, between citizens of the same State claiming lands under grants of different States, and between a State, or the citizens thereof, and foreign States, citizens, or

subjects.

2. In all cases affecting ambassadors, other public ministers and consuls, and those in which a State shall be a party, the Supreme Court shall have original jurisdiction. In all the other cases before mentioned the Supreme Court shall have appellate jurisdiction, both as to law and fact, with such exceptions, and under such regulations, as the Congress shall make.

3. The trial of all crimes, except in cases of impeachment, shall be by jury, and such trial shall be held in the State where the said crimes shall have been committed; but when not committed within any State, the trial shall be at such place or places as the Congress may by law have directed.

SECTION 3.

1. Treason against the United States shall consist only in levying war against them, or in adhering to their enemies, giving them aid and comfort. No person shall be convicted of treason unless on the testimony of two witnesses to the same overt act, or on confession in open court.

2. The Congress shall have power to declare the punishment of treason; but no attainder of treason shall work corruption of blood, or forfeiture, except during the life of the person attainted.

ARTICLE IV

SECTION 1.

1. Full faith and credit shall be given in each State to the public acts, records, and judicial proceedings of every other State. And the Congress

may, by general laws, prescribe the manner in which such acts, records, and proceedings shall be proved, and the effect thereof.

SECTION 2.

1. The citizens of each State shall be entitled to all privileges and immunities of citizens in the several States.

2. A person charged in any State with treason, felony, or other crime, who shall flee from justice and be found in another State, shall, on demand of the executive authority of the State from which he fled, be delivered up, to be removed to the State having jurisdiction of the crime.

3. No person held to service or labor in one State under the laws thereof, escaping into another, shall, in consequence of any law or regulation therein, be discharged from such service or labor; but shall be delivered up on claim of the party to whom such service or labor may be due.

SECTION 3.

1. New States may be admitted by the Congress into this Union; but no new State shall be formed or erected within the jurisdiction of any other State, nor any State be formed by the junction of two or more States, or parts of States, without the consent of the Legislatures of the States concerned, as well as of the Congress.

2. The Congress shall have power to dispose of, and make all needful rules and regulations respecting the territory or other property belonging to the United States; and nothing in this constitution shall be so construed as to prejudice any claims of the United States, or of any particular State.

SECTION 4.

1. The United States shall guaranty to every State in this Union a republican form of Government, and shall protect each of them against invasion; and, on application of the Legislature, or of the Executive, (when the Legislature cannot be convened), against domestic violence.

ARTICLE V

1. The Congress, whenever two-thirds of both Houses shall deem it necessary, shall propose amendments to this constitution; or, on the application of the Legislatures of two-thirds of the several States, shall call a convention for proposing amendments, which, in either case, shall be valid to all intents and purposes as part of this constitution, when ratified by the Legislatures of three-fourths of the several States, or by conventions in three-fourths thereof, as the one or the other mode of ratification may be proposed by the Congress: *Provided*, That no amendment which may be made prior to the year one thousand eight hundred and eight, shall in any manner affect the first and fourth clauses in the ninth section of the first article; and that no State, without its consent, shall be deprived of its equal suffrage in the Senate.

ARTICLE VI

1. All debts contracted, and engagements entered into, before the adoption of this constitution, shall be as valid against the United States under this constitution as under the confederation.

2. This constitution, and the laws of the United States which shall be made in pursuance thereof, and all treaties made, or which shall be made, under the authority of the United States, shall be the supreme law of the land; and the judges in every State shall be bound thereby, any thing in the constitution or laws of any State to the contrary notwithstanding.

3. The Senators and Representatives before mentioned, and the members of the several State Legislatures, and all executive and judicial officers, both of the United States and of the several States, shall be bound by oath or affirmation to support this constitution; but no religious test shall ever be required as a qualification to any office or public trust under the United States.

ARTICLE VII

1. The ratification of the conventions of nine States shall be sufficient for the establishment of this constitution between the States so ratifying the same.

Done in Convention, by the unanimous consent of the States present, the seventeenth day September, in the year of our Lord one thousand seven hundred and eighty-seven, and of the independence of the United States of America the twelfth. In witness whereof we have hereunto subscribed our names.

Bill of Rights

PREAMBLE

Congress of the United States begun and held at the City of New-York, on Wednesday the fourth of March, one thousand seven hundred and eighty nine.

THE Conventions of a number of the States, having at the time of their adopting the Constitution, expressed a desire, in order to prevent misconstruction or abuse of its powers, that further declaratory and restrictive clauses should be added: And as extending the ground of public confidence in the Government, will best ensure the beneficent ends of its institution.

RESOLVED by the Senate and House of Representatives of the United States of America, in Congress assembled, two thirds of both Houses concurring, that the following Articles be proposed to the Legislatures of the several States, as amendments to the Constitution of the United States, all, or any of which Articles, when ratified by three fourths of the said Legislatures, to be valid to all intents and purposes, as part of the said Constitution; viz.

ARTICLES in addition to, and Amendment of the Constitution of the United States of America, proposed by Congress, and ratified by the Legislatures of the several States, pursuant to the fifth Article of the original Constitution.

Amendment I

Congress shall make no law respecting an establishment of religion, or prohibiting the free exercise thereof; or abridging the freedom of speech, or of the press; or the right of the people peaceably to assemble, and to petition the government for a redress of grievances.

Amendment II

A well regulated militia, being necessary to the security of a free state, the right of the people to keep and bear arms, shall not be infringed.

Amendment III

No soldier shall, in time of peace be quartered in any house, without the consent of the owner, nor in time of war, but in a manner to be prescribed by law.

Amendment IV

The right of the people to be secure in their persons, houses, papers, and effects, against unreasonable searches and seizures, shall not be violated, and no warrants shall issue, but upon probable cause, supported by oath or affirmation, and particularly describing the place to be searched, and the persons or things to be seized.

Amendment V

No person shall be held to answer for a capital, or otherwise infamous crime, unless on a presentment or indictment of a grand jury, except in cases arising in the land or naval forces, or in the militia, when in actual service in time of war or public danger; nor shall any person be subject for the same offense to be twice put in jeopardy of life or limb; nor shall be compelled in any criminal case to be a witness against himself, nor be deprived of life, liberty, or property, without due process of law; nor shall private property be taken for public use, without just compensation.

Amendment VI

In all criminal prosecutions, the accused shall enjoy the right to a speedy and public trial, by an impartial jury of the state and district wherein the crime shall have been committed, which district shall have been previously ascertained by law, and to be informed of the nature and cause of the accusation; to be confronted with the witnesses against him; to have compulsory process for obtaining witnesses in his favor, and to have the assistance of counsel for his defense.

Amendment VII

In suits at common law, where the value in controversy shall exceed twenty dollars, the right of trial by jury shall be preserved, and no fact tried by a jury, shall be otherwise reexamined in any court of the United States, than according to the rules of the common law.

Amendment VIII

Excessive bail shall not be required, nor excessive fines imposed, nor cruel and unusual punishments inflicted.

Amendment IX

The enumeration in the Constitution, of certain rights, shall not be construed to deny or disparage others retained by the people.

Amendment X

The powers not delegated to the United States by the Constitution, nor prohibited by it to the states, are reserved to the states respectively, or to the people.

End Notes

Chapter 1

[1] Thomas Hobbes, *Leviathan*

[2] Thomas Hobbes, *Leviathan*

[3] Thomas Hobbes, *Leviathan*

[4] Thomas Hobbes, *Leviathan*

[5] Thomas Hobbes, *Of Man, Being the First Part of Leviathan,* Of Other Laws of Nature

[6] Thomas Hobbes, *Leviathan,* On the Liberty of Subjects

[7] [7] JOHN LOCKE, *The Second Treatise of Government*

[8] JOHN LOCKE, *The Second Treatise of Government,* Of Political Power

[9] JOHN LOCKE, *The Second Treatise of Government,* Of Political Power

[10] JOHN LOCKE, *The Second Treatise of Government,* Of Slavery

[11] JOHN LOCKE, *The Second Treatise of Government,* Of Slavery

[13] JOHN LOCKE, *The Second Treatise of Government*

[12] JOHN LOCKE, *The Second Treatise of Government,* Of Slavery

[14] JOHN LOCKE, *A Letter Concerning Toleration*

[14.5] David L. Holmes, *The Faiths of the Founding Fathers,* 2006

[15] Benjamin Rush, *The Selected Writings of Benjamin Rush*, Dagobert D. Runes

[16] *The Works of John Adams*, Charles Francis Adams

[17] *The Works of Benjamin Franklin*, Jared Sparks

[18] Richard Frothingham, *The Rise of the Republic of the United States*

[19] Letter to the House of Representatives, in Veto of *Federal Public Works* bill, March 3, 1817

[20] Federalist Paper 41 on *Specified Government Powers*

[21] *Piqua Branch Bank vs. Knoup*, 6 Ohio St. 393. Black's Law Dictionary, Revised Fourth Edition

[22] Federalist Papers, No. 39, January, 1788

[23] Thomas Jefferson, *Resolutions Relative to the Alien and Sedition Acts*

[24] Thomas Paine, *First Principles of Government*

[25] James Madison, letter to Henry Lee, 1824

[26] Thomas Jefferson, Letter to Judge William Johnson, 1823

[27] Elliot's Debates, *Remarks on the U.S. House of Representatives, at the New York state convention on the adoption of the Federal Constitution,* volume 2

[28] Federalist Papers, No. 44, January 25, 1788

[29] Thomas Jefferson, letter to C. Hammond, 18 August 1821

[30] Benjamin Constant, *The Liberty of the Ancients compared with the Liberty of the Moderns* (1816)

[31] Mike Farrell, Huffington Post, *A Civilized Society*, July, 8, 2013

[32] Nelson Mandela, *Long Walk to Freedom*, 1995

[33] http://www.prisonpolicy.org/global/

[33.5] http://mic.com/articles/8558/why-we-need-prison-reform-victimless-crimes-are-86-of-the-federal-prison-population

[34] Albert Einstein in a letter to a fatherly friend, 1901

[35] Alexander Hamilton, "Speech on the Constitutional Convention on a Plan of Government," in *Selected Writings and Speeches of Alexander Hamilton*, edited by Morton J. Frisch

[36] Thomas Jefferson, letter to James Madison, 1787

[37] Thomas Jefferson, letter to William C. Jarvis in 1820

[38] http://press-pubs.uchicago.edu/founders/documents/v1ch18s35.html

[39] http://4brevard.com/choice/Public_Education.htm

[39.2] *Education: Free and Compulsory*, Murray Rothbard, pg. 53

[39.4] *Education: Free and Compulsory*, Murray Rothbard, pg. 53

[39.5] http://jewishworldreview.com/cols/sowell080514.php3#.U-DDY6zLeT0

[40] http://www.campusreform.org/?ID=5696

[41] http://www.the-free-foundation.org/tst9-9-2013.html

[42] Letter to Archibald Stewart, December 1791

[43] Frederick Bastiat, The Law, 1850

[44] Alexander Hamilton, Letter of Instructions to the Commanding Officers of the Revenue Cutters, June

1791
[44.5] Thomas Jefferson letter to Isaac Tiffany 1819
[45] Sam Adams, *The Rights of the Colonists*,1772
[46] http://jonathanturley.org/2014/03/14/aca/
[46.5] http://jonathanturley.org/2014/12/31/gruber-in-2009-warned-that-obamacare-was-not-designed-to-reduce-costs-as-opposed-to-guarantee-coverage/
[47] Hale v. Henkel, 201 U.S. 43 (1906) Page 201 U. S. 74
[48] http://www.theblaze.com/stories/2014/03/20/what-two-words-do-those-seeking-to-increase-tyranny-and-totalitarianism-tend-to-use/
[49] Thomas Jefferson to Spencer Roane, 1819
[50] http://press-pubs.uchicago.edu/founders/documents/a2_2_2-3s15.html
[51] http://press-pubs.uchicago.edu/founders/documents/a2_2_2-3s15.html
[51.5] https://www.youtube.com/watch?v=T9BQDJZ42w0
[52] http://jonathanturley.org/2014/03/10/the-constitutional-tipping-point/
[53] Fredrick Bastiat, *The State in Journal des débats (1848)*
[54] Frederick Bastiat, *Justice and Fraternity*, in Journal des Economistes (15/06/1848)
[55] *James vs. United States*
[56] Woodrow Wilson, *Constitutional Government Chapter III*: The President of the United States 1908
[57] *Duplex Printing Press Co. vs. Deering* 1921
[58] Dorsey Richardson, *Constitutional Doctrines of Justice Oliver Wendell Holmes* 1924
[60] Charles A. Beard, The Supreme Court and the Constitution 1912, pg.39
[59] JOHN LOCKE, *The Second Treatise of Government*, Of Paternal Power
[61] The Kentucky Resolutions of 1798

Chapter 2

[1] Michael Badnarik, *Good to be King*, 2004
[2] Murray Rothbard, *The Ethics of Liberty*, 1982
[3] James Madison, *Federalist Paper* essay #62, 1788
[4] Thomas Jefferson, Letter to William Jarvis, 1820
[5] Thomas Jefferson, "A View on the Rights of British America" (1774) in *The Portable Jefferson*, Merrill D. Peterson (editor), pp. 17-18
[6] Stanley N. Katz, *Republicanism and the Law of Inheritance in the American Revolutionary Era*, 1977
[6.5] Thomas Jefferson in a letter to James Madison on *Equality* 1785
[7] John Adams, Letter to John Jebb,
[8] Thomas Jefferson, Letter to George Wythe, 1786
[9] 28 US Title Code 3002 (15), (A)
[10] http://oll.libertyfund.org/titles/808
[11] http://www.salon.com/2014/07/04/we_the_people_are_violent_and_filled_with_rage_a_nation_spinning_apart_on_its_independence_day/
[12] Thomas Jefferson to Isaac McPherson, 1813
[13] Thomas Jefferson: Batture at New Orleans, 1812
[14] Thomas Jefferson: Batture at New Orleans, 1812
[15] http://www.constitution.org/jm/17870416_wash.htm
[16] John Locke, *Second Treatise of Government*, Of Civil Government
[17] John Locke, *Second Treatise of Government*, Of the Extent of the Legislative Power
[18] Thomas West, *Vindicating the Founders*, chapter 2
[19] Thomas Jefferson, Letter to Joseph Milligan, April 6, 1816
[20] James Wilson, "On Property," in Works of James Wilson, Harvard University Press, ed. Robert McCloskey, vol. 2, pg. 719
[21] James Madison speech in the Virginia Constitutional Convention, 1830
[22] Thomas Jefferson to Edward Bancroft, 1788
[23] Locke, *The Second Treatise of Government*
[23.5] *Women and Taxes*, written by Edward J. McCaffery, 2002, via the National Center for Policy Analysis

[24] Thomas Hobbes, *Leviathan,* Of Those Things that Weaken or Tend to the Dissolution of a Commonwealth

[25] http://reason.com/archives/2014/03/27/probable-cause-warrants-and-the-nsa

[26] Terry vs. Ohio

[27] Federalist Paper 51

[28] Julian Waterman, *Thomas Jefferson and Blackstone's Commentaries*, 1933

[29] Thomas Jefferson, Letter to James Madison, 1826

[30] William W. Freehling, *Prelude to Civil War* 1966

[31] James Madison, "Charters," in *James Madison*, Hunt

[32] Timothy Sandefur, *Property Rights in 21st Century America*, 2006

[33] Timothy Sandefur, *Property Rights in 21st Century America*, 2006

[34] Billings vs. Hall, CA 1857

[35] http://hosted.ap.org/dynamic/stories/E/EU_REL_VATICAN_UN?SITE=AP&SECTION=HOME&TEMPLATE=DEFAULT&CTIME=2014-05-09-06-31-28

[35.5] https://www.princeton.edu/%7Emgilens/Gilens%20homepage%20materials/Gilens%20and%20Page/Gilens%20and%20Page%202014-Testing%20Theories%203-7-14.pdf

[36] http://www.dailykos.com/story/2014/05/09/1298205/-Sanders-asks-Yellen-if-America-is-an-Oligarchy#

[37] http://www.dailykos.com/story/2014/05/09/1298205/-Sanders-asks-Yellen-if-America-is-an-Oligarchy#

[37.5] http://www.nytimes.com/2014/07/27/business/the-typical-household-now-worth-a-third-less.html?_r=0

[38] http://www.bls.gov/cex/

[39] Henry George, *Progress and Poverty: An Inquiry into the Cause of Industrial Depressions and of Increase of Want with Increase of Wealth: The Remedy*, 1879

[40] http://www.washingtonsblog.com/2014/06/neofeudal-neoliberal-arrangement-since-need.html

[41] http://www.nationaljournal.com/tech/here-s-how-nasa-thinks-society-will-collapse-20140318

[42] http://www.cnbc.com/id/101046937

[43] http://www.alternet.org/economy/joe-stiglitz-people-who-break-rules-have-raked-huge-profits-and-wealth-and-its-sickening-our

[44] http://www.economonitor.com/lrwray/2012/07/23/why-were-screwed/

[45] http://www.washingtonsblog.com/2008/09/what-time-is-it.html

[46] http://www.businessinsider.com/harry-dent-demographic-cliff-2013-12

[47] John Locke, *Second Treatise of Government*, Of the State of Nature

[47.5] nlchp.org/documents/No_Safe_Place

[48] Benjamin Franklin, *On the Price of Corn and Management of the Poor*, 1766

[49] Benjamin Franklin to Robert Morris, 1783

[50] Thomas Jefferson, Letter to James Madison on Equality 1785

[51] Speech, House of Representatives, during the debate "On the Memorial of the Relief Committee of Baltimore, for the Relief of St. Domingo Refugees"

[51.2] Behold A Pale Horse, by William Cooper, pg 43

[51.5] http://www.itep.org/whopays/executive_summary.php

[52] http://www.monticello.org/site/jefferson/no-freeman-shall-be-debarred-use-arms-quotation

[53] http://www.fda.gov/Drugs/DevelopmentApprovalProcess/DevelopmentResources/DrugInteractionsLabeling/ucm114848.htm

[54] National Vital Statistics Report 2010 – May, 2013

[55] Thomas Jefferson quoting criminologist Cesare Beccaria

[56] www.pewsocialtrends.org/files/2013/05/firearms_final_05-2013.pdf

[57] http://www.detroitnews.com/article/20140716/METRO01/307160034

[58] CNN 06 10 2014 17 08 29

[59] http://www.loc.gov/law/help/firearms-control/australia.php

[60] I Annals of Congress at 750, August 17, 1789

[60.5] J. Elliot's, "Debates in the Several State Conventions", 45, 2d ed. Philadelphia, 1836

[61] Thomas Jefferson in a letter to Major John Cartwright, 1824

[62] http://www.washingtonpost.com/blogs/worldviews/wp/2013/10/17/this-map-shows-where-the-worlds-30-million-slaves-live-there-are-60000-in-the-u-s/

[63] Frederick Douglass, *My Escape from Slavery*

[64] James Madison, Federalist Paper 54
[65] http://en.wikipedia.org/wiki/Slavs
[66] David Livingstone, *Expedition to the Zambesi and its Tributaries*, CH 10
[67] Synopsis from "Freedomain Radio," Stefan Molyneux, *The Truth about Slavery*
[68] James Madison, State of the Union, 1810
[69] James Madison, Federalist Paper No. 42
[70] John Jay, letter to R. Lushington, March 15, 1786
[71] Benjamin Franklin in a 1773 letter to Dean Woodward
[72] Thomas Jefferson, The Writings of Thomas Jefferson, Albert Ellery Bergh, editor (Washington, D. C.: Thomas Jefferson Memorial Association, 1903), Vol. I, p. 34.
[73] John Quincy Adams, *The Crime of Slavery*
[74] John Adams, letter to Robert Evans, June 8, 1819
[75] Reconstruction, America's Unfinished Revolution, Eric Foner, pg. 258-59
[75] Reconstruction, America's Unfinished Revolution, Eric Foner, pg. 258-59
[75] Reconstruction, America's Unfinished Revolution, Eric Foner, pg. 258-59
[76] Reconstruction, America's Unfinished Revolution, Eric Foner, pg. 258-59
[77] Reconstruction, America's Unfinished Revolution, Eric Foner, pg. 489
[78] John Locke, *Second Treatise of Government,* Of Property
[79] Thomas Jefferson, Letter to Roger C. Weightman, 1826
[80] http://www.forbes.com/sites/instituteforjustice/2014/06/05/cops-in-texas-seize-millions-by-policing-for-profit/
[80.5] http://thedea.org/prohibhistory.html
[81] http://www.ij.org/policing-for-profit-the-abuse-of-civil-asset-forfeiture-4
[82] http://endforfeiture.com/what-is-forfeiture-more/
[83] http://online.wsj.com/news/article_email/SB10001424052702304753504579282940412941998-lMyQjAxMTA0MDEwMDExNDAyWj
[84] https://ecf.utd.uscourts.gov/cgi-bin/show_public_doc?211cv0652-78

Chapter 3

[1] http://www.washingtonpost.com/opinions/restore-balancing-among-the-branches-of-government-in-washington/2014/06/27/81440022-f49d-11e3-b633-0de077c9f768_story.html
[2] http://www.chattanoogan.com/2014/1/16/267593/Alexander-Says-Omnibus-Spending-Bill.aspx
[3] Ayn Rand, *The Virtue of Selfishness*, Man's Rights
[4] http://consortiumnews.com/2014/05/09/how-the-us-propaganda-system-works/
[5] http://time.com/2976711/obama-press-surveillance/
[6] Daniel Webster, speech at Niblo's Saloon, New York, March 15, 1837
[7] https://www.princeton.edu/%7Emgilens/Gilens%20homepage%20materials/Gilens%20and%20Page/Gilens%20and%20Page%202014-Testing%20Theories%203-7-14.pdf
[8] Thomas Jefferson, Letter to William Charles Jarvis, 1820
[9] David Brin, *The Postman*, 1997
[10] Letter to Christopher Tolkien 1943
[11] https://www.commondreams.org/view/2009/10/16-2
[12] http://otec.uoregon.edu/intelligence.htm
[13] http://otec.uoregon.edu/intelligence.htm
[14] http://psychology.about.com/od/profilesmz/p/robert-sternberg.htm
[15] Speech, Constitutional Convention (1787-06-29), from Max Farrand's Records of the Federal Convention of 1787, vol. I [1] (1911), p. 465
[16] Letters and Other Writings of James Madison (1865), Vol. II, p. 141
[17] www.ipc.on.ca/images/Resources/2014-05-06%20-%20Ryerson%20OneEleven%20%28Final%29.pdf
[18] http://business.financialpost.com/2014/02/26/beware-big-brother-culture-will-have-adverse-effect-on-creativity-productivity/
[19] https://www.youtube.com/watch?feature=player_embedded&v=G_syFFvefh0
[20] Thomas Jefferson, *Writings of Thomas Jefferson*, Albert Ellery Bergh

[21] James Madison, *Property* 1792

[22] Karl Marx, A Contribution to the Critique of Political Economy

[23] http://www.washingtonpost.com/world/national-security/in-nsa-intercepted-data-those-not-targeted-far-outnumber-the-foreigners-who-are/2014/07/05/8139adf8-045a-11e4-8572-4b1b969b6322_story.html

[24] http://www.wingia.com/en/services/about_the_end_of_year_survey/global_results/7/33/

[25] www.wingia.com/web/files/news/139/file/139.pdf

[26] http://www.washingtontimes.com/news/2014/jun/18/no-kumbaya-here-us-now-101st-most-peaceful-nation-/

[27] http://www.washingtontimes.com/news/2014/jun/18/no-kumbaya-here-us-now-101st-most-peaceful-nation-/#ixzz355ZT9hXe

[28] http://www.washingtontimes.com/news/2014/jun/18/no-kumbaya-here-us-now-101st-most-peaceful-nation-/

[29] http://www.nytimes.com/2014/06/14/upshot/the-lack-of-major-wars-may-be-hurting-economic-growth.html?_r=1

[30] http://www.nakedcapitalism.com/2014/07/noam-chomsky-americas-real-foreign-policy-corporate-protection-racket.html

[31] James Madison, Federalist Paper #48, 1788.

[32] Pennsylvania Assembly: Reply to the Governor, Printed in Votes and Proceedings of the House of Representatives, 1755-1756 (Philadelphia, 1756), pp. 19-21.

[33] Letters of John Quincy Adams; to his son on the Bible and Its Teachings, James M. Alden, 1850

[34] www.supremecourt.gov/opinions/13pdf/13-132_8l9c.pdf

[35] www.supremecourt.gov/opinions/13pdf/13-132_8l9c.pdf

[36] www.supremecourt.gov/opinions/13pdf/13-132_8l9c.pdf

[37] http://www.chron.com/news/politics/article/Police-ready-to-abide-by-court-s-cellphone-ruling-5580402.php

[38] http://www.c-span.org/video/?206206-1/reaction-supreme-court-ruling-dc-gun-law

[39] http://www.theguardian.com/commentisfree/2014/jul/11/the-ultimate-goal-of-the-nsa-is-total-population-control

[40] http://mobile.nytimes.com/blogs/bits/2014/07/05/they-have-seen-the-future-of-the-internet-and-it-is-dark/?emc=edit_ee_20140706&nl=todaysheadlines&nlid=4536558

[41] *The Rapid Rise of Delayed Notice Searches, and the Fourth Amendment 'Rule Requiring Notice'*, Jonathan Witmer-Rich - Cleveland State University - Cleveland-Marshall College of Law, Sept, 2013

[42] http://www.law.cornell.edu/supremecourt/text/10-1259

[43] http://www.phibetaiota.net/2013/02/2013-robert-steele-answers-to-ma-in-uk-osint-and-terrorism/

[44] *Open Source Intelligence* (OSINT).doc, Robert David Steele, pg. 3

[45] http://mobile.nytimes.com/blogs/opinionator/2014/01/19/fifty-states-of-fear/?_php=true&_type=blogs&_r=0

[46] Brzezinski, Zbigniew. *The Grand Chessboard: American Primacy And Its Geostrategic Imperatives.* 1997. P. 211.

[46.5] http://www.theburningplatform.com/2014/08/13/ron-paul-on-iraq-the-sooner-we-get-out-of-there-the-better/

[47] http://www.alternet.org/story/15935/leo_strauss%27_philosophy_of_deception

[48] http://www.thefederalistpapers.org/us/does-usda-need-submachine-guns-republicans-seek-to-demilitarize-federal-agencies

[49] http://fox13now.com/2014/06/03/prosecutor-swallow-investigation-in-a-very-fruitful-period/

[50] http://fox13now.com/2014/06/03/prosecutor-swallow-investigation-in-a-very-fruitful-period/

[50.5] http://www.salon.com/2014/08/22/researchers_police_likely_provoke_protestors_%E2%80%94_not_the_other_way_around/

[51] https://www.rutherford.org/publications_resources/john_whiteheads_commentary/are_police_in_america_now_a_military_occupying_force

[51.5] http://www.vox.com/2014/8/14/6002451/ferguson-police-militarization-seattle

[52] http://time.com/2907307/aclu-swat-local-police/

[52.5] http://time.com/3111474/rand-paul-ferguson-police/

[53] http://privacysos.org/swat

[54] http://www.washingtonpost.com/news/the-watch/wp/2014/06/09/war-comes-to-pulaski-county-indiana/

[55] https://www.hawaii.edu/powerkills/20TH.HTM

[55.5] http://www.businessinsider.com/police-militarization-ferguson-2014-8#ixzz3ADwtPM3N

[56] https://www.rutherford.org/publications_resources/john_whiteheads_commentary/has_the_dept_of_homeland_security_become_americas_standing_army

[57] James Madison Speech, Constitutional Convention, from Max Farrand's Records of the Federal Convention of 1787

[58] https://www.rutherford.org/publications_resources/john_whiteheads_commentary/has_the_dept_of_homeland_security_become_americas_standing_army

[59] *Why Societies Need Dissent*, by Cass Sunstein, 2003

[60] Ohio Univ. Press, 1984

[61] Federalist papers #31

[62] Abraham Lincoln, Speech given at the Young Men's Lyceum of Springfield, Illinois January 27, 1838

[63] https://en.wikipedia.org/wiki/Domestic_terrorism_in_the_United_States

[64] http://www.foxnews.com/politics/2014/06/22/louisiana-gov-jindal-claims-rebellion-brewing-against-washington/

[65] http://minerva.dtic.mil/funded.html

[66] http://www.ijreview.com/2014/06/147235-17-things-kill-often-far-right-extremism-chart-make-media-feel-silly/

[67] START consortium at the University of Maryland

[68] http://www.hrw.org/node/127456

[69] media.oregonlive.com/pacific-northwest-news/other/NoFlyOpinion.pdf

[70] http://www.studioprey.com/snowy.html

[71] Federalist Paper 57

[72] http://consortiumnews.com/2014/07/08/escalating-domestic-warfare/

[73] http://www.washingtonpost.com/news/opinions/wp/2014/02/10/some-justice-in-texas-the-raid-on-henry-magee/

[74] http://jonathanturley.org/2014/07/10/virginia-police-secure-warrant-to-force-teen-to-be-photographed-with-erect-penis/

[75] http://abc11.com/news/i-team-dpd-accused-of--faking-911-calls/172684/

[76] Letter to Messrs, the Abbes Chalut, and Arnaud, 17 April 1787

[77] http://www.examiner.com/article/connecticut-judge-declares-no-one-should-have-guns

[78] http://www.fbi.gov/about-us/investigate/civilrights/color_of_law

[79] http://www.law.cornell.edu/uscode/text/18/242

[80] Timothy Sandefur, *The Right to Earn a Living*, pg. 145

[81] http://www.nytimes.com/2014/07/29/nyregion/port-authority-of-new-york-and-new-jersey-tells-store-to-drop-9-11-items-.html?_r=0

[82] Jay Giedd, psychiatrist leading the National Institutes of Health Study, 2005

[83] Thomas Jefferson to W. H. Torrance, 1815

[84] http://www.hawaii.edu/powerkills/DBG.CHAP2.HTM

[85] http://www.pixiq.com/article/ohio-congressman-bans-cameras-from-town-hall-meeting

[85.5] http://nypost.com/2015/01/11/no-time-off-for-nypd-until-cops-get-back-to-work/

[86] http://thenewspaper.com/rlc/docs/2011/ma-tixappeal.asp

[87] John Emerich Edward Dalberg-Acton, 1st Baron Acton

Chapter 4

[0] Ralph Waldo Emerson, *Self-Reliance*, RWE-Selected Essays, edited by Robert Richardson, pg. 154-155

[1] Sam Adams Letter to James Warren, 1779

[2] *The American Story* by Robert A. Divine and T. H. Breen

[3] Letter from Thomas Jefferson to F. von Humboldt, 1817

[4] Thomas Jefferson to M. D'Ivernois, 1795

[5] http://press-pubs.uchicago.edu/founders/documents/v1ch4s10.html

[6] Letter from Thomas Jefferson to J. Taylor, 1816

[7] Thomas Jefferson to Annapolis Citizens, 1809

[8] http://press-pubs.uchicago.edu/founders/documents/v1ch18s9.html

[9] http://kdvr.com/2014/08/02/medical-examiner-cops-choke-hold-not-asthma-killed-new-york-man/

[9.5] http://www.nbclosangeles.com/news/local/Woman-Punched-by-CHP-Officer-Settles-for-15M-277029691.html

[10] http://www.huffingtonpost.com/2014/08/19/sunil-dutta-police-washington-post_n_5692266.html

[11] Kentucky Resolutions of 1798

[12] http://www.theguardian.com/environment/earth-insight/2014/jun/19/open-source-revolution-conquer-one-percent-cia-spy

[13] http://www.theguardian.com/environment/earth-insight/2014/jun/19/open-source-revolution-conquer-one-percent-cia-spy

[14] http://www.phibetaiota.net/2014/05/robert-steele-at-libtechnyc-the-open-source-everything-manifesto/

[15] http://www.phibetaiota.net/2014/05/robert-steele-at-libtechnyc-the-open-source-everything-manifesto/

[16] http://www.phibetaiota.net/2014/05/robert-steele-at-libtechnyc-the-open-source-everything-manifesto/

[17] http://www.phibetaiota.net/2014/05/robert-steele-at-libtechnyc-the-open-source-everything-manifesto/

[18] http://www.politico.com/magazine/story/2014/06/the-pitchforks-are-coming-for-us-plutocrats-108014.html#.U-qsV6zLeDE

[19] http://finance.yahoo.com/blogs/daily-ticker/why-the-rich-are--mistakenly--worried-about-the-middle-class-151842954.html

[19.5] http://releases.jhu.edu/2014/09/15/when-rulers-cant-understand-the-ruled/

[20] http://www.dailymail.co.uk/sciencetech/article-2614780/How-FARMERS-fitter-athletes-Human-strength-speed-peaked-7-300-years-ago-declining-rapidly.html

[21] http://www.collegenews.com/article/sat_scores_continue_their_downward_spiral

[22] http://www.huffingtonpost.com/2013/05/22/people-getting-dumber-human-intelligence-victoria-era_n_3293846.html

[23] *Conspiracy Theory in America*, written by Lance deHaven-Smith, professor at FSU

[23.5] *Trance: Formation of America, 1995*, by Cathy O'Brien, Mark Phillips

[24] Stephan Molyneux, *The Handbook of Human Ownership*, pg. 3-4

[25] Stephan Molyneux, *The Handbook of Human Ownership*, pg. 4-5

[26] *The Works of Friedrich Nietzsche*, edited by Alexander Tille, translated by William A. Hausemann, pg. 47-48

[27] Stephan Molyneux, *The Handbook of Human Ownership*, pg. 4-5

[28] Stephan Molyneux, *The Handbook of Human Ownership*, pg. 5-6

[29] Stephan Molyneux, *The Handbook of Human Ownership*, pg. 5-6

[30] Frances Bacon, *The New Oregon*, XLIX, pg. 44

[31] Ralph Waldo Emerson, *Self-Reliance*, RWE-Selected Essays, edited by Robert Richardson, pg. 151-152

[32] Thomas Jefferson, Bill 79, *A Bill for the More General Diffusion of Knowledge.*

[32.5] Chuck Norris, *The Secret Power Within*, pg.30

[33] http://www.dailyfinance.com/2013/07/04/money-lessons-founding-fathers/

[34] http://www.24hgold.com/english/contributor.aspx?article=4031300362G10020&contributor=Mike+Maloney

[35] http://goldsilverworlds.com/price/gold-price-reflecting-mike-maloneys-first-deflation-then-inflation/

[36] Thomas Paine, *First Principles of Government*, 1795

[37] Thomas Woods Jr., Nullification, pg.3

[38] http://drhyman.com/blog/2011/08/04/new-research-finds-diabetes-can-be-reversed/#close

[39] http://www.medicaldaily.com/80-police-officers-are-overweight-why-theyre-more-likely-die-heart-disease-fighting-crime-298336

[40] npc.umich.edu/publications/u/2013-06-npc-working-paper.pdf

[41] http://www.caseyresearch.com/articles/corporations-join-droves-renouncing-us-citizenship-1

[42] http://www.orlandosentinel.com/news/breaking-news/os-mayor-tosses-man-for-not-standing-for-pledge-of-20140829,0,80941.story

43 An Inquiry Concerning The Principles of Morals, Edited by Tom L. Beauchamp, pg. 158-159